Contents

MW01612077

1 Preparing for Level 1

2 Complete Step-by-Step Lesson Plans

3 Appendices

4 Index

All About® Spelling

The program that takes the struggle out of spelling

Level 1

Color Edition

by Marie Rippel

Printed in the United States of America

Color Edition
v.2.0.1

All About® Learning Press, Inc.
615 Commerce Loop
Eagle River, WI 54521

ISBN 978-1-935197-90-4

Editor: Renée M. LaTulippe
Contributors: Samantha Johnson, Renée M. LaTulippe
Cover Illustration and Design: Dave LaTulippe
Graphics: Shanna Behrens, Donna Goeddaeus, Emily F. Johnson, Dave LaTulippe

The *All About® Spelling* Level 1 Teacher's Manual is part of the *All About® Spelling* program.

For more books in this series, go to www.AllAboutSpelling.com.

1

Preparing for Level 1

Start Here!

To prepare for teaching *All About Spelling* Level 1, you can either watch our short videos or follow the checklist on the subsequent pages. Do whichever works best for you!

Option 1: Watch the Videos

Go to www.aalp.tv/spelling-level-1 on your phone, tablet, or computer, or scan the QR code to be taken directly to the videos.

Let us show you how to get set up for success!

After watching the videos, turn to page 37 of this Teacher's Manual to start teaching the first lesson.

Option 2: Read the Following Pages

Check off each page as you complete it.

Find Out If Your Student Is Ready for Spelling

Before beginning Level 1, be sure your student is comfortable with these prerequisite concepts.

☐ **Your student should be able to name the letters of the alphabet.**

To test, have your student tell you the names of the following letters.

k r w e j u f

If your child doesn't know the letter names yet, visit blog.allaboutlearningpress.com/letter-knowledge for some fun ways to work on them as you start *All About Spelling* Level 1.

It is not essential that your student know the *sounds* of the letters before beginning. The sounds will be taught in Lesson 1.

☐ **Your student should be able to read the following words.**

snack	**glass**
bunch	**stem**
wishes	**sandbox**

If reading the words listed above was difficult for your student, complete *All About Reading* Level 1 before starting spelling instruction.

Having a strong start in reading will help your student in three ways:

1. While learning to read, students pick up basic skills that will enable them to spell more easily.
2. It is easier to decode words than it is to encode words, giving your student more confidence with words.
3. Reading helps establish a visual memory of many words, making spelling much easier.

Gather the Materials

In addition to this Teacher's Manual, you will need the following items:

1 Student Packet

The Student Packet contains:

- *Zip into Spelling* activity book
- Flashcards
- Stickers for the Progress Chart

2 Letter Tiles Kit or Letter Tiles App

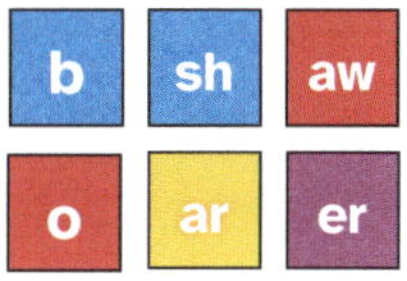

You can use either the physical letter tiles or the Letter Tiles app. See Appendix O for guidance in choosing which option to use.

3 Spelling Review Box with Divider Cards

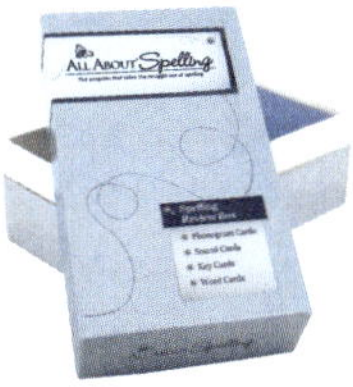

The review box is the perfect size to organize your student's flashcards.

4 Magnetic Whiteboard (Optional)

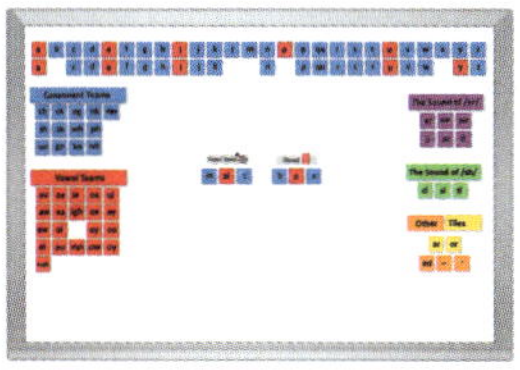

If you choose to use the physical letter tiles, a 2' x 3' magnetic whiteboard is highly recommended. See Appendix Q for information on selecting a whiteboard.

5 Notebook or Our Free Spelling Dictation Sheets

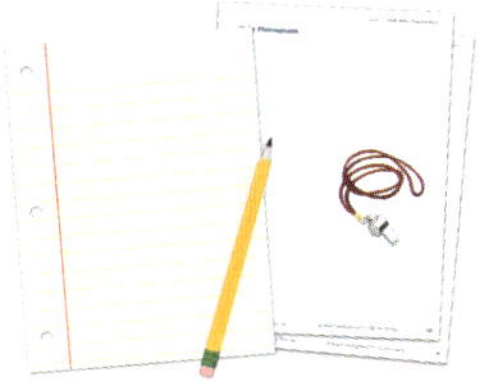

Your student will need a notebook with lined paper for spelling practice. Or you may choose to print our free dictation sheets. Go to www.allaboutlearningpress.com/dictation-sheets or scan the QR code.

Regular-ruled Dictation Sheets

Wide-ruled Dictation Sheets

Learn about the *All About Spelling* Method

First of all, you can do this! *All About Spelling* is a scripted, open-and-go program developed for busy parents, teachers, and tutors who want to teach spelling in the most effective way possible. This program doesn't require long periods of study, you don't have to develop your own lesson plans, and you don't have to stress over what to teach next—because everything is laid out for you, step by step. You'll get solid grounding in how to teach spelling without being overwhelmed.

Your student will be actively involved in the learning process. This is a truly multisensory program; your student will learn through sight, sound, and touch. Everything is taught in context and your student will apply what he has learned right away. Your student will be engaged in thinking, processing, comparing, and learning.

Students who use the *All About Spelling* method tend to feel a sense of excitement in learning. And they should! They are learning how to think, explore, and grow in their abilities. They feel successful as they see continual progress.

There are no gaps in this program. Your student will be taught everything he or she needs to know about spelling, so no guessing is required. Each new concept builds upon the previous one, and no steps are skipped.

***All About Spelling* is a mastery-based program.** As such, the levels don't correspond to grade levels. In mastery-based learning, students master one concept before moving on to a more advanced concept, regardless of age or grade level.

Most importantly, *All About Spelling* is committed to results. The *All About Spelling* program has a very focused mission: to enable you to teach your student to spell while guaranteeing retention and enjoyment. Our approach to spelling focuses on helping students become confident, fluent spellers who can absorb and retain new information.

> If you ever have a question as you are teaching, please feel free to contact us at support@allaboutlearningpress.com or 715-477-1976.
>
> We're here to help!

Preview the Teacher's Manual

Lesson Plans

Turn to Part 2 of this teacher's manual, beginning on page 35. You'll see that the lessons are laid out for you, step by step. Lessons consist of five parts:

1. **Before You Begin.** This cream-colored box contains an overview of the lesson and is meant only for you, the teacher. It takes just a few minutes to read it so you'll be well equipped to teach the lesson confidently.

2. **Review.** Beginning with Lesson 2, you'll give your student a quick review of previously taught concepts. You will need your student's Spelling Review Box for this part of the lesson.

3. **New Teaching.** This is the hands-on, multisensory portion of the lesson. Your student will work with the letter tiles and activity sheets while learning and practicing new spelling concepts.

4. **Advanced Application.** If you have older students who need more of a challenge, the Advanced Application section provides the opportunity to practice new concepts with higher-level, multisyllable words. This section begins in Lesson 7.

5. **Track Your Progress.** At the end of each lesson, you'll record your student's progress on the Progress Chart.

Appendices

Take a few minutes to flip through the Appendices section starting on page 233. The Appendices are full of extra resources, tips, and activities to help you and your student get the most out of your spelling lessons. This is where you will find creative ideas for reviewing concepts, tips and troubleshooting help, and lists of concepts covered in the program.

Preview the Activity Book

The *Zip into Spelling* activity book contains:

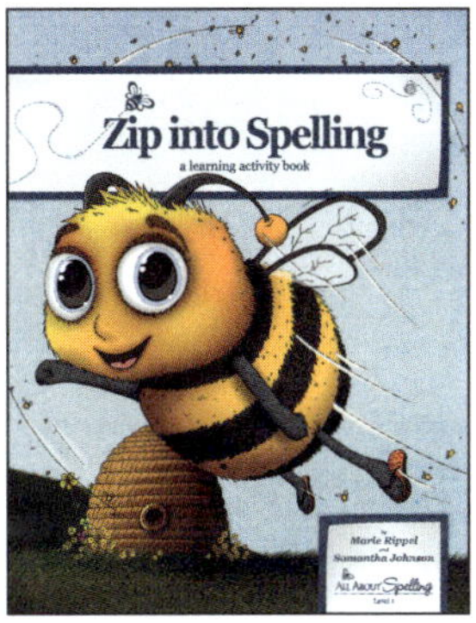

- Progress Chart
- Phonograms Chart
- Activity Sheets
- Advanced Application Sheets
- Word Banks
- Rule Posters
- Certificate of Achievement

The lesson plans in the Teacher's Manual will tell you which pages you need for each lesson. The pages in the activity book are perforated for easy removal.

Let's take a quick look at each part of the activity book.

Progress Chart

The Progress Chart can be found on page 5 of the activity book.

This chart is a motivating part of the lessons for many students because it is a visual reminder of the progress they have made toward spelling independently.

Remove the chart on the perforation and decide where to place it. Choose a prominent place like a bulletin board, the refrigerator, the back of a door, or another easily accessible area.

After each lesson has been completed, have your student color in or place a sticker over the next circle on the chart.

Activity Sheets

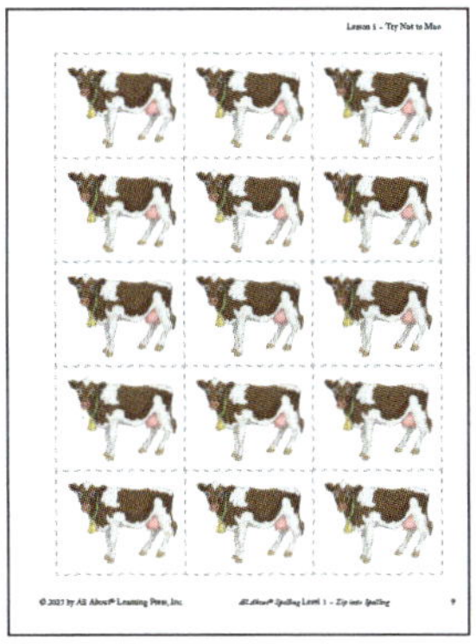

The activity sheets are very motivating for most students. They provide a variety of ways to practice the new concepts taught in the lessons. Flashcards and word banks have their place, but it is nice to break out of the "serious" learning and have a little fun applying it!

Take a look at the activity called "Try Not to Moo" on page 9 of the activity book. When you get to Lesson 1, the lesson plan will prompt you to cut out the cow cards and place them in a pile. Your student will choose a card, flip it over, and say the sound(s) of the phonogram indicated. But if he draws a Moo card, he will have to moo like a cow instead.

Although the activity sheets are optional, you may find that students of all ages enjoy the mental break that they provide.

Advanced Application Sheets

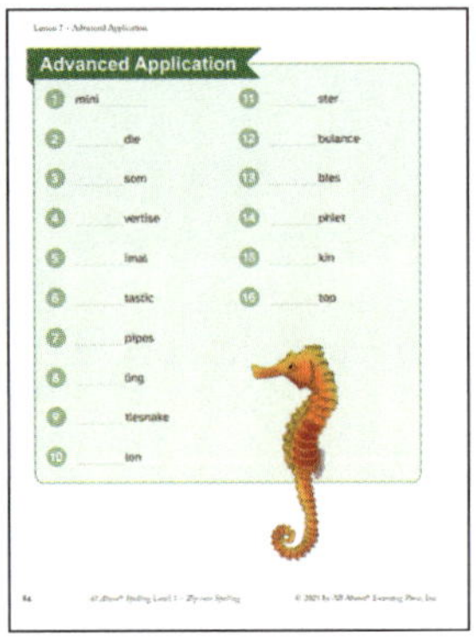

Starting in Lesson 7, Advanced Application is included at the end of each lesson to meet the needs of older students who already know how to spell simple words.

As an example, turn to page 84 of this teacher's manual and page 54 of the activity book. Instead of spelling words like *fan, am,* and *nap*, older students can practice the same concepts while completing multisyllabic words such as *fantastic*, *ambulance*, and *napkin*.

Spelling Rule Posters

Level 1 teaches eight spelling rules. These rules have been illustrated on posters that you can display in a prominent area as visual reminders for your student.

The first Spelling Rule poster is taught in Lesson 4. For a list of all Spelling Rules introduced in Level 1, see Appendix C.

Learn about Phonograms

Understanding phonograms is vital to your child's success in spelling. Fortunately, phonograms are simple to understand and easy to teach.

Let's start with a quick definition.

What Are Phonograms?

A phonogram is a letter or combination of letters that represent a sound. For example:

- **CK** is a phonogram that says /k/ as in *clock*.
- **S** is a phonogram that says /s/ as in *sat* or /z/ as in *has*.
- **OY** is a phonogram that says /oi/ as in *boy*.

The word *phonogram* comes from Greek and is literally translated as the "written symbol for a sound."

Why Do We Teach Phonograms?

Phonograms make learning to read and spell much easier!

Take a look at the word *shed*. If you pronounce the word slowly to hear the individual sounds, you will hear three different sounds: /sh/–/ĕ/–/d/. As we say each sound, we can write down the corresponding phonogram.

sh-e-d

That was an easy example, but the same principle applies to multisyllable words as well. For the word *winter*, for example, we say the individual sounds in each syllable and write the corresponding phonograms.

w-i-n   t-er

As you can see, your student doesn't need to remember w-i-n-t-e-r as a random string of letters. Instead, just segment the word and represent each sound with a phonogram.

Phonograms Are Like Building Blocks

Phonograms are the building blocks of almost every English word. In fact, a study of 17,000 words showed that the vast majority of words follow the regular phonogram sounds. Only 3% of the words are completely irregular (such as *said* and *of*).[1] This means that there are very few words that must be learned through repetition and rote memorization.

Since phonograms represent sounds, the number of letters in a word doesn't necessarily correspond to the number of phonograms. Look at these examples.

h igh

Since *high* has two sounds, it is represented by two phonograms.

sh ee p

Sheep has three sounds, so it is represented by three phonograms.

Preview the Phonogram Sounds

The lesson plans will prompt you to preview the sounds of new phonograms before you teach them to your student. Below are three ways you can preview the sounds.

Phonogram Sounds app. This free app can be used on your computer, tablet, or phone. Go to www.allaboutlearningpress.com/phonogram-sounds-app to download. Simply tap the phonogram to hear the sound.

Letter Tiles app. If you own the Letter Tiles app, "long hold" on a letter tile to hear the sound(s).

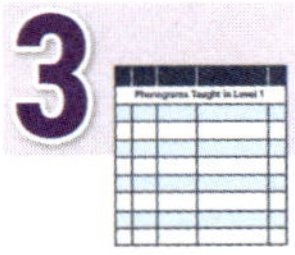

Chart in Appendix B. Key words are given for each phonogram.

Using the method you prefer, take a moment to preview the first two Phonogram Cards: m and s. You'll discover that m has one sound (/m/), while s has two sounds (/s/–/z/). Try out a few more letters, being sure to pronounce them clearly. Practice saying the pure sound without adding a noticeable /uh/ sound at the end. A common problem is to say /tuh/ instead of /t/ or /nuh/ instead of /n/.

> **For letters with more than one sound,** we always say the sounds in a particular order, starting with the most common sound. Say one sound after the other, with only a slight pause in between. For example, for the letter c, say "/k/–/s/."

[1]Hanna, P.R., Hanna, J.S., Hodges, R.E., & Rudorf, E.H. (1966). *Phoneme-grapheme correspondences as cues to spelling improvement.* Washington, DC: United States Office of Education Cooperative Research.

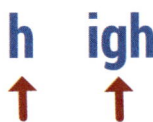

Learn about the Flashcards

We will be using four types of flashcards. Below is an introduction to each type.

Phonogram Cards are used to teach and review the phonograms.

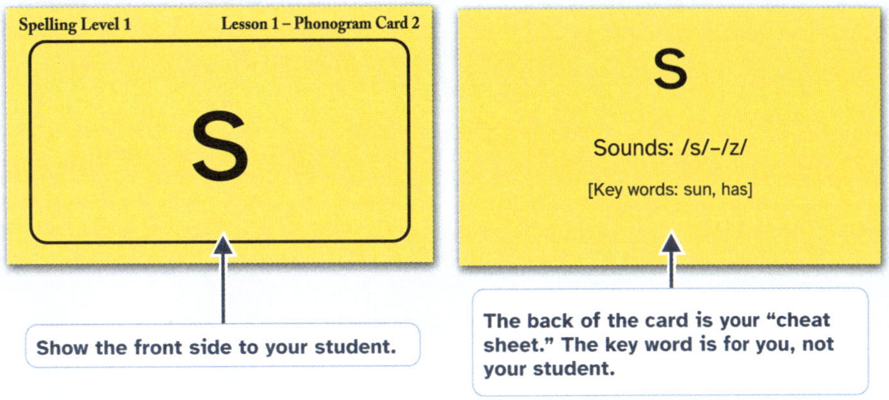
Spelling Level 1
Lesson 1 – Phonogram Card 2
s
s
Sounds: /s/–/z/
[Key words: sun, has]
Show the front side to your student.
The back of the card is your "cheat sheet." The key word is for you, not your student.

Sound Cards are used to practice writing phonograms from dictation. You'll dictate the sound(s) listed on the flashcard and your student will write the corresponding phonogram.

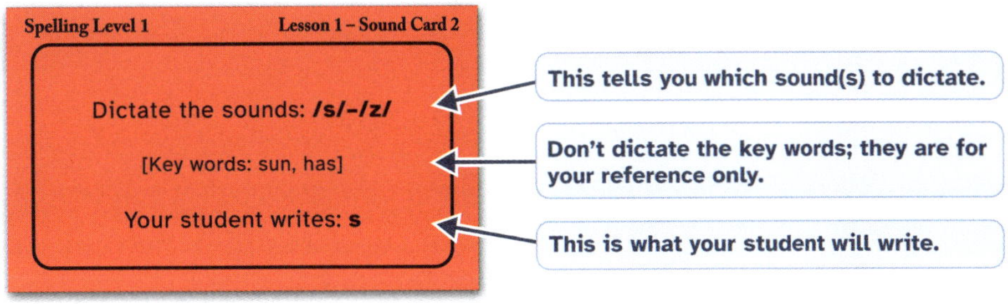
Spelling Level 1
Lesson 1 – Sound Card 2
Dictate the sounds: /s/–/z/
[Key words: sun, has]
Your student writes: s
This tells you which sound(s) to dictate.
Don't dictate the key words; they are for your reference only.
This is what your student will write.

Word Cards are used to teach and review spelling words. You'll dictate the word and your student will write the word in his dictation notebook.

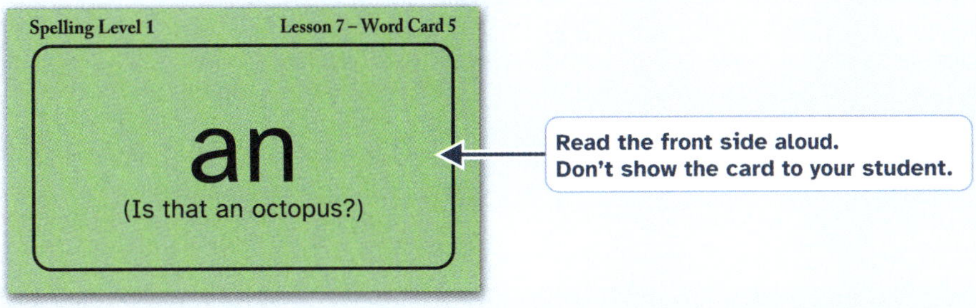
Spelling Level 1
Lesson 7 – Word Card 5
an
(Is that an octopus?)
Read the front side aloud.
Don't show the card to your student.

Some Word Cards contain a sentence like the one under the word *an* above. This is to distinguish it from the word *Ann*. You can read the sentence aloud for clarity, but **don't have your student write the sentence**. Your student will only write the word *an*. Sentences are added to all cards containing homophones (words that sound alike but are spelled differently).

Rule Cards contain spelling rules and generalizations.

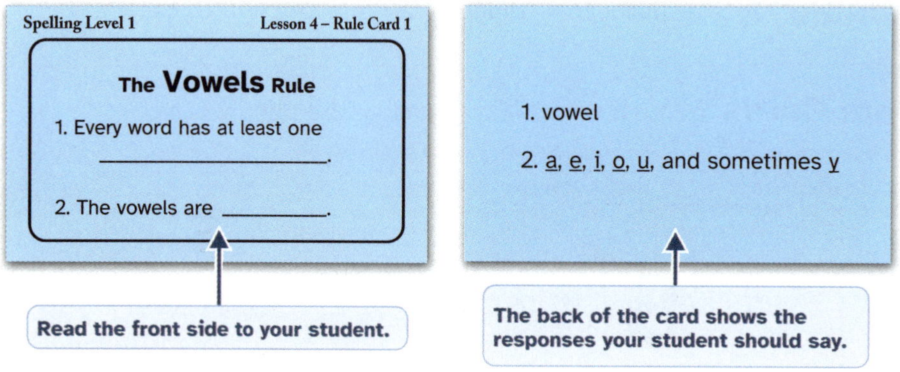

Spelling Level 1
Lesson 4 – Rule Card 1
The Vowels Rule
1. Every word has at least one ________.
2. The vowels are ________.
Read the front side to your student.
1. vowel
2. a, e, i, o, u, and sometimes y
The back of the card shows the responses your student should say.

Prepare Your Spelling Review Box

The Spelling Review Box will help you keep the flashcards organized. Follow the instructions below to set up your Spelling Review Box.

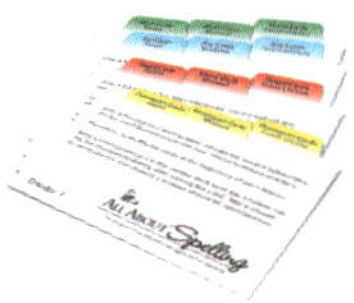

1. **Place the divider cards in your box.** The divider cards are numbered 1-12 so you can be sure to get them in the correct order. Foam spacers are also provided to allow the cards to stand upright. As you need more room for cards, simply remove a foam spacer.

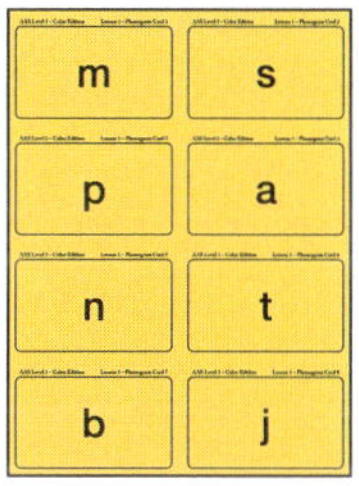

2. **Locate the yellow Phonogram Cards** in the Student Packet. Separate the perforated cards and place them behind the yellow tabbed divider called *Phonogram Cards–Future Lessons.*

3. **Locate the red Sound Cards** in the Student Packet. Separate the perforated cards and place them behind the red tabbed divider called *Sound Cards–Future Lessons.*

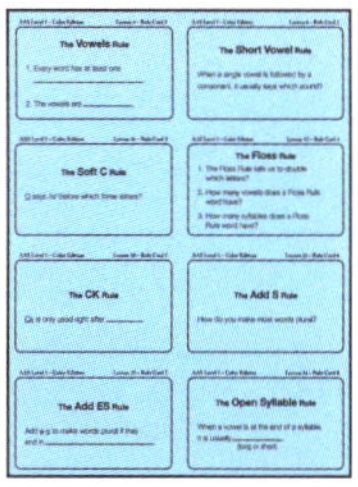

4. **Locate the blue Rule Cards** in the Student Packet. Separate the perforated cards and place them behind the blue tabbed divider called *Rule Cards–Future Lessons.*

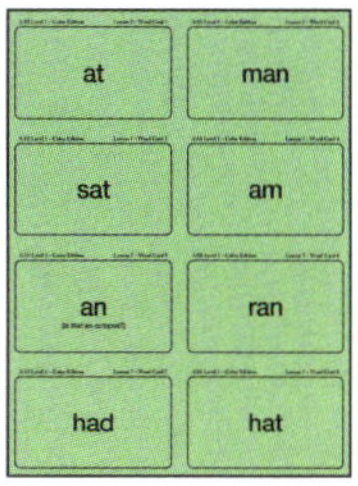

5. **Locate the green Word Cards** in the Student Packet. Separate the perforated cards and place them behind the green tabbed divider called *Word Cards–Future Lessons.*

Set Up the Letter Tiles

Starting with Lesson 4, letter tiles are used in every lesson to help your student quickly and easily grasp new concepts. You have the option to use either the Letter Tiles app or the physical letter tiles. See Appendix O if you need help deciding which format to use.

If You Will Be Using the Letter Tiles App

Visit www.allaboutlearningpress.com/letter-tiles-app to purchase the app for your tablet, or scan the QR code. (Please note that the Letter Tiles app is only available for tablets and touch-enabled Chromebooks. There is no version for phones because the tiles would be too small to be useful.)

Short tutorial videos are available in the app menu to show you everything you need to know about using the app in your lessons.

If You Will Be Using the Physical Letter Tiles

1. **Take out the Letter Tiles kit.** Locate Sheets 1-3. Do not separate the tiles yet. (Sheets 4-13 will be used in future levels.)

2. **Apply the magnets to the back of the sheets you removed in Step 1.** Stick one magnet in each gray box.

3. **Separate the tiles** on the perforations.

4. **Set up your whiteboard for Lesson 4.** Set up the letter tiles on your magnetic whiteboard as shown below.

Set the board aside until letter tiles are introduced in Lesson 4.

5. **Place the remaining Level 1 items in the small zip storage bag provided with the Letter Tiles kit.** The lessons will tell you when to add these items to your whiteboard. For safekeeping, store the baggie in the larger zip storage bag provided with the kit.

Answers to Common Questions about Letter Tiles

What do the different colors mean?

b Blue tiles are consonants and consonant teams.

u Red tiles are vowels and vowel teams.

er Purple tiles are for the sound of /er/.

or Yellow tiles are for Bossy R combinations that don't say /er/.

ci Green tiles are for alternate spellings of /sh/: ti, ci, si.

ed Orange tiles are for miscellaneous symbols and letters.

You'll learn about each category when you get to it in the lessons.

Why are there two different y's?

- Y can be a consonant or a vowel, depending on the word.
- When it is a consonant, it says /y/.
- When it is a vowel, it can say /ĭ/, /ī/, or /ē/.

Why are q and u together on a tile?
Since q is always followed by a u in English words, they are placed together on a single tile.

What will happen with the other items that are left in my Level 1 baggie?

- Starting in Lesson 13, the lessons will prompt you to add the remaining letter tiles to the board.
- To see what the board will look like by the end of Level 1, see Appendix P.

What if I don't have a magnetic whiteboard?
A magnetic whiteboard makes it easier and faster to set up for your spelling lessons, but if you don't have a magnetic whiteboard, you can set up the letter tiles right on your table.

What do all these funny marks and symbols mean?
As a shorthand way to represent the sounds of letters in this Teacher's Manual, we use slashes. For example, /m/ stands for the spoken sound *mmm* as in *monkey*.

You will also see two other sound symbols:

- A straight line above a letter, as in /ā/, represents the long vowel sound. This symbol is called a *macron*.
- A "smile" above a letter, as in /ă/, represents the short vowel sound. This symbol is called a *breve*.

Prepare for Spelling Dictation

1. Prepare a notebook with lined paper or use whichever type of paper your student uses for handwriting lessons.

   Alternatively, download our free Level 1 Dictation Sheets at www.allaboutlearningpress.com/dictation-sheets or scan one of the QR codes on page 11.

2. When the lesson prompts you to take out your student's dictation notebook, you can use either the notebook you've prepared, the printed dictation sheets, or loose-leaf paper.

   - **Starting in Lesson 5,** your student will be writing phonograms from dictation.
   - **Starting in Lesson 7,** your student will be writing words from dictation.
   - **Starting in Lesson 12,** your student will be writing phrases from dictation.
   - **In Lesson 24,** the last new-concept lesson of Level 1, your student will write complete sentences from dictation.

Read This If You Are Teaching an Older Student

All About Spelling is frequently used with older students, including teens and adults. The words in Level 1 may be easy to spell, but many students have not learned the concepts behind them—and these concepts are crucial for success throughout the program. For example, most struggling students will know how to spell *cat*, but they don't know why *cat* is spelled with a c instead of a k. They may not need to practice spelling the word *cat*, but they do need to learn the concept so they can apply it to words like *emergency* and *concentrate*. Level 1 fills in important gaps like this.

Other Level 1 concepts that older learners may not be familiar with include

- the sounds of the vowels;
- how to segment words; and
- how to make words plural.

Here are five tips for working with older students who need remedial work.

1 Be ready to explain why you're working in Level 1 instead of a higher level.

Compare learning to spell to something they can relate to, like video games or swimming lessons. Your student may understand that even though the first level of a game (or of swimming lessons) may seem easy, that doesn't mean he should jump ahead to the fifth level. But it does mean that he can go quickly through the earlier levels, learning what he needs to know so that when he does get to the higher levels, he isn't overwhelmed by having to learn too much at once.

2 Look for the section called "Can You Skip This Lesson?"

> **Can You Skip This Lesson?**
>
> Many students who begin *All About Spelling* have already completed *All About Reading* Level 1 (or can read at an equivalent level) and know the sounds of letters a through z. If your student already knows the sounds on Phonogram Cards 1-26 without hesitation, place the Phonogram Cards behind the **Mastered** divider in the Spelling Review Box and move on to Lesson 2.

This section, located in the Before You Begin box of the first six lessons, will help you decide if your student needs to complete that particular lesson.

3 Take advantage of Advanced Application.

Starting in Lesson 7, Advanced Application sheets are provided especially for older students. These students may already know how to spell small words such as *fan* and *nap*, and this section helps them use those words to create longer words, such as *fantastic* and *napkin*.

4 **Adjust the speed for your student.**

With older learners, you will probably go much faster than you would with a younger child, but be prepared to slow down if you reach a concept that your student doesn't understand. Your goal is to achieve mastery. Anna Gillingham, co-founder of the Orton-Gillingham approach, put it this way: "Go as fast as you can, but as slow as you must."

5 **Use the activity sheets.**

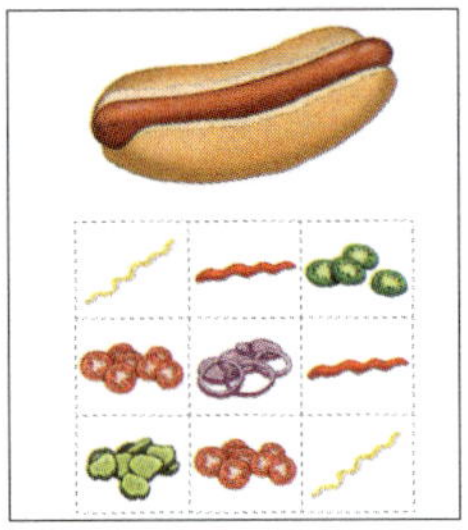

Although the activity sheets are optional, you may find that students of all ages enjoy the mental break that they provide.

Decide How Much Time to Spend on Spelling

All About Spelling lessons are designed so that you can work at your student's pace. Following are general guidelines.

Spend 20 minutes per day teaching spelling.

We recommend spending about 20 minutes per day, five days a week, on spelling instruction, but you can adjust this if necessary for younger students or for older remedial students.

It can be helpful to set a timer. When 20 minutes are up, mark the spot in the lesson where you stopped. When you begin teaching the next day, briefly review some of the daily review cards and then begin in the Teacher's Manual wherever you left off previously.

Short daily lessons are much more effective than longer, less frequent lessons. Your student's attention is less likely to wander, and you can accomplish more when your student is actively engaged in the lesson.

If you aren't done with the lesson when the 20 minutes are up, don't worry! This next tip is for you.

Lessons often take more than one day to complete.

Please know that the lessons in *All About Spelling* are **not** meant to be completed in one day.

In fact, some lessons may take a week or more to finish. A number of variables including your student's age, attention span, prior experience, the difficulty of the concept being taught, and the length of the lesson all play a part in how quickly a lesson can be completed.

Bring a Great Attitude!

Teaching your student can be a wonderful way to show him that he has great value in your eyes. You can view this as an opportunity to build him up and help him develop skill and character. Can you see yourself as a calm, uncritical coach with the worthy goal of helping this child fulfill his natural potential? Imagine the type of teacher *you* would want: friendly, supportive, with a you-can-do-it attitude. Smile. Point out what your student has done *right* more often than you point out his mistakes. Treat lesson time as a special time between the two of you.

Praise your student when he does well. We can get so used to correcting students that sometimes we overlook opportunities to let them know when they are doing something right. Listen to yourself to see if you need to fit in more expressions of approval. Here are some ideas to get you started:

"Wow, you catch on fast!"

"Excellent—you did so well!"

"Very good! You are a quick learner!"

"I love to work with you."

"Hey, you got that the first time!"

"You are doing great!"

"That was a tough one, and you got it!"

"Good for you!"

"You're getting it!"

"Awesome job!"

"You remembered that from yesterday—great!"

"I can tell that you tried hard to figure that out."

"Way to go!"

"Just last week you couldn't have done that!"

> *"Kind words can be short and easy to speak,*
> *but their echoes are truly endless."*
> –Mother Teresa

2

Complete Step-by-Step Lesson Plans

Hello there!
My name is Bumble and I'll BEE humming through the lessons with you, giving you pep talks and helping you study along the way.
So adjust your antennae and fluff up your fuzz, because it's time for us to
BUZZ OFF!

Lesson 1 Mastering the First 26 Phonograms

Objective

This lesson teaches the sounds of the first 26 phonograms.

You Will Need

- ☐ Phonogram Cards 1-26
- ☐ Progress Chart
- ☐ *Zip into Spelling* pages 7-19

Before You Begin

At the beginning of each lesson, you will find a cream-colored Before You Begin section like this one. Review these instructions before you begin the lesson.

The actual lesson plan you will teach to your student begins *after* the Before You Begin section.

Can You Skip This Lesson?

If your student already knows the sounds on Phonogram Cards 1-26 without hesitation, place the Phonogram Cards behind the **Mastered** divider in the Spelling Review Box and move on to Lesson 2. However, students who haven't completed *All About Reading* Level 1 may not know all the sounds of letters a to z and should not skip this important lesson.

Preview the Phonogram Cards

In this lesson, you'll figure out which phonograms your student knows and which still need to be taught. The quickest way to do this is with Phonogram Cards.

Let's take a look at the first Phonogram Card

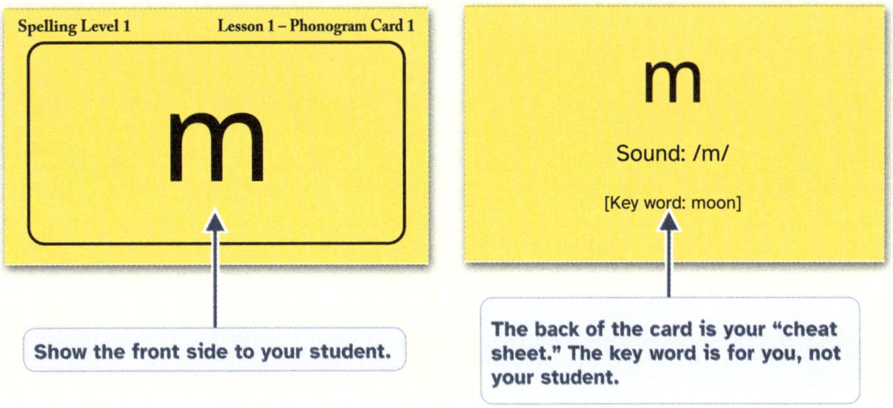
Spelling Level 1
Lesson 1 – Phonogram Card 1
m
m
Sound: /m/
[Key word: moon]
Show the front side to your student.
The back of the card is your "cheat sheet." The key word is for you, not your student.

Before You Begin
(continued)

How many phonograms should you teach in a day? For some students, especially younger ones, learning four new Phonogram Cards at a time will be enough. Other students, especially those who are good readers, will be able to learn many more in a day. You will have to judge the attention span and previous experience of your student and adjust the number of cards to teach in a session. You don't want to frustrate your student by trying to teach too many in a day, yet you don't want to hold her back by not teaching *enough*, either.

What order should the Phonogram Cards be taught in? It is best to teach the phonograms in numerical order, according to the Phonogram Card number shown in the upper right corner of the card. Some phonograms, like b and d, sound alike to the untrained ear and teaching them together could result in confusion. By teaching them in the numerical order shown on the cards, the following sets of phonograms are split up and taught in separate learning sessions:

b, d • a, e, i, o, u • p, b • m, n

How should you teach phonograms with multiple sounds? When a phonogram has more than one sound, we say the sounds in a particular order, starting with the most common sound. For example, for the letter s we say /s/–/z/ with only a slight pause in between. For a demonstration of how this is done, refer to the free Phonogram Sounds app, described on page 20, or the paid Letter Tiles app described on page 25 and in Appendix O.

How do you know when your student has mastered a Phonogram Card? Look for these three signs that a phonogram has been mastered:

- Your student says the pure, clipped sound(s) without adding /uh/ at the end (for example, she says /p/, not /puh/).
- Your student responds quickly and easily when you hold up the card.
- You have no doubt that your student knows the card thoroughly.

Using the Spelling Review Box

Throughout *All About Spelling*, you'll use the Spelling Review Box to keep track of what has been mastered and what still needs to be reviewed. If a card has been mastered, the lessons will prompt you to place it behind the **Mastered** divider. If the card has not yet been mastered, you will place it behind the **Review** divider so it can be reviewed again in the next learning session.

Now you are ready to teach the first lesson!

This lesson provides the foundation for all spelling lessons that follow, so take as many teaching sessions as your student needs to master it.

Evaluation

Set Your Timer

Remember that each teaching session should be short—no more than twenty minutes per day. If this is your student's first introduction to phonograms, it will take multiple sessions to complete Lesson 1.

This lesson is the foundation for all future spelling lessons. Spend as many days on this lesson as your student needs.

Determine Which Phonograms Need to Be Taught

Take out Phonogram Cards 1-26.

"Let's find out which of these cards you know and which of them we should work on. We will sort them into two piles: *cards you know* and *cards you need to learn*."

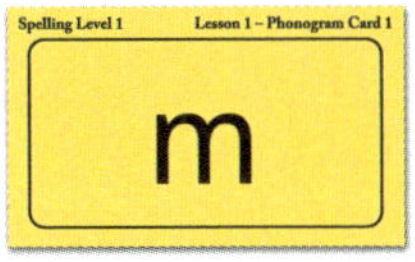

Show your student the front side of Phonogram Card 1.

"Most letters have one sound. For example, the letter m says /m/."

Return the card to the back of the deck. Your student does *not* write the phonogram.

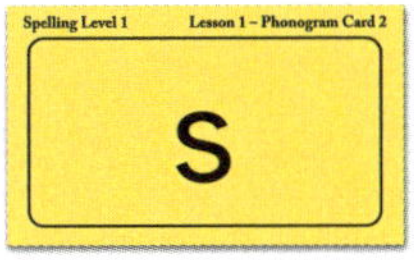

Show your student the front side of Phonogram Card 2.

"But some letters can say *more* than one sound, depending on the word it is found in. For example, the letter s can say /s/ or /z/, depending on the word."

"When I show you a letter that can say more than one sound, tell me all the sounds. For this card, you would say */s/–/z/*."

Go through all the Phonogram Cards with your student and sort them into two piles: **Need to Learn** and **Mastered**.

Evaluation
(continued)

When you get to Phonogram Card 25, you may need to give the following explanation to your student:

Tip!

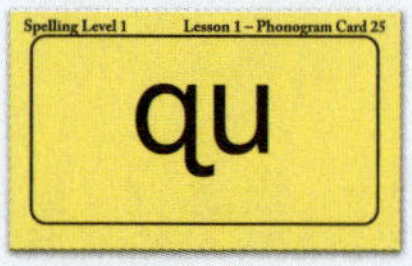

"You can see that there are two letters on this card. In English, q is always followed by a u. Together, they say the sound of /kw/. Repeat after me: /kw/."

The u does not act like a vowel in this phonogram.

Organize the Phonogram Cards in the Review Box

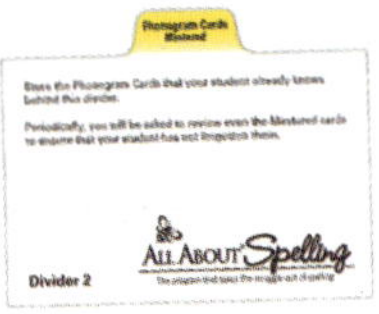

Now you have two piles of cards. Place the "Mastered" pile behind the divider labeled Mastered.

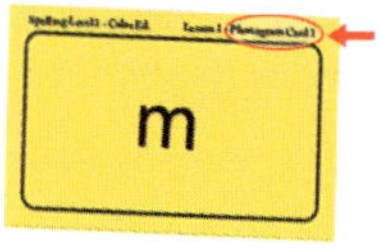

Next, arrange the cards in the "Need to Learn" pile in numerical order as indicated by the Phonogram Card number shown in the upper right corner of the card.

Place those cards behind the divider labeled Future Lessons.

New Teaching

Teach the Phonograms

Now that you have identified which phonograms your student needs to learn, **teach four phonograms at a time**. Be sure to teach them in numerical order and not in alphabetical order. Use the following procedure for each card.

1. Show the front of the Phonogram Card to your student.
2. Say the sound or sounds.
3. Have your student repeat the sound or sounds.

If a phonogram has several sounds, you can give your student a hint by holding up the appropriate number of fingers.

After several repetitions, see if your student can say the sound(s) without your prompting. The goal is that as you flip through the flashcards, your student will be able to say the phonograms without pausing to think.

New Teaching
(continued)

File the four Phonogram Cards that you are working on behind the **Phonogram Cards Review** divider in your student's Spelling Review Box. Review them at the beginning of each teaching session until each card is Mastered.

Keep Track of Which Phonogram Cards Have Been Mastered

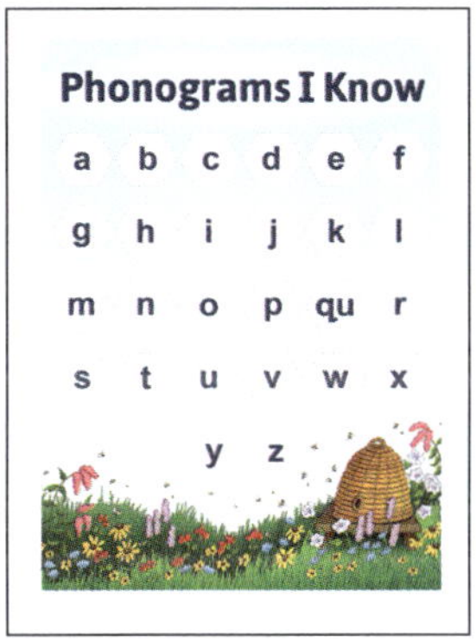

Remove the Phonograms I Know chart from page 7 of the *Zip into Spelling* activity book and post it in a prominent place. Have your student color in mastered phonograms with colored pencil.

Update the chart each time a Phonogram Card is moved to the Mastered pile.

Practice with Games and Activities *(Optional)*

If your student would benefit from additional practice with the phonogram sounds, choose from any of the following activities.

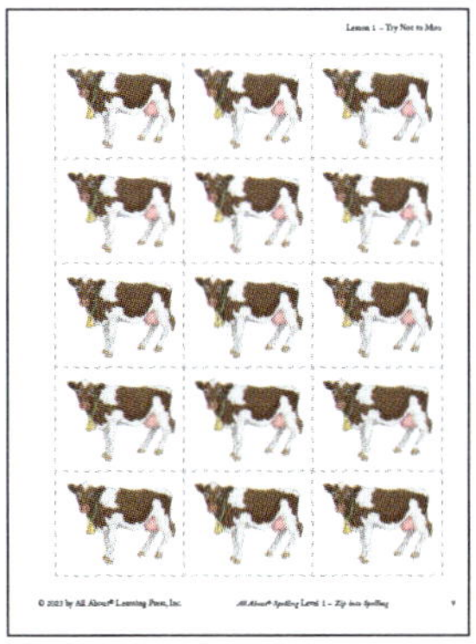

Try Not to Moo

Remove pages 9-12 from the activity book.

Cut out the cow cards, mix them up, and place them in a pile with the phonograms facing down.

Have your student select a card, turn it over, and look at the phonogram next to the cow's face. She should then say the sound(s) of that phonogram. If your student needs a hint, the number of sounds is represented by the number on the cow's bell. If your student draws a Moo card, she should moo like a cow instead of saying the phonogram sounds.

Continue until all the cards have been completed.

New Teaching
(continued)

Splash!

Remove pages 13-15 from the activity book.

Cut out the penguin cards and place them at the top of the iceberg. Select a Phonogram Card and show it to your student. Have your student say all the sounds the phonogram makes. If it makes one sound, your student can help one penguin slide down the iceberg into the pool of water. If the phonogram makes two sounds, your student can help two penguins slide down, and so on.

Continue until all the penguins have made it safely down the iceberg and into the pool.

Jungle Phonograms

Remove page 17 from the activity book.

Give your student something fun to use for markers, like popcorn, raisins, mini marshmallows, coins, or Bingo chips.

Place the appropriate number of markers in each square, referring to the number located in the lower right corner. For example, place eight markers in the first square (representing eight sounds), three in the next square (representing three sounds), and so on.

Have your student choose a square and say the sound(s) of each phonogram in that square. If she says the sounds correctly, she can keep the markers. Continue until all the markers have been collected.

You may wish to check your student's responses by listening to the sounds of the phonograms on the Letter Tiles app or referring to the phonograms chart in Appendix B.

New Teaching
(continued)

Climb the Mountain

Remove page 19 from the activity book.

Cut out the animal cards at the bottom of the page. Have your student choose her favorite animal (bobcat, wolf, mountain goat, or bear).

Show a Phonogram Card to your student and have her say the sound(s) of that phonogram. If she says the sound(s) correctly, the animal may advance up the mountain by one green space. If she says the sound(s) incorrectly, return the card to the pile to try again.

Continue until the animal has climbed the mountain and reached the top.

> For more activities for practicing the Phonogram Cards, see Appendix M.

Track Your Progress

Mark the Progress Chart

Once your student has a firm grasp on all the sounds of the first 26 phonograms, you can consider this lesson mastered and have your student mark Lesson 1 on the Progress Chart.

Well, flap my flip-flops!! Look at that ... you're already done with Lesson 1!
Now that you know all the phonograms, it won't be long before you can spell lots of important words ... you know, like BUMBLE and BEE.
So what are we waiting for? Let's zip off to Lesson 2!

Lesson 2 Identifying Initial and Final Sounds

Objective

This lesson teaches how to identify initial and final sounds in a word.

You Will Need

☐ *Zip into Spelling* pages 21-23

Before You Begin

Can You Skip This Lesson?

This lesson teaches how to identify the initial and final sounds in a spoken word. The exercises in the New Teaching section are phonemic awareness activities that are covered in the *All About Reading* Pre-reading program. If your student has completed the Pre-reading program, he is already familiar with this concept. If your student can easily answer the following questions, you can move on to Lesson 3.

- "What is the first sound in the word *van*?" *Student replies: /v/.*
- "What is the last sound in the word *stop*?" *Student replies: /p/.*

Look Ahead to the Review Section

Starting with this lesson, you'll find a Review section at the beginning of each lesson. Continual review is an essential part of learning to spell.

Preview Initial Sounds

In the first New Teaching activity, you will ask your student to repeat the first, or initial, sound in a word. You are not asking for the name of the first letter; you are asking for the first *sound*. For example, the first sound in the word *map* is /m/. Your student, therefore, should respond by saying /m/, not the letter m.

When you say the word, elongate the first sound if possible, as in *fff-ish*. This will make it easier for your student to identify the first sound. The sounds of the following letters—called *continuant sounds*—are easy to hold: f, l, m, n, r, s, v, z, and the vowels.

Some sounds—called *stop sounds*—cannot be held. They include the consonants c, b, d, g, j, k, p, and t. To help your student hear the first sound in words that start with stop sounds, repeat the first sound several times, as in *b-b-bear*.

Before You Begin
(continued)

Preview Final Sounds

The second New Teaching activity focuses on the final sound in a word. As with the initial sound, your student should say the sound and not the name of the letter. For example, the last sound in the word *sap* is /p/. Your student should respond by saying /p/, not the letter p.

Review

Review Phonogram Cards

Phonogram Cards

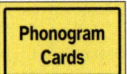

Spend several minutes reviewing the Phonogram Cards to keep them fresh in your student's mind. You can either flip through the flashcards as shown in Appendix D or choose one of the activities from Appendix M.

> You may wish to bookmark the two appendices mentioned above for easy future reference.
>
> **Tip!**

New Teaching

Repeat the First Sound in a Word

Turn toward your student so he can see your mouth as you speak.

"The first sound we hear in the word *floor* is /f/. What is the first sound you hear in the word *sun*?" */s/.*

"What is the first sound you hear in the word *ball*?" */b/.*

Repeat this activity with the words below.

Easier words (with continuant sounds): **map lid zip foot nice**

Harder words (with stop sounds): **pan top cat banana garden**

> If your student needs extra help, try these strategies:
>
> **Tip!**
>
> - Hold or repeat the first sound of the word.
> - Have your student watch your mouth.
> - Have your student say the word s-l-o-w-l-y and then go back and repeat the first sound he said.

New Teaching
(continued)

Complete Activity Sheet *(Optional)*

"Let's explore some animals!"

Explore the Animals

Remove page 21 from the *Zip into Spelling* activity book.

Cut out the animal cards and identify each animal with your student. (The animal names are on the back of the cards for your reference. The student is not expected to read the animal names.)

Place the cards in a pile with the animals facing up.

Have your student select a card, say the name of the animal, and then repeat the first sound in the word. If he gets it right, he can keep the card. If not, he should return the card to the bottom of the pile for another try.

Remember that your student should say the first *sound* he hears, not the name of the letter.

Continue until all the animal cards have been collected.

Answer Key

baboon:	/b/	dolphin:	/d/	octopus:	/ŏ/
lion:	/l/	snake:	/s/	goat:	/g/
rhinoceros:	/r/	tiger:	/t/	elephant:	/ĕ/
giraffe:	/j/	hippopotamus:	/h/	zebra:	/z/

If you feel your student needs additional practice, repeat this activity in your next session. For variety, you can point to objects in the room, such as *table* and *window,* and have your student identify the first sound in the word. Illustrations in magazines or books can also be used.

Once identifying the first sound in a word becomes easy for your student, continue on to the next activity.

New Teaching
(continued)

Repeat the Last Sound in a Word

"Now you are going to say the *last* sound in a word. The last sound in the word *jam* is /m/. What is the last sound you hear in the word *glass*?" */s/.*

Repeat this activity with the words below.

Easier words (with continuant sounds): **bell fuzz dragonfly car candle**

Harder words (with stop sounds): **sap bed rag start mound**

Complete Activity Sheet *(Optional)*

"Now let's explore some delicious foods."

Explore the Foods

Remove page 23 from the activity book.

Cut out the food cards and place them in a pile on the table. Have your student select a card, say the name of the food, and then repeat the last sound in the word. If he gets it right, he can keep the card. If not, he should return the card to the bottom of the pile for another try.

Continue until all the food cards have been collected.

Answer Key

pepper:	/r/	peanuts:	/s/	pineapple:	/l/
avocado:	/ō/	fig:	/g/	beet:	/t/
yam:	/m/	orange:	/j/	banana:	/ah/
coffee:	/ē/	garlic:	/k/	watermelon:	/n/

For additional practice, go for a walk and have your student identify the last sound in various objects.

Track Your Progress

Mark the Progress Chart

After identifying the first and last sounds in spoken words has been mastered, have your student mark Lesson 2 on the Progress Chart.

Lesson 3 Segmenting Words

Objective

This lesson teaches how to segment words containing up to three sounds.

You Will Need

- ☐ *Zip into Spelling* pages 25-31
- ☐ three tokens*

Before You Begin

Can You Skip This Lesson?

The New Teaching portion of this lesson helps students master segmenting. If your student has completed the Pre-reading program, she is already familiar with this concept. If your student can easily answer the following questions, you can move on to Lesson 4.

- "Break up the word *leg* into three sounds." *Student replies: /l/–/ĕ/–/g/.*
- "Break up the word *mop* into three sounds." *Student replies: /m/–/ŏ/–/p/.*

Preview Segmenting

Segmenting is the ability to hear the individual sounds in words. It is a crucial skill that improves phonological awareness and long-term spelling ability.

Think of segmenting as the opposite of blending. When we speak, we blend sounds together very quickly to form words. In segmenting, we take the individual sounds apart and say each one separately. For example, there are three separate sounds in the word *ham*: /h/–/ă/–/m/. In this lesson, your student will learn how to hear the sounds in short words so that later she can represent each sound with a written phonogram. A student who can segment words into their basic sounds can spell much more easily. In later lessons, your student will move from segmenting with tokens to segmenting with letter tiles.

Throughout this lesson, your student will be segmenting the words orally; **she will not be writing the words.** If this is your student's first exposure to segmenting, spend as much time as your student needs in order to master this important concept.

*Tokens for segmenting are included in the Letter Tiles kit. If you are using the Letter Tiles app, you can create tokens by following the instructions in this lesson.

Review

Review Phonogram Cards

Phonogram Cards

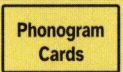

Spend several minutes reviewing the Phonogram Cards to keep them fresh in your student's mind. You can either flip through the flashcards as shown in Appendix D or choose one of the activities from Appendix M.

New Teaching

Segment Words with Two Sounds

"Let's break some words apart."

Breaking Words Apart: Two Sounds
Remove pages 25-27 from the *Zip into Spelling* activity book.

Cut apart the segmenting cards. Place the tie card in front of your student to demonstrate the activity.

"This is a tie. Say *tie*." *Tie.*

"Watch as I break up the word *tie*." Working from left to right, touch a circle for each sound as you say it: "/t/–/ī/. Tie."

Place the hoe card in front of your student. "Now it's your turn. This is a hoe. Say *hoe*." *Student repeats the word.*

"Segment the word *hoe*." *Student touches a circle as she says each sound: /h/–/ō/.*

Repeat for the remaining cards. Name each item so your student doesn't have to guess what it is.

Answer Key

1. tie: /t/–/ī/	6. bee: /b/–/ē/
2. hoe: /h/–/ō/	7. knee: /n/–/ē/
3. tea: /t/–/ē/	8. pie: /p/–/ī/
4. key: /k/–/ē/	9. eat: /ē/–/t/
5. hay: /h/–/ā/	10. pea: /p/–/ē/

New Teaching
(continued)

> Once your student can easily segment words with two sounds, move on to the next activity. **Tip!**

Segment Words with Three Sounds

"Let's break some more words apart."

Breaking Words Apart: Three Sounds
Remove pages 29-31 from the activity book.

Cut apart the segmenting cards. Place the pig card in front of your student to demonstrate the activity.

"This is a pig. Say *pig*." *Pig.*

"Watch as I break up the word *pig*." Working from left to right, touch a circle for each sound as you say it: "/p/–/ĭ/–/g/. Pig."

Have your student repeat the exercise with the remaining cards. Name each item so your student doesn't have to guess what it is.

Answer Key

1. pig: /p/–/ĭ/–/g/
2. bed: /b/–/ĕ/–/d/
3. bus: /b/–/ŭ/–/s/
4. rat: /r/–/ă/–/t/
5. sun: /s/–/ŭ/–/n/
6. mop: /m/–/ŏ/–/p/
7. bat: /b/–/ă/–/t/
8. leg: /l/–/ĕ/–/g/
9. fan: /f/–/ă/–/n/
10. map: /m/–/ă/–/p/

Segment Words with Tokens or the App

If your student would benefit from additional hands-on segmenting activities, you can use either the colored tokens or the Letter Tiles app.

New Teaching
(continued)

Tokens: Lay three colored tokens on the table. Give your student a word that has three sounds, such as *mud.* The student should repeat the word and then say the individual sounds. As she says each sound, she pulls a token toward herself as indicated below.

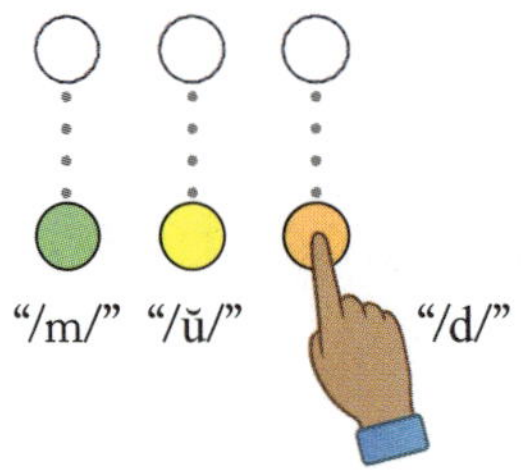

Letter Tiles App: Select *All About Spelling* Level 1, Lesson 3. Create "tokens" by tapping the work area on the screen to create gray squares. Give your student a word that has three sounds. The student should repeat the word and then say the individual sounds. As she says each sound, she pulls a square down.

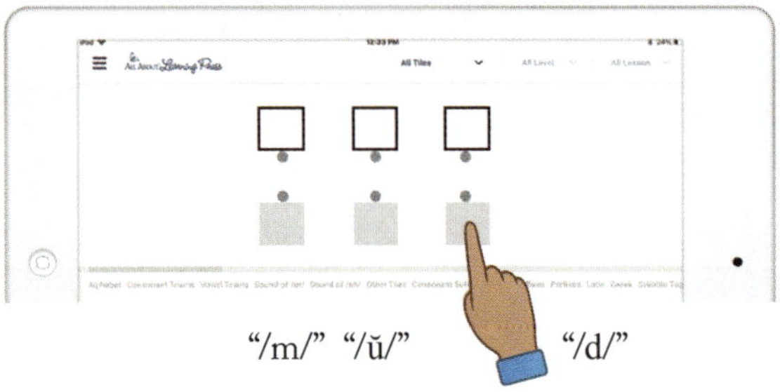

Whichever method you choose, practice with a selection of the following words.

lip	**mat**	**win**	**jam**	**get**	**zip**	**gum**
bug	**log**	**leg**	**nod**	**men**	**rib**	**yes**

Track Your Progress

Mark the Progress Chart

After segmenting words with three sounds has been mastered, have your student mark Lesson 3 on the Progress Chart.

Lesson 4 Working with Letter Tiles

Objective

This lesson introduces the letter tiles, teaches how to alphabetize them, and teaches how to identify vowels and consonants.

You Will Need

- ☐ three tokens
- ☐ letter tiles a to z, including red y and blue y
- ☐ Rule Card 1
- ☐ *Zip into Spelling* pages 33-39

Before You Begin

Can You Skip This Lesson?

If your student has used the *All About Reading* program, he can probably already identify vowels and consonants, and it is possible that he already knows how to alphabetize. To test, ask your student these questions:

- "What are the names of the vowels?" *Student replies: a, e, i, o, u, and sometimes y.*
- "Can you name a few consonants?" *Student replies with consonants such as b, c, d.*
- "Can you put these letters in alphabetical order?" *Using either the Letter Tiles app or the physical letter tiles, your student places the tiles in alphabetical order.*

If these concepts have already been mastered, place Rule Card 1 behind the appropriate Mastered divider in the Spelling Review Box and move on to Lesson 5.

Preview the Letter Tiles

Whether you're using the Letter Tiles app or physical tiles, letter tiles help you explain spelling concepts very clearly so your student can quickly and easily grasp them. Letter tiles also make spelling rules and abstract ideas more concrete in your student's mind because he is able to actually see and manipulate them.

It is important for your student to use his dominant hand when working with letter tiles.

In this lesson, your student will learn that the red letter tiles are vowels and the blue letter tiles are consonants.

Before You Begin
(continued)

Preview Alphabetizing

Your student will also learn how to alphabetize the letter tiles. Learning alphabetical order will make it easier to work with the letter tiles and locate letters quickly.

Alphabetizing is an essential literacy skill used in many areas of our lives, such as:

- looking up a friend's phone number in your contact list
- locating a store using a mall directory
- finding your favorite song on a playlist
- locating a book on a library shelf.

There are four stages of alphabetizing:

1. putting letters in order
2. alphabetizing to the first letter
3. alphabetizing to the second and third letters
4. advanced rules

In this lesson, your student will be working on the first stage of alphabetizing.

Preview The Vowels Rule

The Vowels Rule
grass
leg
kick
hop
up
happy
Every word has at least one vowel.
The vowels are A, E, I, O, U, and sometimes Y.

Remove the Vowels Rule poster from page 33 of the activity book and keep it handy for use in the lesson.

This rule explains that the vowels are <u>a</u>, <u>e</u>, <u>i</u>, <u>o</u>, <u>u</u>, and sometimes <u>y</u>, and that every word has at least one vowel.

For a list of all the spelling rules taught in Level 1, see Appendix C.

Before You Begin
(continued)

Preview the Rule Cards

The Rule Cards contain rules and generalizations about spelling and are used to **reinforce new concepts**. After a new concept is introduced in the lesson, you read the Rule Card with your student.

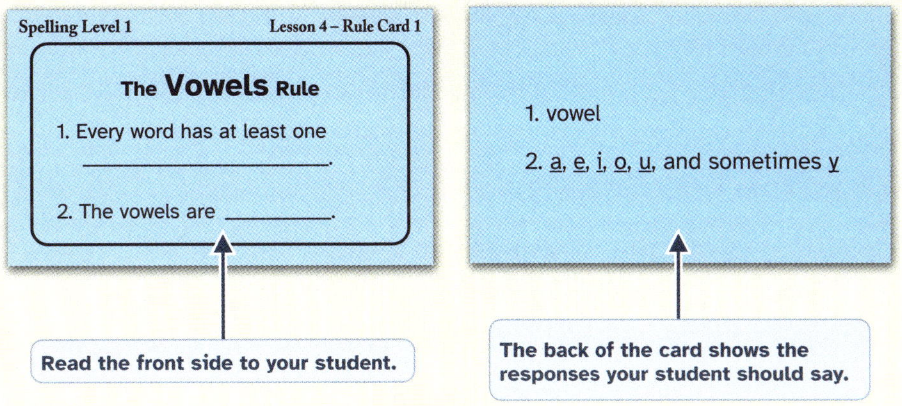
Spelling Level 1
Lesson 4 – Rule Card 1
The Vowels Rule
1. Every word has at least one ______.
2. The vowels are ______.
1. vowel
2. a, e, i, o, u, and sometimes y
Read the front side to your student.
The back of the card shows the responses your student should say.

Rule Cards are then placed behind the appropriate Review divider in the Spelling Review Box. You will be prompted to review them in subsequent lessons.

Review

Review Phonogram Cards

Phonogram Cards

Spend several minutes reviewing the Phonogram Cards to keep them fresh in your student's mind. You can either flip through the flashcards as shown in Appendix D or choose one of the activities from Appendix M.

Review Segmenting

Set out three tokens or create them in the Letter Tiles app. Have your student segment the following words aloud, pulling down a token for each sound.

ten **pan** **hot** **gum** **sit**

New Teaching

Introduce the Letter Tiles

Open the Letter Tiles app or set out letter tiles a to z. Move the b tile into the workspace.

"These letter tiles contain the same letters as the flashcards. Can you tell me the sound that this tile makes?" */b/.*

Move several more tiles into the workspace and ask your student to identify the sounds.

Teach Spelling Rule 1: The Vowels Rule

"The red tiles are vowels. The vowels are a, e, i, o, u, and sometimes y."

"The blue tiles are consonants. Can you name some of the consonants?" *Student names several consonants.*

Move the blue y and red y tiles into the workspace.

"The letter y is special. Sometimes it is a vowel and sometimes it is a consonant. When it says /y/, it is a consonant. When it says /ĭ/, /ī/, or /ē/, it is a vowel."

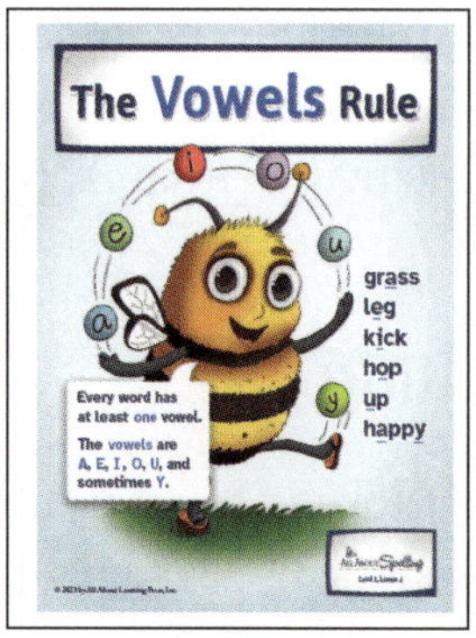
The Vowels Rule
grass
leg
kick
hop
up
happy
Every word has at least one vowel.
The vowels are A, E, I, O, U, and sometimes Y.

Take out the Vowels Rule poster and explore it with your student.

Point to the example words. "Every word has at least one vowel. Can you find the vowels in each of these words?"

You may wish to hang the poster in your lesson area for future reference.

New Teaching
(continued)

Take out Rule Card 1 and read it with your student.

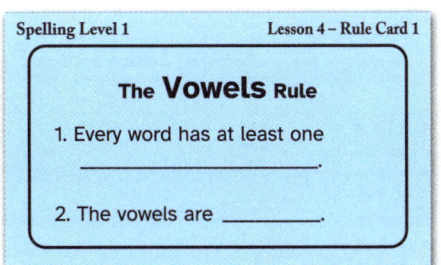

Spelling Level 1 | **Lesson 4 – Rule Card 1**

The Vowels Rule

1. Every word has at least one ____________.

2. The vowels are ________.

1. vowel

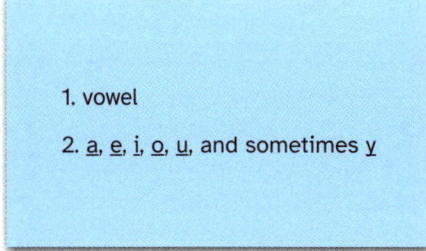

2. a, e, i, o, u, and sometimes y

File Rule Card 1 behind the **Rule Cards Review** divider in your student's Spelling Review Box. Review it at the beginning of each teaching session.

After your student has mastered the Rule Card, you will move it behind the **Rule Cards Mastered** divider.

Complete Activity Sheets *(Optional)*

"Let's help the jugglers pack their trunks for the show!"

Pack the Trunks

Remove pages 35-38 from the *Zip into Spelling* activity book.

Cut slits in the trunks as indicated by the dotted lines. Cut out the equipment cards and place them in a pile with the letters facing down.

"Romi wants to pack all the vowels in his red trunk, and Samuel wants to pack all the consonants in his blue trunk." Have your student select a card, determine whether it's a vowel or a consonant, and place the card in the appropriate trunk. For the letter y, your student may choose to put it either with the consonants or with the vowels.

Continue until all the cards have been sorted and the trunks are packed.

New Teaching
(continued)

"Now let's help this juggler catch his pins."

Catch the Pins

Turn to page 39 in the activity book.

Have your student use a red pencil or crayon to color the squares that contain vowels.

Continue until all the vowels have been colored red and your student has helped the juggler catch the pins.

Answer Key

Teach How to Alphabetize the Letter Tiles

You can use either the physical letter tiles or the Letter Tiles app for this activity.

Physical Letter Tiles: Lay out letter tiles a to z in random order. Use the blue y tile for this activity. Demonstrate how to alphabetize the letter tiles and then have your student do it. He may sing the alphabet song if necessary.

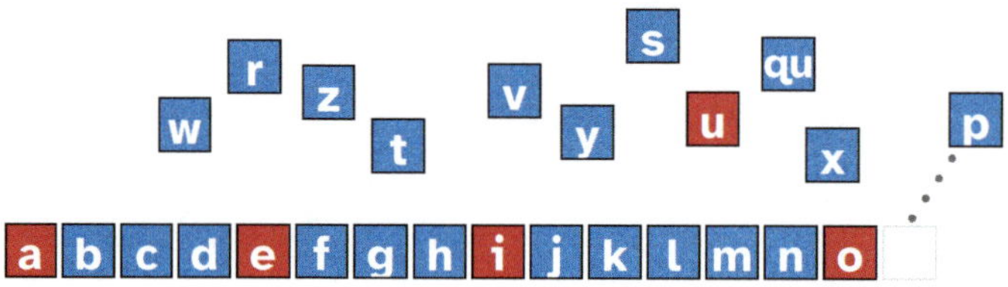

"a - b - c - d - e - f - g - h - i - j - k - l - m - n - o - p -"

New Teaching
(continued)

Letter Tiles App: From the drop-down menus, select Alphabetize and All Letters.

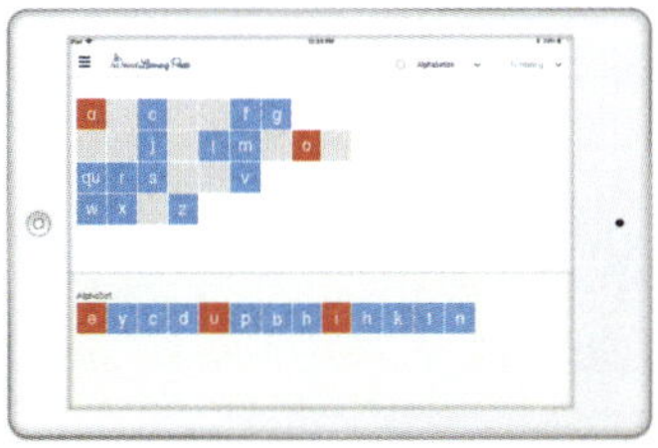

The letters of the alphabet will appear in random order and your student will be prompted to alphabetize them. He may sing the alphabet song if necessary.

Track Your Progress

Mark the Progress Chart

After recognizing vowels and consonants and alphabetizing have been mastered, have your student mark Lesson 4 on the Progress Chart.

Hi, again!
You've been a busy bee ...
learning to alphabetize, to recognize
first and last sounds, and even how to
segment words.
Hey, you know what else is segmented? ME!
That's right—I'm an insect, so my buzzy
body is made up of segments,
just like words.
We have so much
in common!

Lesson 5 Writing Phonograms from Dictation

Objective

This lesson introduces the Sound Cards and teaches how to write the phonograms from dictation.

You Will Need

- ☐ three tokens
- ☐ Sound Cards 1-26
- ☐ *Zip into Spelling* pages 41-42
- ☐ dictation notebook

Before You Begin

Can You Skip This Lesson?

Probably not! Unlike the first four lessons, which contained concepts that are covered in the *All About Reading* program, this lesson is very specific to spelling. Completing this lesson will ensure that your student is confident in writing the phonograms.

If you are certain that your student already knows how to write phonograms from dictation, turn to page 66 and complete the activity Write Phonograms from Dictation for a quick review before moving to Lesson 6.

Preview the Sound Cards

This lesson introduces the first 26 Sound Cards. You'll dictate the sound(s) listed on the flashcard and your student will write the phonogram that makes the sound(s).

Let's take a look at the first Sound Card.

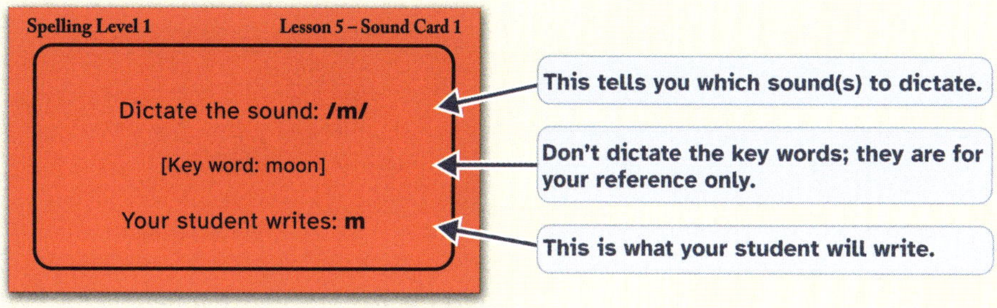
Spelling Level 1
Lesson 5 – Sound Card 1
Dictate the sound: /m/
[Key word: moon]
Your student writes: m
This tells you which sound(s) to dictate.
Don't dictate the key words; they are for your reference only.
This is what your student will write.

When you dictate phonograms that have more than one sound, such as the letter s, say the sounds in succession with only a slight pause between them, as demonstrated on the Letter Tiles app or the Phonogram Sounds app.

Before You Begin
(continued)

Your student will repeat the sounds as she writes the phonogram. This engages the three main pathways to the brain simultaneously:

- sight (seeing the phonogram)
- sound (hearing the phonogram)
- touch (feeling the process of forming the letters and feeling the vocal cords as the sound is repeated)

In conjunction with *All About Spelling*, you may use whichever handwriting program you like best.

If you notice that your student reverses letters while writing—particularly similar letter pairs like b and d or p and q—see Appendix F for more information about how to handle letter reversals.

Preview Dictation

Starting in this lesson, your student will be writing phonograms from dictation. In subsequent lessons, she will also write words, phrases, and sentences from dictation.

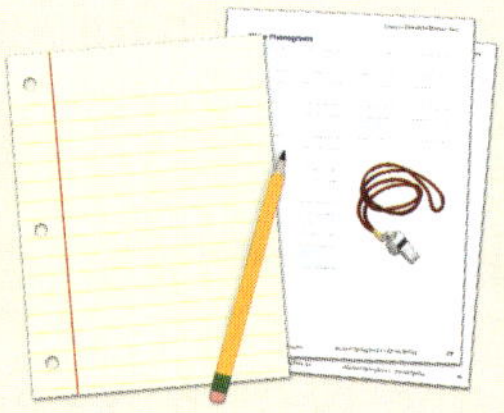

Your student may use a regular-lined notebook or loose-leaf paper for the dictation activities, or you may prefer to download the free printable dictation sheets for each lesson. See page 11 for information on where to obtain the dictation sheets.

For tips on dictation, see Appendix L: Procedure and Troubleshooting for Spelling Dictation.

Review

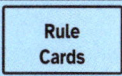

Review a selection of Phonogram Cards from behind the Mastered divider in your student's Spelling Review Box.

Review the Rule Card from behind the Mastered divider.

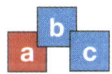

Set out three tokens or create them in the Letter Tiles app. Have your student segment the following words aloud, pulling down a token for each sound.

job **tan** **mug** **pin** **rat**

Have your student alphabetize using either the Letter Tiles app or the physical letter tiles.

New Teaching

Introduce the Sound Cards

Take out Sound Cards 1-26 and the Letter Tiles app or physical letter tiles.

Move letter tiles **m**, **s**, **p**, and **a** into the workspace.

"Which letter says /m/?" *Student points to the* **m**.

"Good! Now I'll dictate more sounds and you will point to the correct letter tile."

Dictate Sound Card 2: "/s/–/z/." *Student points to the* **s**.

Dictate Sound Card 3: "/p/." *Student points to the* **p**.

Dictate Sound Card 4: "/ă/–/ā/–/ah/." *Student points to the* **a**.

Continue with Sound Cards 5-26 and the corresponding letter tiles, working with four to six Sound Cards at a time. Take as many days as you need to complete this lesson, practicing until your student can easily match the correct letter tile with the sound(s).

New Teaching
(continued)

Write Phonograms from Dictation

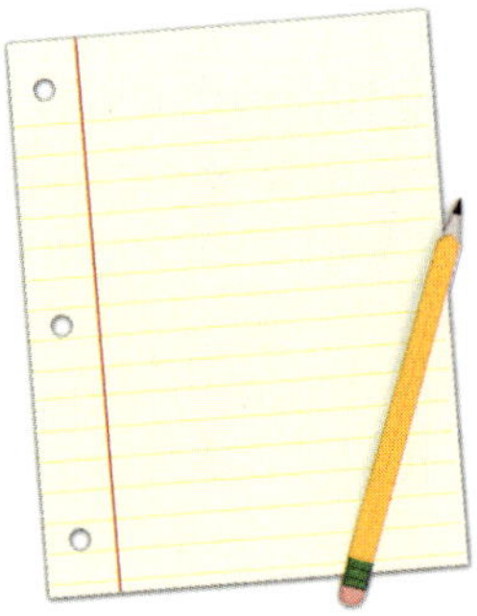

"Take out your dictation notebook."

"I am going to dictate a sound and you will write the letter that makes that sound. As you write the letter, repeat the sound."

Dictate Sound Card 1: "/m/." *Student writes m on the first line as she says /m/.*

Dictate Sound Card 2: "/s/–/z/." *Student writes s on the second line as she says /s/–/z/.*

If a phonogram has more than one sound, dictate all the sounds that appear on the Sound Card, adding a slight pause between sounds.

Continue with the remaining Sound Cards. With younger students you may choose to practice only a few per day, while with older students you may be able to go through the stack several times.

Practice over as many days as necessary until your student can easily write down the dictated phonograms.

During the days you are working on this lesson, file Sound Cards 1-26 behind the **Sound Cards Review** divider in your student's Spelling Review Box. Review them daily at the start of each session.

Once your student is able to write a phonogram from dictation without hesitation, you can consider that card mastered. At that point, you will move the mastered Sound Card behind the **Sound Cards Mastered** divider.

New Teaching
(continued)

Complete Activity Sheet *(Optional)*

"Now let's shoot some hoops!"

Slam Dunk

Remove pages 41-42 from the *Zip into Spelling* activity book.

Cut out the basketball cards and the basketball hoop. Create the basketball hoop by taping the ends together as indicated.

Choose eight Sound Cards that you would like your student to practice. For each phonogram you dictate, your student should repeat the sound(s) and write the phonogram on the back of a basketball card.

Once your student has written the phonogram correctly, have her crumple the basketball card and toss it into the basketball hoop.

Continue until your student has written all eight phonograms and all the basketballs have gone through the hoop.

Twenty-four additional basketballs are included on pages 43-46. You can use these for later practice sessions.

Track Your Progress

Mark the Progress Chart

If your student still has a lot of Sound Cards to master, spend more days on this lesson.

However, if she has just a few left to master, you can file them behind the Review divider and continue to practice them daily as you move on to the next lesson.

Have your student mark Lesson 5 on the Progress Chart.

Zzzzzz ...
Oh, sorry! Guess I dozed off on that last phonogram. Zzzzzzz is such a soothing sound, isn't it?
But now I'm awake and ready to zip into some vowels. Whee!

Lesson 6 Choosing the Correct Vowel

Objective

This lesson teaches the short vowel sounds and how to choose the correct vowel.

You Will Need

- ☐ three tokens
- ☐ Rule Card 2
- ☐ Phonogram Cards 4, 16, 20, 23, 24
- ☐ *Zip into Spelling* pages 47-49

Before You Begin

Can You Skip This Lesson?

If your student has used the *All About Reading* program, he can probably identify the short vowel sounds. To test, dictate the following short vowels and have your student write the corresponding letter.

/ĕ/ /ă/ /ŭ/ /ĭ/ /ŏ/

If your student already knows how to write the short vowel sounds from dictation, turn to page 74 and complete the Vowel Hunt activity for a quick review. Place Rule Card 2 behind the appropriate Mastered divider in the Spelling Review Box and move on to Lesson 7.

Preview the Short Vowel Sounds

In this lesson we will concentrate on the short vowel sounds. As you know, each vowel has more than one sound. Your student will learn that the **first sound** of each vowel is called its **short sound**.

a The first sound of a is /ă/ as in *apple*.

e The first sound of e is /ĕ/ as in *echo*.

i The first sound of i is /ĭ/ as in *itchy*.

o The first sound of o is /ŏ/ as in *otter*.

u The first sound of u is /ŭ/ as in *udder*.

We are concentrating on the short sounds because they are the most frequently used of the vowel sounds. It is important that your student be able to choose the correct vowel when he hears it in a word.

Before You Begin (continued)

Preview The Short Vowel Rule

Remove the Short Vowel Rule poster from page 47 of the activity book and keep it handy for use in the lesson.

This rule explains that when a single vowel is followed by a consonant, it usually says its short sound. Read the following examples and listen for the short vowel sounds.

ant pet grin moss hug

The short vowel can be at the beginning or middle of a word, and it can be followed by one or more consonants. This concept also applies to syllables in multisyllable words, as in *pumpkin* (*pump–kin*) and *helmet* (*hel–met*).

Note that the Short Vowel Rule applies to single vowels only; it does not apply to multi-letter phonograms like ai and oo.

> In Level 2, your student will learn the Find Gold Rule, which explains that i and o followed by two consonants may say their long sounds, as in *told* and *grind*.

Review

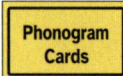

Phonogram Cards — Review a selection of Phonogram Cards from behind the Mastered or Review divider in your student's Spelling Review Box.

Sound Cards — Review a selection of Sound Cards from behind the Mastered or Review divider. Have your student write the phonograms in his dictation notebook.

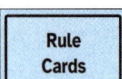

Rule Cards — Review the Rule Card from behind the Review divider.

Review
(continued)

Set out three tokens or create them in the Letter Tiles app. Have your student segment the following words aloud, pulling down a token for each sound.

ham **zip** **rob** **tug** **bed**

Alphabetize letter tiles a to z with your student.

New Teaching

Introduce Short Vowel Sounds

Take out Phonogram Cards 4, 16, 20, 23, and 24. These are the cards for the vowels.

Hold up Phonogram Card 4.

"What sounds does this letter make?" */ă/–/ā/–/ah/.*

"Good. The first sound you said, /ă/, is called the **short sound of a**."

Hold up Phonogram Card 24.

"What sounds does this letter make?" */ĕ/–/ē/.*

"Good. The first sound you said, /ĕ/, is called the **short sound of e**."

Repeat this activity with Phonogram Cards 16, 20, and 23 to demonstrate that the first sound of each vowel is the short sound.

Practice Short Vowels

Move letter tiles **a**, **e**, **i**, **o**, and **u** into the workspace.

"I am going to dictate a vowel sound and you will point to the vowel that makes that sound. Usually I dictate all the sounds the vowel makes, but today I am only going to say the short vowel sound."

> The key word in brackets is for your reference only. Do not dictate the key word.

New Teaching
(continued)

"/ă/." [as in *apple*] *Student points to the* a.

"/ĕ/." [as in *echo*] *Student points to the* e.

"/ĭ/." [as in *itchy*] *Student points to the* i.

"/ŏ/." [as in *otter*] *Student points to the* o.

"/ŭ/." [as in *udder*] *Student points to the* u.

Practice until your student can easily match up the correct tile with the sound.

Once your student is able to select the correct vowel tile, dictate the following sounds and have your student write the corresponding vowel in his dictation notebook.

/ĕ/ /ă/ /ŭ/ /ĭ/ /ŏ/

Teach Spelling Rule 2: The Short Vowel Rule

"As you know, vowels can make different sounds. The sound a vowel makes depends on where it is in the word."

Build the word b a t.

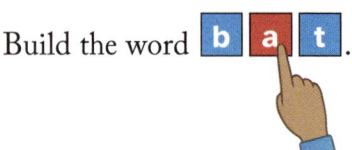

"When a single vowel is followed by a consonant, it usually says its short sound. What sound does a say in *bat*?" */ă/.*

"Good. A is followed by a consonant, so it says its short sound."

Build the word s i t.

"Point to the single vowel." *Student points to the i.*

"Is the vowel followed by a consonant?" *Yes.*

"What sound does i say in *sit*?" */ĭ/, or its short sound.*

New Teaching
(continued)

Take out the Short Vowel Rule poster and explore it with your student.

Read the sample words and point out the following details:

- In each word, the single vowel is followed by a consonant. The vowel is short in each word.
- A short vowel can be followed by more than one consonant, as in *bell* and *socks*.
- A short vowel can be at the beginning of the word, as in *and*.

You may wish to hang the poster in your lesson area for future reference.

> If your student is curious, you can show that vowels make their long sound when they are at the end of a word or syllable, as in *be*, *no*, and *hi*. This pattern will be taught in Lesson 24.

Take out Rule Card 2 and read it with your student.

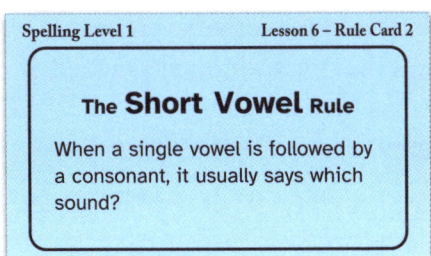

Spelling Level 1 — Lesson 6 – Rule Card 2

The Short Vowel Rule

When a single vowel is followed by a consonant, it usually says which sound?

short sound

New Teaching
(continued)

Complete Activity Sheet *(Optional)*

"Uh-oh! These words are missing their vowels. You need to put these vowels in the words where they belong!"

Vowel Hunt

Remove page 49 from the *Zip into Spelling* activity book.

Cut out the vowel tiles at the bottom of the page and distribute them on the table in front of your student.

Point to the illustration of the lid on the activity sheet.

"This is supposed to say *lid*. Find the vowel that completes this word." *Student looks around the table until he finds an i and places it in the blank to correctly spell the word.*

Continue with each item pictured. Your student should then read each word, pronouncing the vowel sound slowly and distinctly.

A second Vowel Hunt activity is provided on page 51 of the activity book. You can save this for additional practice, if necessary.

Answer Key

Vowel Hunt #1		
lid	mud	web
ham	bag	zip
mop	fan	pot

Vowel Hunt #2		
cat	tub	bed
pop	bug	rug
map	lip	pan

New Teaching
(continued)

Exchange Vowels to Make New Words

Build the word **h** **i** **t**.

"I can change *hit* to *hot* like this."

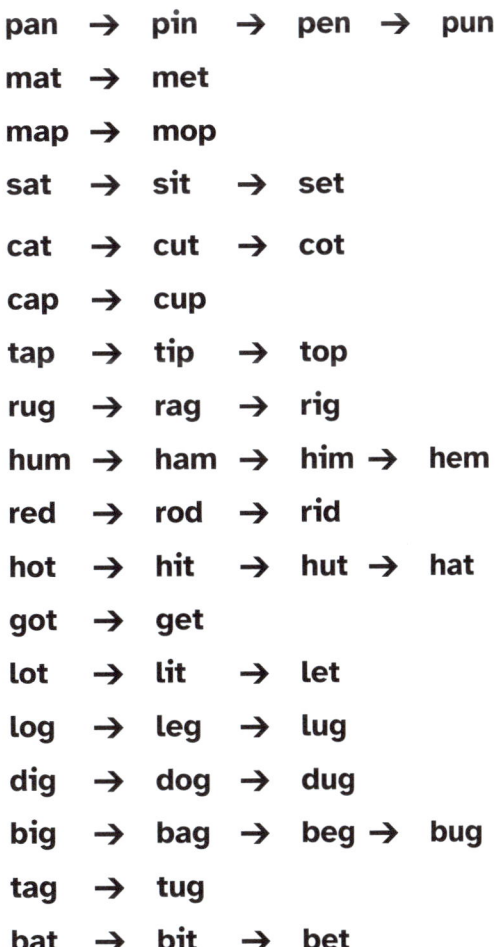

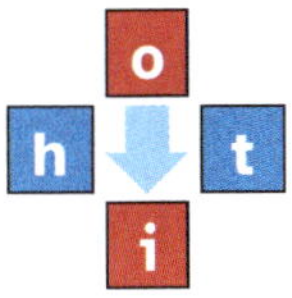

Build the word **r** **u** **n**.

"Now it's your turn. Change the word *run* to *ran* by switching one of the tiles." *Student exchanges the u tile for an a tile.*

If your student needs more practice with this concept, use the following sets of words. Build the first word in each set and have your student change the vowel to spell the word you specify.

pan → pin → pen → pun
mat → met
map → mop
sat → sit → set
cat → cut → cot
cap → cup
tap → tip → top
rug → rag → rig
hum → ham → him → hem
red → rod → rid
hot → hit → hut → hat
got → get
lot → lit → let
log → leg → lug
dig → dog → dug
big → bag → beg → bug
tag → tug
bat → bit → bet

Track Your Progress

Mark the Progress Chart

After choosing the correct vowel has been mastered, have your student mark Lesson 6 on the Progress Chart.

Lesson 7 Short A

Objective

This lesson teaches how to segment words using letter tiles and how to spell words with short a.

You Will Need

- ☐ three tokens
- ☐ Word Cards 1-10
- ☐ *Zip into Spelling* pages 53-58

Before You Begin

Preview the Word Cards

Starting today, each lesson includes ten Word Cards. You'll dictate the word and your student will segment and write the word.

Take a look at Word Card 5. See the sentence under the word *an*? This is to distinguish it from the word *Ann*. You can read the sentence aloud for clarity, but **don't have your student write the sentence**. Your student will only write the word *an*. Sentences are added to all cards containing homophones (words that sound alike but are spelled differently).

At the end of the lesson, you'll be prompted to file the Word Cards behind the appropriate Review divider until they are mastered.

Preview the Practice More Words Section

Starting with this lesson, all lessons contain a **Practice More Words section.** This section dramatically expands the number of words your student learns. Instead of knowing just the ten words on the spelling list, she knows many more because she is learning the concepts behind spelling.

Many lessons also contain a **Word Search section**, which includes even more words to expand your student's spelling list.

The Practice More Words and Word Search sections can be used in two ways, so you can tailor them to meet your student's needs.

Before You Begin
(continued)

Method #1: Teach the words the same way you taught the words on the Word Cards, having your student spell first with letter tiles and then on paper. This method works well with younger students and with older students who struggle with spelling. They gain the extra practice they need with a concept instead of being pushed ahead before they are ready.

Method #2: Have your student read the Practice More Words and Word Search lists. Point out that she can now spell these words as well as the words she learned from the spelling list. Dictate a selection of words to make sure she can apply the concept taught in the lesson to new words.

This method works well with most older students and advanced younger students. They are introduced to the words they are able to spell and can quickly move on to the next step. They are not held back with unnecessary repetition.

The Word Search section also includes a word search activity, which is optional.

Preview the Advanced Application Sheet

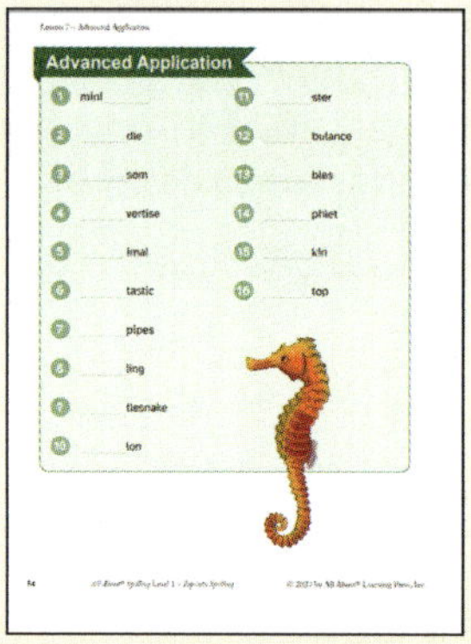

Does your student already know how to spell simple words such as *fan* and *nap*? If so, the Advanced Application sheets in Lessons 7-24 are for you!

Work very quickly through the main part of the lesson to make sure your student understands all the concepts, and then move on to the Advanced Application to practice those concepts with higher-level words. Your student will complete multisyllable words such as *fantastic* and *napkin*.

Review

Review a selection of Phonogram Cards from behind the Review divider in your student's Spelling Review Box.

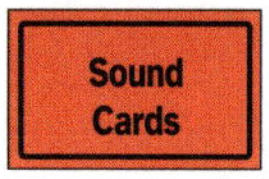

Review a selection of Sound Cards from behind the Review divider. Have your student write the phonograms in her dictation notebook.

Review
(continued)

Rule Cards

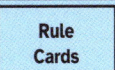

Review a selection of Rule Cards from behind the Review divider.

> **Tip!** If there are no cards behind a Review divider, either skip that part of the review or choose cards from behind the Mastered divider, according to your student's needs.

Set out three tokens or create them in the Letter Tiles app. Have your student segment the following words aloud, pulling down a token for each sound.

mud **bit** **van** **hem** **mom**

Alphabetize letter tiles a to z with your student.

New Teaching

Introduce Segmenting with Letter Tiles

Move letter tiles a, b, c, and d into the workspace.

"Let's spell some words using the letter tiles."

"I will say a word and you will repeat it slowly, one sound at a time, like you did with the tokens. Instead of pulling down a token for each sound, you will choose the correct letter tile."

"The word is *cab*." Point to the letter tiles. *Student segments the word aloud, pulling down the correct letter tile for each sound.*

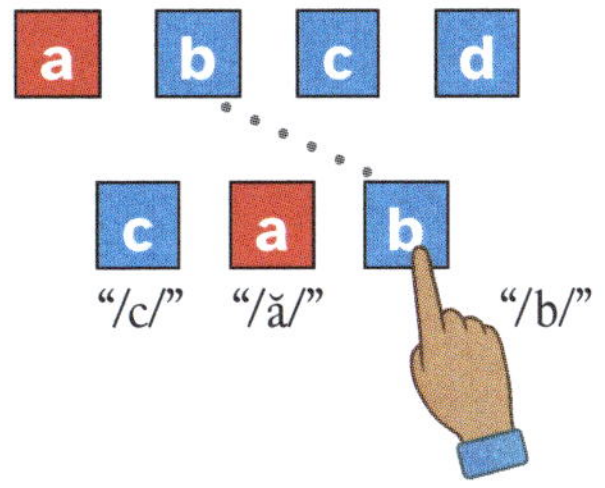

"Read the word you just spelled." *Cab.*

Put the letter tiles back into alphabetical order in the workspace.

New Teaching
(continued)

"The next word is *bad.*" Point to the letter tiles. *Student segments the word aloud, pulling down the correct letter tile for each sound.*

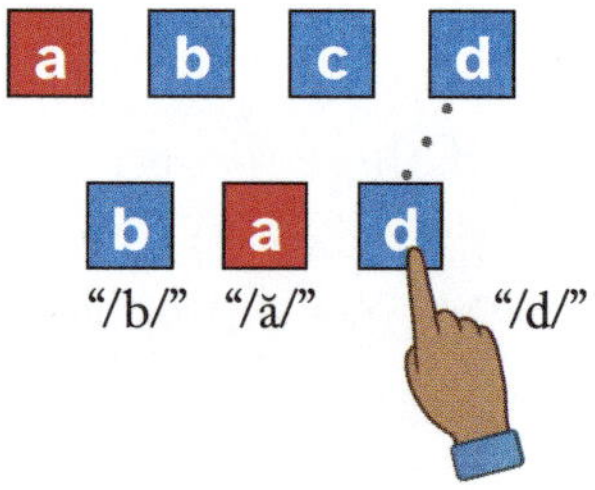

"Read the word you just spelled." *Bad.*

"Good! Now clear the workspace." *Student either puts the tiles back into alphabetical order (if using the physical tiles) or drags a tile upward (if using the app).*

Spell Word Cards 1-10 with Letter Tiles

Take out Word Cards 1-10. "I will dictate a word and you will spell it using the letter tiles. You can choose from all the letters of the alphabet."

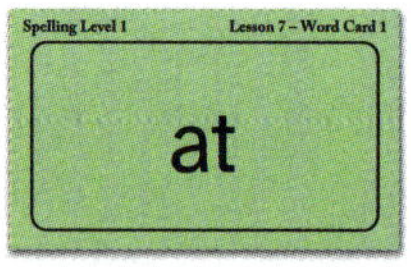

"The first word is *at.*" Point to the letter tiles to prompt your student to begin using them. *Student segments the word* at, *placing the letter tiles in the workspace as she says the sounds: /ă/–/t/.*

"Read the word." *At.*

"Good! Now clear the workspace to prepare for the next word."

You just walked your student through the Procedure for Spelling with Letter Tiles, which is summarized in Appendix E. We will use this routine throughout Level 1.

Continue with Word Cards 2-10, following the same procedure.

New Teaching
(continued)

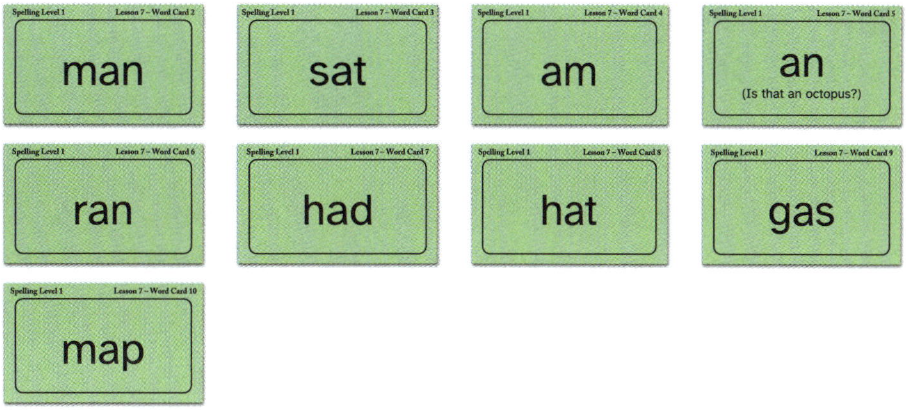

> If your student has a hard time distinguishing between *am* and *an* when you dictate the words, have her watch your lips.

Spell on Paper

Once your student is able to spell the words using the letter tiles, she will write the words on paper.

"Take out your dictation notebook."

"I will dictate a word and you will spell it on paper."

"The first word is *at*." *Student writes the word.*

"Read the word." *At.*

"Good!"

Continue with Word Cards 2-10, following the same procedure.

> **Tip!**
>
> If your student misspells a word, don't correct it for her. Have her read the word that she just wrote and guide her toward correcting the error.
>
> For tips on handling spelling mistakes, refer to Appendix K. You may want to bookmark this appendix for future reference.

New Teaching
(continued)

File the Word Cards behind the **Word Cards Review** divider in your student's Spelling Review Box. Review them at the beginning of the next teaching session.

After your student has mastered these Word Cards, you will move them behind the **Word Cards Mastered** divider.

Practice More Words

The following words reinforce the concepts taught in this lesson. For additional practice, have your student spell some of them in her dictation notebook.

bad	**ham**	**bat**	**bag**
dad	**fan**	**lab**	**mad**
jam (grape jam)	**lap**	**fat**	**pat**
mat (welcome mat)	**nap**	**pad**	**sad**
rag	**dab**	**rat**	**wag**
tag	**tap**	**van**	**sap**
pan	**gap**	**fad**	**bam**
ram	**sag**		

New Teaching
(continued)

Complete Word Search

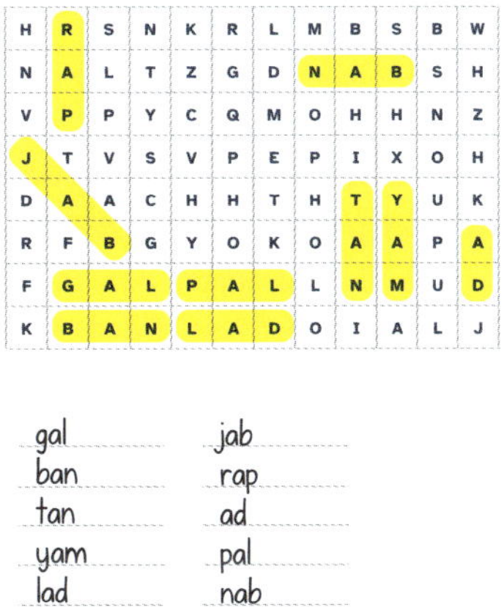

Turn to page 53 in the *Zip into Spelling* activity book.

Part 1: Dictate the following words and have your student write them on the lines provided.

gal	**jab**	**ban**	**nab**
tan	**lad**	**yam**	**pal**
rap (rap on the door)		**ad** (newspaper ad)	

Part 2 *(Optional)*: Have your student find and circle the words hidden in the Word Search.

Complete Activity Sheet *(Optional)*

"Let's put these fish back in their aquarium!"

Fill the Tank!
Remove pages 55-58 from the activity book.

Cut out the aquarium cards and place them in a pile.

Choose nine words from this lesson that you think would most benefit your student to practice. Dictate the words one by one and have your student write each word on the back of one of the aquarium cards. After spelling the word correctly, she may add the card to the aquarium.

Continue until the aquarium is full and the student has practiced all nine words.

Advanced Application

Don't Forget!

Advanced Application is intended only for older or more advanced students who would benefit from a challenge.

For advanced practice, have your student turn to the Advanced Application sheet on page 54 of the activity book.

"You can spell *van*. Now spell *minivan*, as in *Who put the skunk in the minivan?" Student writes* van *on the first line.*

Continue with the remaining words. Dictate the full word, read the sentence, and have your student fill in the missing syllable.

1.	**minivan**	Who put the skunk in the minivan?
2.	**paddle**	My aunt always said, "Paddle your own canoe."
3.	**ransom**	Henry paid Mom a ransom to get his toy back.
4.	**advertise**	Did you advertise the free puppies?
5.	**animal**	There is a large animal under the picnic table.
6.	**fantastic**	Your polka-dot pants are fantastic!
7.	**bagpipes**	They played bagpipes at my cousin's wedding.
8.	**sapling**	We planted the sapling by the porch.
9.	**rattlesnake**	I have a pet rattlesnake named Harold.
10.	**gallon**	Suzie drank a gallon of lemonade.
11.	**hamster**	Jamal's hamster used my best socks for a nest!
12.	**ambulance**	My baby brother's cry sounds like an ambulance.
13.	**dabbles**	Laticia dabbles in yodeling.
14.	**pamphlet**	Where's the pamphlet on how to plant pansies?
15.	**napkin**	You'll need a napkin with that messy sauce.
16.	**laptop**	This laptop computer is top of the line!

Track Your Progress

Mark the Progress Chart

Remember that each lesson may require several sessions to complete. Before moving on, ask yourself these questions:

1. Can your student segment words with letter tiles?

2. Has your student mastered eight out of the ten Word Cards? A Word Card is mastered when your student can spell it quickly and easily, without self-correcting or having to stop and think about it.

If the answer to both is yes, have your student mark Lesson 7 on the Progress Chart and move on to the next lesson!

The hive is all abuzz with the news that you just spelled the first ten words! You know what that means, don't you?
That's right—you are now an official SPELLING BEE!
I'm going to make a honey cake to celebrate! Whoo!

Lesson 8 Short I

Objective

This lesson teaches how to spell words with short i.

You Will Need

- ☐ extra d letter tile
- ☐ Word Cards 11-20
- ☐ *Zip into Spelling* pages 59-65

Before You Begin

Letter Tile Setup

If you are using physical letter tiles, set out an extra d letter tile so your student can spell the word *did.*

Tips to Distinguish between Short I and Short E

Some students have a hard time distinguishing between the sounds of short i (taught in this lesson) and short e (taught in Lesson 11).

Of all the vowel sounds, short i and short e are the most similar, and depending upon where you live, some words containing these vowels may sound identical. Say the following word pairs aloud:

him - hem **tint - tent** **win - when**

Do the words sound very similar to you? There's an official name for this: the *Pin-Pen Merger*. There's nothing wrong with this pronunciation—it is a regional dialect—but it does make it more difficult to spell words that contain short i and short e sounds. See Appendix G for five tips to make it easier, and be sure to take advantage of the activities included in this lesson and in Lesson 11.

Preview the Word Cards Review Section

Beginning with this lesson, the Review section includes an icon for reviewing Word Cards. Each day, review **a small selection** of the Word Cards behind the Review divider. You will dictate the word and your student will spell it on paper. Alternatively, you may use one of the activities listed in Appendix N: Activities for Reviewing Spelling Words.

Before You Begin
(continued)

Once a Word Card is mastered—that is, your student does not hesitate when he spells the word—move it behind the Mastered divider in the student's Spelling Review Box.

As you move through future lessons, a good practice is to keep no more than twenty Word Cards behind the Review divider at a time: the ten cards from the most recent lesson, plus several cards that have not yet been mastered. If you find that the Word Cards for review are stacking up too much, it may be a sign to slow down the lessons and spend more time on review.

Review

Review a selection of Phonogram Cards from behind the Review divider in your student's Spelling Review Box.

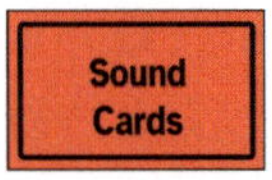

Review a selection of Sound Cards from behind the Review divider. Have your student write the phonograms in his dictation notebook.

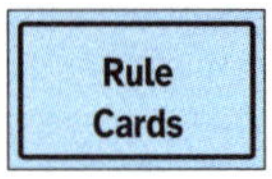

Review a selection of Rule Cards from behind the Review divider.

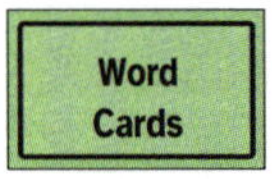

Review a selection of Word Cards from behind the Review divider. Have your student write the words in his dictation notebook.

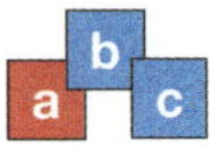

Alphabetize letter tiles a to z with your student.

New Teaching

Introduce Words with Short I

"Today we will be spelling words that have the sound of /ĭ/ in the middle. Point to the vowel that says /ĭ/." *Student points to the* **i**.

"I will dictate a word and you will spell it using the letter tiles."

"The word is *lip*." Point to the letter tiles to prompt your student to begin using the tiles. *Student segments the word* lip, *moving the letter tiles into the workspace as he says the sounds: /l/–/ĭ/–/p/.*

l i p

"Read the word." *Lip.*

"Good!"

Spell Word Cards 11-20 with Letter Tiles

Dictate the words and have your student spell them with letter tiles. Use the **Procedure for Spelling with Letter Tiles** in Appendix E.

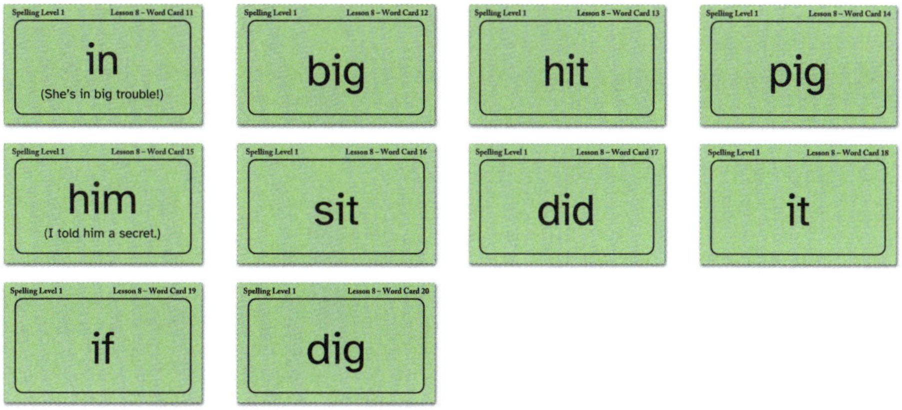

If your student tries to spell the word *sit* with a c̲ (*cit*), tell him that in Level 1, all words beginning with the sound of /s/ are spelled with s̲.

Words with /s/ spelled c̲ will be covered in Level 2.

New Teaching
(continued)

Spell on Paper

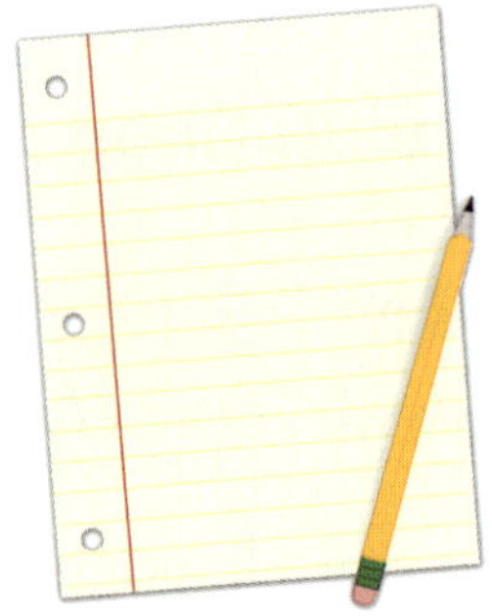

Once your student is able to spell the words using the letter tiles, have him take out his dictation notebook. Dictate Word Cards 11-20 and have your student spell the words on paper.

File the Word Cards behind the Review divider in the Spelling Review Box.

Practice More Words

The following words reinforce the concepts taught in this lesson. For additional practice, have your student spell some of them in his dictation notebook.

bit	**dim**	**pin**	**fit**
tip	**hip**	**rip**	**lip**
zip	**win**	**rib**	**lid**
pit	**hid**	**bid**	**jig**
wit (a sharp wit)	**sip**		

Complete Word Search

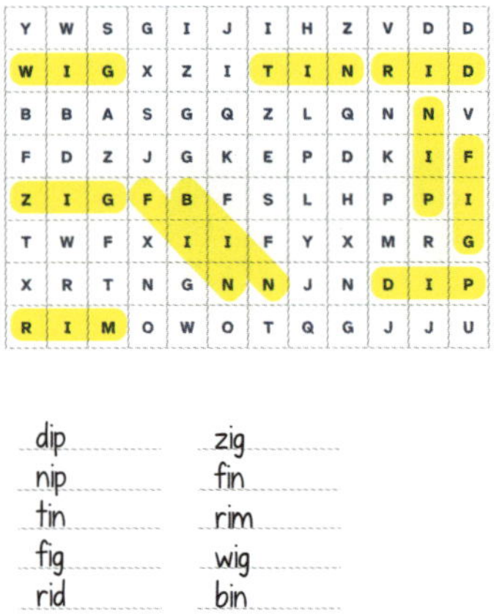

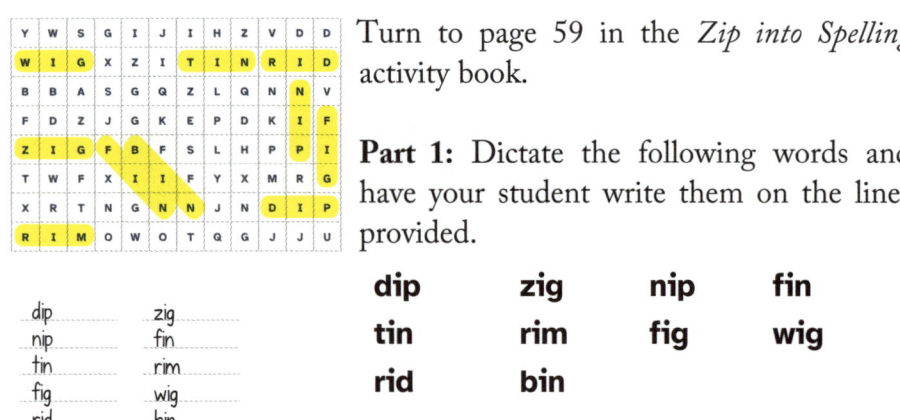

Turn to page 59 in the *Zip into Spelling* activity book.

Part 1: Dictate the following words and have your student write them on the lines provided.

dip	**zig**	**nip**	**fin**
tin	**rim**	**fig**	**wig**
rid	**bin**		

Part 2 *(Optional)*: Have your student find and circle the words hidden in the Word Search.

New Teaching
(continued)

Complete Activity Sheet *(Optional)*

"Let's help these frogs get back on their lily pad."

Frog Hop

Remove pages 61-64 from the activity book.

Cut out the frog cards and place them in a pile.

Choose nine words from this lesson that you think would most benefit your student to practice. Dictate the words one by one and have your student write each word on the back of a frog card. After spelling the word correctly, he may hop the frog onto a lily pad.

Continue until the lily pads are full of frogs and the student has practiced all nine words.

Read Word Bank for Short I

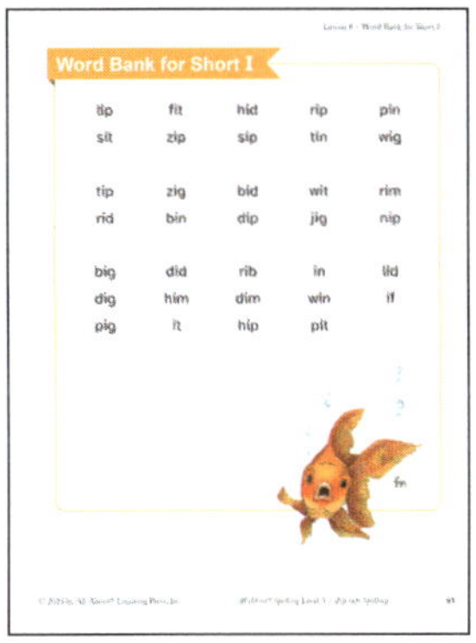

Turn to page 65 in the activity book.

If your student's regional dialect makes it difficult to differentiate between words like *pin* and *pen*, have him read through the Word Bank for Short I now and at the beginning of the next several lessons. This will help him develop a visual memory for how these words are spelled. As your student reads through the Word Bank, he should use his normal dialect.

Advanced Application

For advanced practice, have your student turn to the Advanced Application sheet on page 60 of the activity book.

"You can spell *pig*. Now spell *pigpen*, as in *The sow has escaped from the pigpen!" Student writes* pig *on the first line.*

Continue with the remaining words. Dictate the full word, read the sentence, and have your student fill in the missing syllable.

1.	**pigpen**	The sow has escaped from the pigpen!
2.	**finish**	Did you finish polishing the tubas?
3.	**himself**	He helped himself to a third piece of pie.
4.	**digging**	Fido is digging a hole in the flower bed.
5.	**situation**	Well, this is a strange situation!
6.	**hidden**	There are eighteen eggs hidden in the garden.
7.	**habit**	She has a habit of whistling while she walks.
8.	**fingertip**	My fingertip is numb from playing the guitar.
9.	**candid**	I like taking candid pictures with my camera.
10.	**ribbon**	My pony won a blue ribbon at the fair.
11.	**winner**	And the winner of the race is ... Clara the Cow!
12.	**ripple**	The waves ripple over the rocks.
13.	**lipstick**	What color lipstick should I wear?
14.	**riddle**	He told me a riddle about a frizzy chicken.
15.	**inside**	The goats fell asleep inside the car again.
16.	**outwit**	I must outwit everyone to win the spelling bee!

Track Your Progress

Mark the Progress Chart

Remember that each lesson may require several sessions to complete.

If your student has mastered eight out of the ten Word Cards, have him mark Lesson 8 on the Progress Chart and move on to the next lesson!

Lesson 9 Short O

Objective

This lesson teaches how to capitalize proper names and how to spell words with short o.

You Will Need

- ☐ extra m letter tile
- ☐ *Zip into Spelling* pages 67-71
- ☐ Word Cards 21-30

Before You Begin

Letter Tile Setup

If you are using physical letter tiles, set out an extra m tile so your student can spell the word *mom*.

Preview the "Pronounce for Spelling" Technique

In many regional dialects, *log* is pronounced as *lawg* and *bog* as *bawg*. To make these words easier to spell, you can tell your student to "pronounce for spelling."

"Pronounce for spelling" means to pronounce the word clearly and as it is written. In the case of *bog*, you can demonstrate the technique by overemphasizing the /ŏ/ sound when you pronounce the word. Of course, in everyday conversation your student should continue to pronounce the word as she normally would.

This technique becomes especially helpful in higher levels. For example, most of us say the word *button* as *butn*. The vowel sound in the unaccented syllable gets lost in the normal rhythm of speech. But when learning to spell *button*, it is helpful to pronounce for spelling and enunciate each syllable clearly: *but-ton*. You can use this technique any time your student has difficulty spelling a word because of her pronunciation.

More information on the Pronounce for Spelling technique can be found in Appendix H.

Review

Phonogram Cards

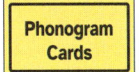

Review a selection of Phonogram Cards from behind the Review divider in your student's Spelling Review Box.

Review
(continued)

Review a selection of Sound Cards from behind the Review divider. Have your student write the phonograms in her dictation notebook.

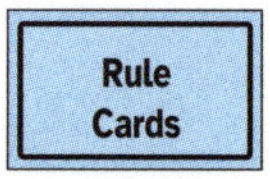

Review a selection of Rule Cards from behind the Review divider.

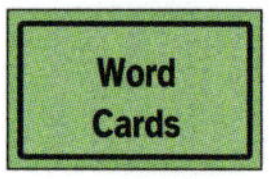

Review a selection of Word Cards from behind the Review divider. Have your student write the words in her dictation notebook.

Read through the Word Bank for Short I.

Alphabetize letter tiles a to z with your student.

How is the daily review going? Are the decks behind the Mastered dividers getting bigger?

Mastered cards will be reviewed in Lesson 11 to keep them fresh in your student's mind.

New Teaching

Introduce Words with Short O

"Today we will be spelling words that have the sound of /ŏ/ in the middle. Point to the vowel that says /ŏ/." *Student points to the* o.

"I will dictate a word and you will spell it using the letter tiles."

"The word is *mop*." Point to the letter tiles to prompt your student to begin using the tiles. *Student segments the word* mop, *moving the letter tiles into the workspace as she says the sounds: /m/–/ŏ/–/p/.*

m o p

"Read the word." *Mop.*

"Good!"

New Teaching
(continued)

Spell Word Cards 21-30 with Letter Tiles

Dictate the words and have your student spell them with letter tiles. Use the **Procedure for Spelling with Letter Tiles** in Appendix E.

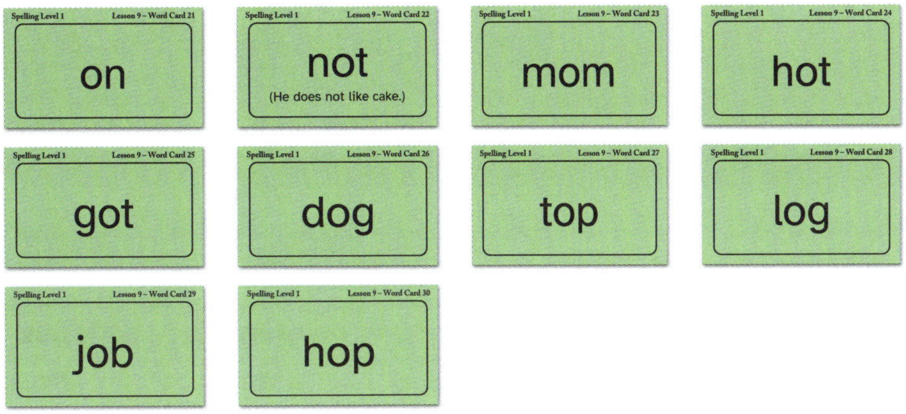

If your student tries to spell the word *job* with a g (*gob*), tell her that in Level 1, all words beginning with the sound of /j/ are spelled with j. Words with /j/ spelled g will be covered in Level 2.

If your student has difficulty spelling words like *log*, tell her to "pronounce for spelling." Demonstrate by using a clear /ŏ/ sound when you pronounce the word.

Spell on Paper

Once your student is able to spell the words using the letter tiles, have her take out her dictation notebook. Dictate Word Cards 21-30 and have your student spell the words on paper.

File the Word Cards behind the Review divider in the Spelling Review Box.

New Teaching
(continued)

Practice More Words

"Names—like *Sarah, Bob, Mr. Twizzle,* and *Fido*—always start with a capital letter. Let's try one."

"Spell the name *Bob*." *Student writes the name with a capital B.*

"Good! From now on when I dictate words, be sure to capitalize all the names."

For additional practice, have your student spell some of the following words in her dictation notebook.

Bob	**Jim** (Uncle Jim)	**pod**	**rot**
God (name)	**Pam**	**Ron**	**Tom**
mop	**rob**	**sod**	**pot**
sob	**fog**	**Sam**	**dot**

lot

Complete Word Search

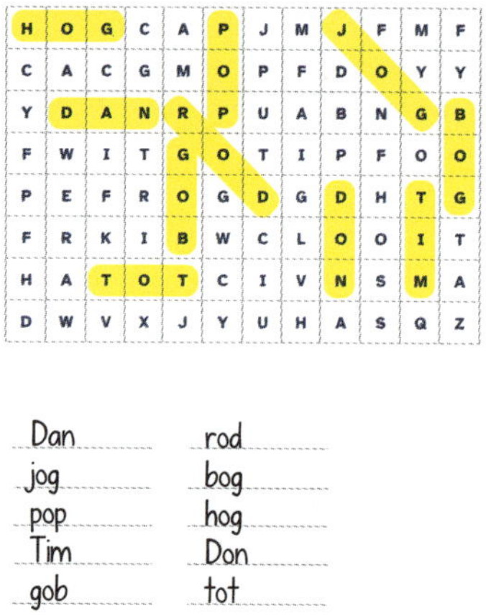

Turn to page 67 in the *Zip into Spelling* activity book.

Part 1: Dictate the following words and have your student write them on the lines provided.

Dan	**rod**	**jog**	**bog**
pop	**hog**	**Tim**	**gob**
tot	**Don** (Uncle Don)		

Part 2 ***(Optional)*****:** Have your student find and circle the words hidden in the Word Search.

New Teaching
(continued)

Complete Activity Sheet *(Optional)*

"Now let's have a hot dog picnic!"

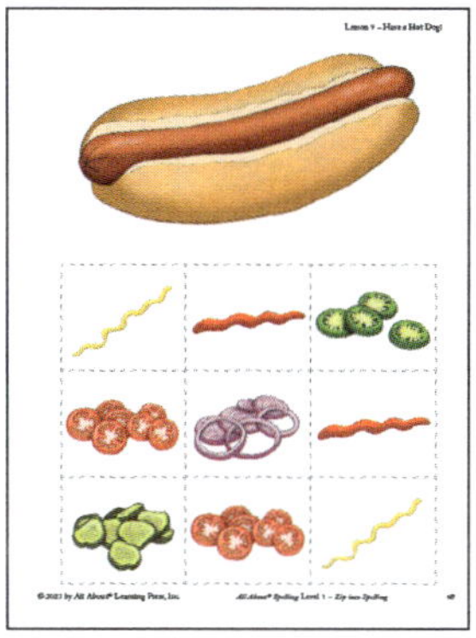

Have a Hot Dog!
Remove pages 69-70 from the activity book.

Cut out the hot dog toppings cards and place them in a pile. Cut a slit in the hot dog as indicated by the dotted lines.

Choose nine words from this lesson that you think would most benefit your student to practice. Include several proper names to give your student practice with capitalization. Dictate the words one by one and have your student write each word on the back of a toppings card. After spelling the word correctly, she may add the topping by inserting the card into the slit on the hot dog.

Continue until the hot dog has all its toppings and the student has practiced all nine words.

Read Word Bank for Short O

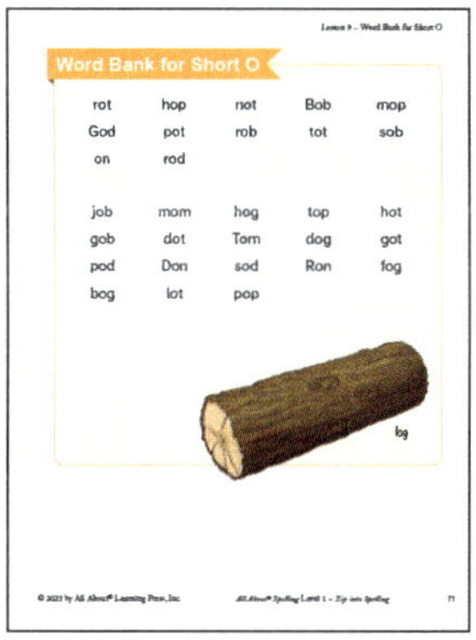

Turn to page 71 in the activity book.

If your student's regional dialect causes words like *dog* and *log* to be difficult to spell, have her read through the Word Bank for Short O now and at the beginning of the next several lessons. This will help her develop a visual memory for how these words are spelled.

Words ending in -og and -on are most likely to be troublemakers. As your student reads the words, she can use her normal dialect; in other words, if she normally says *bog* as *bawg*, she doesn't need to adjust her pronunciation in any way—she can read the word as she normally would say it in everyday conversation.

Advanced Application

For advanced practice, have your student turn to the Advanced Application sheet on page 68 of the activity book.

"You can spell *got*. Now spell *forgot*, as in *I forgot to iron my socks."* *Student writes* got *on the first line.*

Continue with the remaining words. Dictate the full word, read the sentence, and have your student fill in the missing syllable.

1.	**forgot**	I forgot to iron my socks.
2.	**hedgehog**	There's a hedgehog under the rosebush.
3.	**rotten**	Yuck! Those eggs are rotten!
4.	**cannot**	I cannot figure out how I got to Katmandu.
5.	**robber**	The robber stole all our cookies.
6.	**popcorn**	Who wants popcorn?
7.	**foghorn**	Doesn't the foghorn sound lonely in the night?
8.	**jogging**	Hal went jogging with his cat.
9.	**dogwood**	Let's have dinner under the dogwood tree.
10.	**boggle**	This new trick will boggle your mind!
11.	**hopscotch**	We played hopscotch by the river.
12.	**sobbed**	The sad snail sniffled and sobbed all night.
13.	**lottery**	Sarah will never play the lottery again.
14.	**toppings**	My favorite toppings are hot fudge and sprinkles.
15.	**tripod**	The camera fell off the tripod!
16.	**potluck**	We're bringing fruit salad to the potluck picnic.

Track Your Progress

Mark the Progress Chart

Remember that each lesson may require several sessions to complete. Before moving on, ask yourself these questions:

1. Does your student consistently begin names with a capital letter?
2. Has your student mastered eight out of the ten Word Cards?

If the answer to both is yes, have your student mark Lesson 9 on the Progress Chart and move on to the next lesson!

Lesson 10 Short U

Objective

This lesson teaches how to spell words with short u.

You Will Need

☐ *Zip into Spelling* pages 73-76 ☐ Word Cards 31-40

Before You Begin

Look at Your Student's Review Box

Now that you've been adding Word Cards to your student's Review Box for several lessons, let's make sure that you are maximizing its effectiveness. Follow these guidelines:

1. Shuffle and review the cards behind the Review dividers daily. Doing so gives your student practice with a variety of spelling concepts presented in random order.

2. Choose a mix of **no more than twenty** Phonogram, Sound, Rule, and Word Cards to review each day.

3. If your student is misspelling a lot of words during the daily review, slow down the pace of the lessons. Move on to the next lesson only when you are sure your student has mastered the previous one. See also Appendix N: Activities for Reviewing Spelling Words and Appendix K: How to Handle Spelling Mistakes.

Review

Phonogram Cards

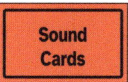

Review a selection of Phonogram Cards from behind the Review divider in your student's Spelling Review Box.

Sound Cards

Review a selection of Sound Cards from behind the Review divider. Have your student write the phonograms in his dictation notebook.

Rule Cards

Review a selection of Rule Cards from behind the Review divider.

Word Cards

Review a selection of Word Cards from behind the Review divider. Have your student write the words in his dictation notebook.

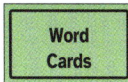

Review
(continued)

Read through the Word Bank for Short O.

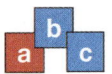

Alphabetize letter tiles a to z with your student.

New Teaching

Introduce Words with Short U

Point to the u.

"What is the first sound of this letter?" */ŭ/.*

"Good! Today we will spell words that have the sound of /ŭ/ in the middle, using the letter u."

"I will dictate a word and you will spell it using the letter tiles."

"The word is *gum.*" Point to the letter tiles to prompt your student to begin using the tiles. *Student segments the word* gum, *moving the letter tiles into the workspace as he says the sounds: /g/–/ŭ/–/m/.*

g u m

"Read the word." *Gum.*

"Good!"

New Teaching
(continued)

Spell Word Cards 31-40 with Letter Tiles

Dictate the words and have your student spell them with letter tiles. Use the **Procedure for Spelling with Letter Tiles** in Appendix E.

Spell on Paper

Once your student is able to spell the words using the letter tiles, have him take out his dictation notebook. Dictate Word Cards 31-40 and have your student spell the words on paper.

File the Word Cards behind the Review divider in the Spelling Review Box.

Practice More Words

The following words reinforce the concepts taught in this lesson. For additional practice, have your student spell some of them in his dictation notebook.

bud	**tug**	**Gus**	**gum**
jug	**hug**	**pup**	**yum**
tub	**mug**	**hum**	**rub**
but (all but one)			

New Teaching
(continued)

Complete Word Search

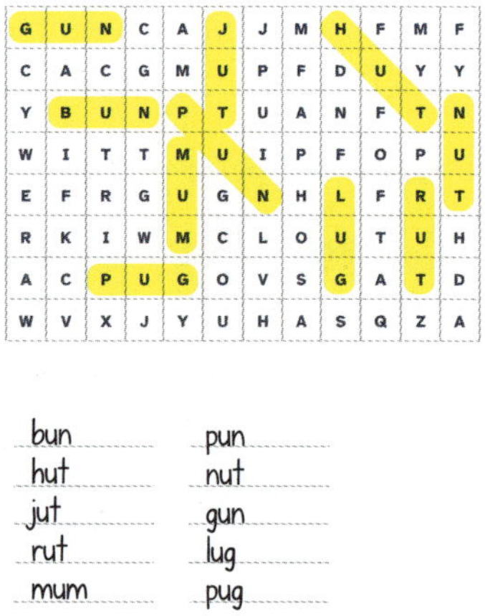

G U N C A J J M H F M F
C A C G M U P F D U Y Y
Y B U N P T U A N F T N
W I T T M U I P F O P U
E F R G U G N H L F R T
R K I W M C L O U T U H
A C P U G O V S G A T D
W V X J Y U H A S Q Z A
bun
pun
hut
nut
jut
gun
rut
lug
mum
pug

Turn to page 73 in the *Zip into Spelling* activity book.

Part 1: Dictate the following words and have your student write them on the lines provided.

bun	**pun**	**hut**	**nut**
jut	**gun**	**rut**	**lug**
mum	**pug**		

Part 2 *(Optional)*: Have your student find and circle the words hidden in the Word Search.

Complete Activity Sheet *(Optional)*

"Let's help these bees get back to their hive."

Busy Bees
Remove pages 75-76 from the activity book.

Cut out the worker bee cards and place them in a pile. Cut a slit in the beehive as indicated by the dotted line.

Choose twelve words from this lesson that you think would most benefit your student to practice. Dictate the words one by one and have your student write each word on the back of a bee card. After spelling the word correctly, he may help the worker bee back to the hive by inserting the card into the slit on the beehive.

Continue until all the worker bees are safely in the hive and the student has practiced all twelve words.

You may wish to point out that some of the worker bees have pollen baskets on their legs. Pollen baskets help honey bees carry pollen back to the hive.

Advanced Application

For advanced practice, have your student turn to the Advanced Application sheet on page 74 of the activity book.

"You can spell *bug*. Now spell *ladybug*, as in *The ladybug landed on a daisy." Student writes* bug *on the first line.*

Continue with the remaining words. Dictate the full word, read the sentence, and have your student fill in the missing syllable.

1.	**ladybug**	The ladybug landed on a daisy.
2.	**sunrise**	Meet me at the tree house at sunrise.
3.	**runner**	I'm the fastest runner in town.
4.	**muddy**	I love sloshing through the muddy meadows!
5.	**rosebud**	Nyah gave me a rosebud in a vase.
6.	**juggle**	Where did you learn to juggle frogs?
7.	**washtub**	The washtub overflowed with bubbles.
8.	**bunny**	That tiny bunny ate my entire lettuce patch.
9.	**butter**	We need more butter for this batter!
10.	**hummingbird**	A hummingbird hovered at my window.
11.	**rubber**	All our rubber tires are flat as pancakes.
12.	**mummy**	I've never seen a mummy do the cha-cha.
13.	**nutcracker**	I loaned our nutcracker to a squirrel.
14.	**tugboat**	Horace wants to be a tugboat captain.
15.	**punish**	It would be silly to punish the pigs for oinking.
16.	**funnel**	I covered a funnel in foil and wore it as a hat.

Track Your Progress

Mark the Progress Chart

Remember that each lesson may require several sessions to complete.

If your student has mastered eight out of the ten Word Cards, have him mark Lesson 10 on the Progress Chart and move on to the next lesson!

Huzzah!
An activity featuring the buzz-erific worker bees!
I even saw some of my friends there, like Bee-atrice, Polly, and Zelda. They are the BEST pollen collectors ever.
Thank you for helping them get back to the hive!

Lesson 11 Short E

Objective

This lesson teaches how to count syllables and how to spell words with short e.

You Will Need

☐ *Zip into Spelling* pages 77-89 ☐ Word Cards 41-50

Before You Begin

Preview Counting Syllables

Words are made up of syllables. A syllable is a "word chunk" that contains a single vowel sound. A word may have one, two, or even more syllables. The number of vowel sounds in a word determines the number of syllables. For example:

- *bat* has one vowel sound and therefore one syllable
- *sticky* has two vowel sounds and therefore two syllables
- *south* has one vowel sound—/ow/—and therefore one syllable

Fortunately, there is an easy way to recognize and count syllables: by clapping. In this lesson, you will demonstrate how to clap syllables and then provide practice for your student. For example:

- *puppy* has two syllables: *pup* [clap]–*py* [clap]
- *tape* has one syllable: *tape* [clap]

Although the clapping method works well with most students, you may also want to try some of the alternative methods listed in Appendix I: Methods for Counting Syllables.

Can You Skip the Activities?

If your student has used the *All About Reading* Pre-reading program, she probably already knows how to count syllables. To test, ask your student how many syllables are in the following words:

pizza (two) **alligator** (four) **truck** (one)

If counting syllables has already been mastered, skip the first two activities and start the lesson on page 112 with Introduce Words with Short E.

Review

It's time to review the cards behind the Mastered dividers to ensure they stay fresh in your student's mind. Shuffle the cards and choose a selection for review.

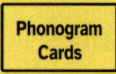

Phonogram Cards — Review a selection of Phonogram Cards from behind the **Mastered** divider in your student's Spelling Review Box.

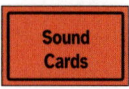

Sound Cards — Review a selection of Sound Cards from behind the **Mastered** divider. Have your student write the phonograms in her dictation notebook.

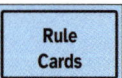

Rule Cards — Review a selection of Rule Cards from behind the **Mastered** divider.

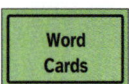

Word Cards — Review a selection of Word Cards from behind the **Mastered** divider. Have your student write the words in her dictation notebook.

Word Banks — Read through the Word Banks for Short I and Short O.

Alphabetize letter tiles a to z with your student.

Tip!

How many flashcards should you review each day?
By now you may have quite a few flashcards behind the Review dividers, and more will be added as the lessons progress. To avoid overwhelming your student, choose a mix of no more than twenty Phonogram, Sound, Rule, and Word Cards to review each day.

However, if you feel too many cards are stacking up, take a day or even several days, as needed, to just work on review. Then you can continue on to new lessons when your student is ready.

New Teaching

Teach Counting Syllables

In this exercise, you will demonstrate what a syllable is by clapping your hands as you say the syllables.

"Words are made up of syllables. A word might have one, two, or even more syllables."

"*Reading* has two syllables: *read* [clap]–*ing* [clap]."
"*Blue* has one syllable: *blue* [clap]."
"*Pumpkin* has two syllables: *pump* [clap]–*kin* [clap]."

"Now you try. Clap your hands for each syllable in the word *pig*." *Student claps her hands one time as she says* pig.

Read the following words aloud and have your student practice counting syllables by clapping.

seven **purple** **elephants** **went** **swimming**

Complete Activity Sheet *(Optional)*

"Let's sort some objects!"

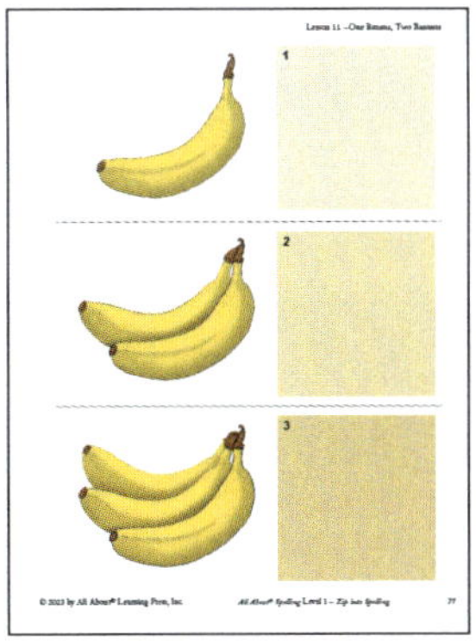

One Banana, Two Bananas
Remove pages 77-83 from the *Zip into Spelling* activity book.

Cut out the object cards, mix them up, and place them in a pile with the illustrations facing up.

Place the banana page in front of your student. "Let's use these bananas to help us sort items into bunches."

Your student should select an object card, name the item or animal, and determine the number of syllables by clapping. Then she may place the card in the appropriate box next to the banana bunch that represents that number. For example, if she collects a card for an item with one syllable, she'll place it in the box next to the illustration of the single banana.

Continue until all the cards have been sorted.

New Teaching
(continued)

<u>Answer Key</u>
One syllable: kite, snake, ax, drum, cat, grapes, car, fish, dog, cap, bee, fox

Two syllables: zebra, lemon, wagon, mittens, monkey, pumpkin, giraffe, tractor, rabbit, football, balloon, carrot

Three syllables: kangaroo, volcano, tomato, spaghetti, dinosaur, umbrella, octopus, violin, banana, hamburger, butterfly, elephant

It's perfectly acceptable if your child identifies an item by a name that differs from the answer key, such as saying *puppy* instead of *dog*. In that case, she would clap the number of syllables for *puppy*.

Introduce Words with Short E

"Today we will be spelling words that have the sound of /ĕ/ in the middle. Point to the vowel that says /ĕ/." *Student points to the* e.

"I will dictate a word and you will spell it using the letter tiles."

"The word is *net*." Point to the letter tiles to prompt your student to begin using the tiles. *Student segments the word* net, *moving the letter tiles into the workspace as she says the sounds: /n/–/ĕ/–/t/.*

n e t

"Read the word." *Net.*

"Good!"

New Teaching
(continued)

Spell Word Cards 41-50 with Letter Tiles

Dictate the words and have your student spell them with letter tiles. Use the **Procedure for Spelling with Letter Tiles** in Appendix E.

Spell on Paper

Once your student is able to spell the words using the letter tiles, have her take out her dictation notebook. Dictate Word Cards 41-50 and have your student spell the words on paper.

File the Word Cards behind the Review divider in the Spelling Review Box.

Practice More Words

The following words reinforce the concepts taught in this lesson. For additional practice, have your student spell some of them in her dictation notebook.

bed	**Jeb**	**hem**	**bet**	**Jed**
met	**den**	**Ben** (name)	**Deb**	**let**
Ned	**beg**	**Ed**	**jet**	**Peg**
hen				

New Teaching
(continued)

Complete Word Search

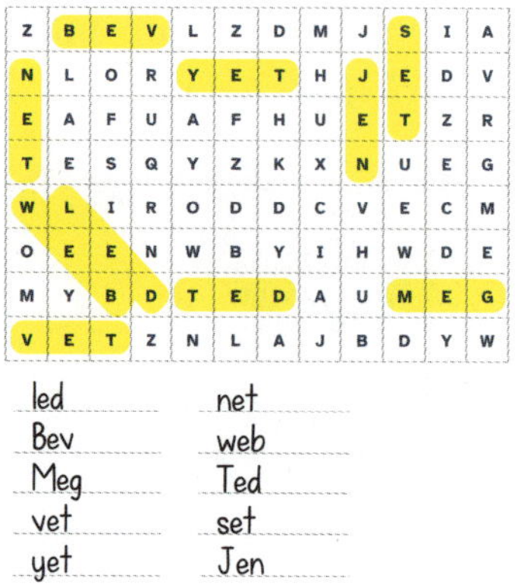

Turn to page 85 in the activity book.

Part 1: Dictate the following words and have your student write them on the lines provided.

net	**Bev**	**web**	**Meg**
vet	**Ted**	**set**	**yet**
Jen	**led** (led a parade)		

Part 2 *(Optional)*: Have your student find and circle the words hidden in the Word Search.

Complete Activity Sheet *(Optional)*

"These monkeys can't wait to jump on the bed. Let's help them up!"

Monkeys Jumping on the Bed
Remove pages 87-88 from thc activity book.

Cut out the monkey cards and place them in a pile.

Choose eight words from this lesson that you think would most benefit your student to practice. Dictate the words one by one and have your student write each word on the back of a monkey card. After spelling the word correctly, she may let the monkey jump on the bed.

Continue until all the monkeys are jumping on the bed and the student has practiced all eight words.

New Teaching
(continued)

Read Word Bank for Short E

Turn to page 89 in the activity book.

If your student's regional dialect makes it difficult to differentiate between words like *pin* and *pen*, have her read through the Word Bank for Short E now and at the beginning of the next several lessons. This will help her develop a visual memory for how these words are spelled.

Words ending in -en and -em are most likely to be troublemakers. As your student reads the words, she can use her normal dialect; in other words, if she normally says *Ben* as *bin*, she doesn't need to adjust her pronunciation in any way—she can read the word as she normally would say it in everyday conversation.

Advanced Application

For advanced practice, have your student turn to the Advanced Application sheet on page 86 of the activity book.

"You can spell *ten*. Now spell *tenacious*, as in *The bear has a tenacious grip on the salmon." Student writes* ten *on the first line.*

Continue with the remaining words. Dictate the full word, read the sentence, and have your student fill in the missing syllable.

1.	**tenacious**	The bear has a tenacious grip on the salmon.
2.	**forget**	Don't forget to feed the rabbits.
3.	**carpet**	Rule #1: No muddy shoes on the carpet!
4.	**setback**	Losing that game is a real setback for the team.
5.	**metropolis**	The superhero saved the metropolis from evildoers.
6.	**federal**	Bank robbery is a federal crime.
7.	**network**	Look at that intricate network of spiderwebs!
8.	**letter**	I wrote a letter to Horuko, my pen pal in Japan.
9.	**veterinarian**	My cat meowed menacingly at the veterinarian.
10.	**hemlock**	Be careful! That hemlock is a poisonous herb.
11.	**yesterday**	Did you practice ballet yesterday?
12.	**mentor**	My mentor taught me how to write a poem.
13.	**pegboard**	Hang my tools neatly on the pegboard, please!
14.	**nutmeg**	Did you put cinnamon and nutmeg in the pie?
15.	**pencil**	Terrell sharpened every colored pencil in my case.
16.	**garden**	A family of lizards moved into our garden.

Track Your Progress

Mark the Progress Chart

Remember that each lesson may require several sessions to complete. Before moving on, ask yourself these questions:

1. Can your student count syllables by clapping or by some other method?

2. Has your student mastered eight out of the ten Word Cards?

If the answer to both is yes, have your student mark Lesson 11 on the Progress Chart and move on to the next lesson!

Lesson 12 X, QU, and S

Objective

This lesson teaches how to spell words with x, qu, and the second sound of s.

You Will Need

- ☐ *Zip into Spelling* pages 91-95
- ☐ Word Cards 51-60

Before You Begin

Preview Phonograms X, QU, and S

x In Level 1, the sound of /ks/ is spelled with x, as in *box*. In Lesson 22, your student will also hear /ks/ in plural words that end in ck, such as *ducks*.

qu The sound of /kw/ is spelled qu. Listen for the sound of /kw/ in these words:

quick **queen** **quiet** **quack**

If your student ever spells the sound of /kw/ with k-w, remind him that in English the /kw/ sound is spelled qu. (The word *Kwanzaa* may appear to be an exception, but it comes from Swahili.)

s The letter s is the most common way to spell the sound of /z/ at the end of words. Listen for the sound of /z/ in these words:

has	**wings**	**cheese**	**wise**	**is**
as	**his**	**lose**	**waves**	**bruise**

There are thousands of words in which the final /z/ sound is spelled with the letter s. In contrast, very few common words end with the letter z: *quiz, buzz, frizz, fuzz, jazz, topaz, glitz, quartz, waltz, pizzazz,* and *whiz.*

Preview the Dictate Phrases Activity

Starting with this lesson, you will dictate several phrases each day. The phrases reinforce concepts taught in both current and previous lessons.

Your student should repeat the phrase and then write it on a line in his dictation notebook. Having your student repeat the phrase before he writes it will help him develop a good routine for future lessons.

Later in the program we will be dictating whole sentences, not just phrases. The sentences are longer and you will be reading them aloud one time. Having your student repeat the phrases and sentences aloud helps him remember them more easily and write them down accurately.

Review

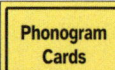

Review a selection of Phonogram Cards from behind the Review divider in your student's Spelling Review Box.

Review a selection of Sound Cards from behind the Review divider. Have your student write the phonograms in his dictation notebook.

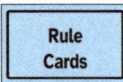

Review a selection of Rule Cards from behind the Review divider.

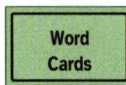

Review a selection of Word Cards from behind the Review divider. Have your student write the words in his dictation notebook.

Read through the Word Bank for Short E.

Alphabetize letter tiles a to z with your student.

New Teaching

Introduce Words with X

"Today we will be spelling words that have the sound of /ks/ at the end. Point to the consonant that says /ks/." *Student points to the* x.

"Repeat these words after me and listen for the /ks/ sound: *six, fox, wax.*" *Student repeats the words.*

"I will dictate a word and you will spell it using the letter tiles."

"The word is *ox.*" Point to the letter tiles to prompt your student to begin using the tiles. *Student segments the word* ox, *moving the letter tiles into the workspace as he says the sounds: /ŏ/–/ks/.*

o x

"Read the word." *Ox.*

"Good!"

New Teaching
(continued)

Introduce Words with QU

"We will also be spelling words that begin with the sound of /kw/. Point to the letter tile that says /kw/." *Student points to the* **qu**.

"Repeat these words after me and listen for the /kw/ sound: *quick, quiet, quilt.*" *Student repeats the words.*

"I will dictate a word and you will spell it using the letter tiles."

"The word is *quit.*" Point to the letter tiles to prompt your student to begin using the tiles. *Student segments the word* quit, *moving the letter tiles into the workspace as he says the sounds: /kw/–/ĭ/–/t/.*

qu **i** **t**

"Read the word." *Quit.*

"Good!"

Teach the Most Common Way to Spell Final /z/

"Finally, we will spell words that have the sound of /z/ at the end. Repeat these words after me and listen for the /z/ sound: *has, is, his.*" *Student repeats the words.*

Point to the tiles. "Which two tiles can say /z/?" *S and z.*

> If your student doesn't know the answer, point to the s tile and ask, "What are the two sounds of this tile?"
>
> **Tip!**

"Good! Most of the time, when we hear the sound of /z/ at the end of a word, we use the letter s."

Build the word **h** **a** **s**.

"What sound do you hear at the end of the word *has*?" */z/.*

"What letter did I use to spell the sound of /z/ at the end of the word?" *S.*

"Change the word *has* to *his.*" *Student changes the a to i.*

h **i** **s**

New Teaching
(continued)

Spell Word Cards 51-60 with Letter Tiles

Dictate the words and have your student spell them with letter tiles. Use the **Procedure for Spelling with Letter Tiles** in Appendix E.

Spell on Paper

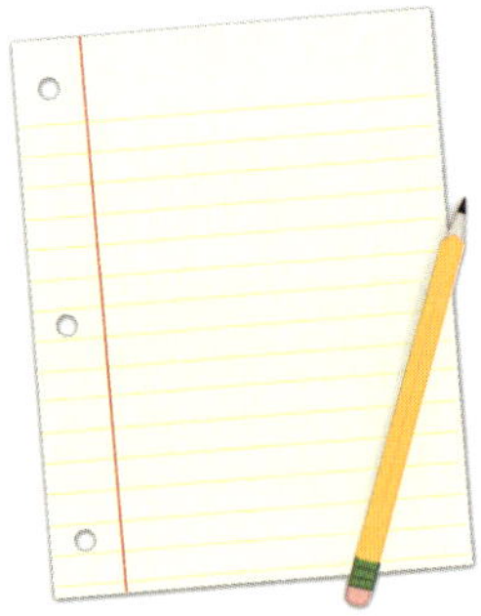

Once your student is able to spell the words using the letter tiles, have him take out his dictation notebook. Dictate Word Cards 51-60 and have your student spell the words on paper.

File the Word Cards behind the Review divider in the Spelling Review Box.

Practice More Words

The following words reinforce the concepts taught in this lesson. For additional practice, have your student spell them in his dictation notebook.

ox | **tax** (pay a tax)
wax (made of wax) | **ax** (wood ax)

New Teaching
(continued)

Complete Activity Sheet *(Optional)*

"Let's help this donkey find its lost tail."

Donkey Tails

Remove pages 91-94 from the *Zip into Spelling* activity book.

Cut out the donkey tail cards and place them in a pile.

Choose twelve words from this lesson that you think would most benefit your student to practice. Dictate the words one by one and have your student write each word on the back of a donkey tail card. After spelling the word correctly, he may try to pin the tail on the donkey using tape.

For an added challenge, blindfold your student before he tries pinning the tails on the donkey!

Continue until all the tails have been pinned and the student has practiced all twelve words.

Dictate Phrases

> For tips on dictation, refer to Appendix L: Procedure and Troubleshooting for Spelling Dictation.

Dictate several phrases each day. Your student should repeat each phrase and write it in his dictation notebook.

big dog	**fix it**	**quit it**
on top	**mix up**	**hot sun**
dig in mud	**fat rat**	**six men**
fox den	**his box**	**sad pig**

Advanced Application

For advanced practice, have your student turn to the Advanced Application sheet on page 95 of the activity book.

"You can spell *fox*. Now spell *foxtrot*, as in *Have you ever danced the foxtrot with a fox?" Student writes* fox *on the first line.*

Continue with the remaining words. Dictate the full word, read the sentence, and have your student fill in the missing syllable.

1.	**foxtrot**	Have you ever danced the foxtrot with a fox?
2.	**toolbox**	The sculptor chose a chisel from his toolbox.
3.	**earwax**	The vet cleaned the earwax out of Milo's ears.
4.	**acquit**	Did the judge acquit the alleged spy?
5.	**sixteen**	We found sixteen marbles under the bed.
6.	**mixture**	What a yucky mixture of mud, twigs, and grass!
7.	**oxen**	Two oxen pulled the cook's covered wagon.
8.	**taxpayer**	The school used taxpayer money to fix the roof.
9.	**fixable**	I don't think this broken robot is fixable.
10.	**axle**	The wooden wheel came loose from its axle.

Track Your Progress

Mark the Progress Chart

Remember that each lesson may require several sessions to complete.

If your student has mastered eight out of the ten Word Cards, have him mark Lesson 12 on the Progress Chart and move on to the next lesson!

Lesson 13 TH, SH, and CH

Objective

This lesson introduces consonant teams th, sh, and ch and teaches how to spell words with these phonograms.

You Will Need

- ☐ letter tiles th, sh, ch
- ☐ Consonant Teams label
- ☐ Phonogram Cards 27-29
- ☐ four tokens
- ☐ Sound Cards 27-29
- ☐ *Zip into Spelling* pages 97-101
- ☐ Word Cards 61-70

Before You Begin

Preview Consonant Teams TH, SH, and CH

Consonant teams are two or more consonants working together to make one sound. For example, s and h work together to make the sound of /sh/. Another common term for this is *consonant digraph*.

Three consonant teams will be taught in this lesson.

th Consonant team th can say two sounds:

- /th/ as in *three*
- /~~th~~/ as in *then*

You will notice that there is a strikethrough on the th in the second sound: /~~th~~/. This strikethrough is used to differentiate between the two sounds of th. The /th/ is considered an *unvoiced* sound, while the /~~th~~/ is considered a *voiced* sound because we use our vocal cords to say it.

sh Consonant team sh says /sh/ as in *ship*.

You may wish to help your student remember the sound of /sh/ by showing her how to hold her finger to her lips and say "shhh."

ch Consonant team ch can say three sounds:

- /ch/ as in *child*
- /k/ as in *school*
- /sh/ as in *chef*

Refer to the Letter Tiles app or Phonogram Sounds app for a demonstration of the th, sh, and ch phonogram sounds.

Before You Begin
(continued)

If you are using the Letter Tiles app, select Lesson 13 from the menu. You'll see that the three new tiles are organized under the Consonant Teams category.

If you are using a magnetic whiteboard, place the Consonant Teams label and the th, sh, and ch tiles below the alphabet row.

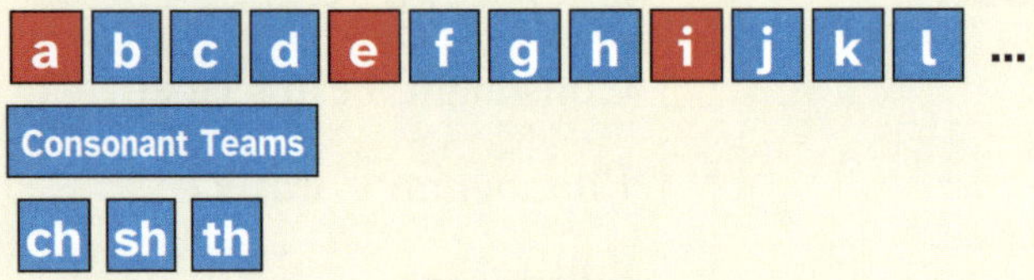

To see what the magnetic whiteboard will look like after all the Level 1 consonant teams have been placed on the board, refer to Appendix P.

Review

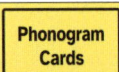

Review a selection of Phonogram Cards from behind the Review divider in your student's Spelling Review Box.

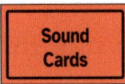

Review a selection of Sound Cards from behind the Review divider. Have your student write the phonograms in her dictation notebook.

Review a selection of Rule Cards from behind the Review divider.

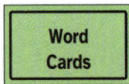

Review a selection of Word Cards from behind the Review divider. Have your student write the words in her dictation notebook.

Read through the Word Bank for Short E.

Alphabetize letter tiles a to z with your student.

New Teaching

Teach Consonant Teams TH, SH and CH

"We have three new tiles today."

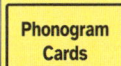

Move the **th** tile into the workspace.

"See how there are two letters on one tile? The two letters work together to make one sound. This one can say /th/, or it can say /~~th~~/. Repeat after me: /th/–/~~th~~/." *Student repeats the sounds.*

Move the **sh** tile into the workspace.

"This one says /sh/. Repeat after me: /sh/." *Student repeats the sound.*

Move the **ch** tile into the workspace.

"This one has three different sounds: /ch/–/k/–/sh/. Repeat after me: /ch/–/k/–/sh/." *Student repeats the sounds.*

"Are the letters on these tiles vowels or consonants?" *Consonants.*

"Good. Since the two consonants work together as a team, we call these tiles consonant teams."

Point to the category label. "They are stored in their own category, Consonant Teams."

Phonogram Cards

Take out Phonogram Cards 27-29 and practice them with your student. Mix in several other Phonogram Cards for mixed review and practice until your student can say the sounds accurately.

Teach Sound Cards 27-29

Sound Cards

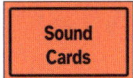

Take out Sound Cards 27-29.

"I am going to dictate a sound. Write the two letters that work together to make that sound."

Dictate the new Sound Cards. Practice until your student can easily write the correct phonograms in her dictation notebook. Mix in several other Sound Cards for mixed review.

If a phonogram has more than one sound, dictate all the sounds that appear on the Sound Card, adding a slight pause between sounds.

Any time you introduce a new flashcard in a lesson—Phonogram, Sound, Word, or Rule Card—remember to file it behind the appropriate **Review** divider in your student's Spelling Review Box. Shuffle the cards before reviewing them with your student.

Segment Words with Consonant Teams

Create four gray token boxes on the app or lay four tokens on the table.

Point to the tokens. "You may not need all of these tokens. Segment the word *rush*." *Student repeats the word and says the individual sounds. As she says each sound, she pulls a token toward herself.*

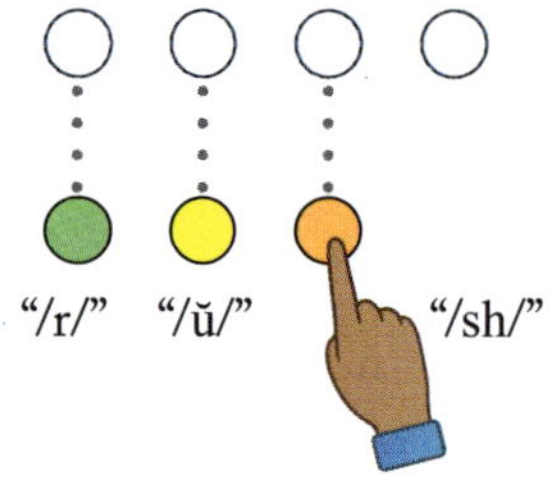

Repeat the activity with the following words.

chip **thin** **dish** **rich** **them**

Your student will only need three tokens to segment each word, but we set out four tokens to encourage her to think through this activity.

Some students—especially if they already know how to spell the word—confuse the number of *letters* in a word with the number of *sounds*. For example, the words *fish* and *fast* both have four letters, but they have a different number of sounds. *Fish* has only three sounds (/f/–/ĭ/–/sh/), while *fast* has four sounds (/f/–/ă/–/s/–/t/). If your student is thinking about the number of letters, you might say, "That's right, *fish* has four letters, but how many sounds does it have?"

New Teaching
(continued)

Spell Word Cards 61-70 with Letter Tiles

Dictate the words and have your student spell them with letter tiles. Use the **Procedure for Spelling with Letter Tiles** in Appendix E.

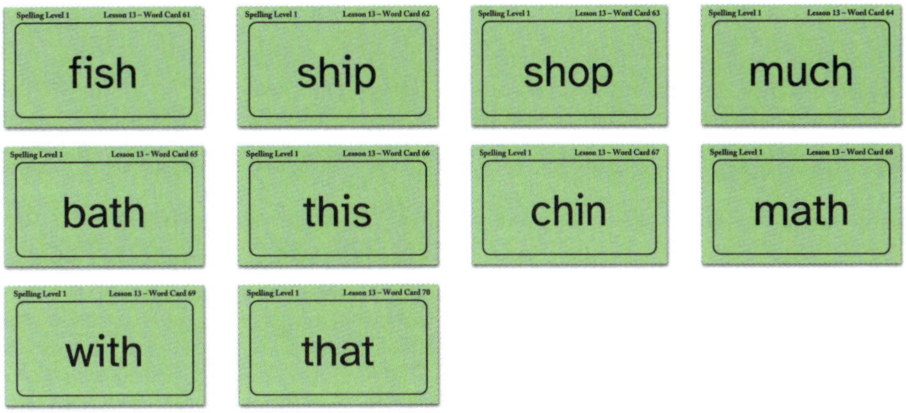

Spell on Paper

Once your student is able to spell the words using the letter tiles, have her take out her dictation notebook. Dictate Word Cards 61-70 and have your student spell the words on paper.

File the Word Cards behind the Review divider in the Spelling Review Box.

Practice More Words

The following words reinforce the concepts taught in this lesson. For additional practice, have your student spell some of them in her dictation notebook.

Beth	**them**	**rash**	**dash**	**shin**
moth	**path**	**chop**	**thud**	**rush**
shed	**dish**	**shot**	**wish**	**such**
than	**then**	**chip**	**thin**	**rich**
shut	**Seth**	**ash**	**hush**	**chat**
gush				

New Teaching
(continued)

Complete Word Search

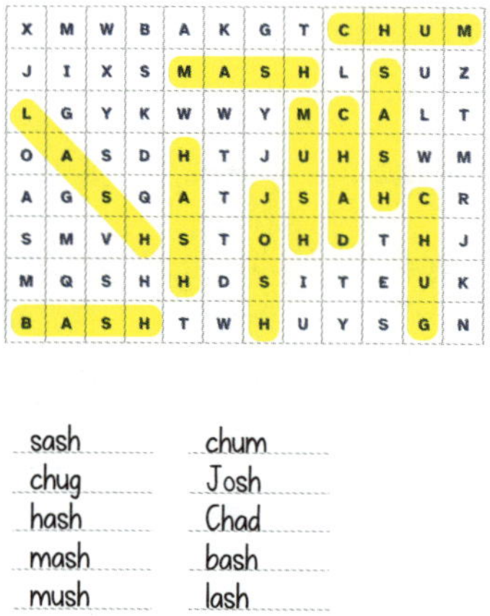

Turn to page 97 in the *Zip into Spelling* activity book.

Part 1: Dictate the following words and have your student write them on the lines provided.

sash	**chum**	**chug**	**Josh**
hash	**Chad**	**mash**	**bash**
mush	**lash**		

Part 2 ***(Optional)*****:** Have your student find and circle the words hidden in the Word Search.

Complete Activity Sheet *(Optional)*

"Someone's calling! Let's answer the phone and see who it is."

Hello, Hello!
Remove pages 99-101 from the activity book.

Cut out the telephone cards and place them in a pile.

Choose twelve words from this lesson that you think would most benefit your student to practice. Have your student answer the phone by selecting a telephone card, saying "Hello," and listening while you dictate a word. She should then write the word in the word bubble next to the telephone. After spelling the word correctly, she may say "Goodbye!" and hang up the phone.

Continue until all the telephones have been answered and the student has practiced all twelve words.

New Teaching
(continued)

Dictate Phrases

Dictate several phrases each day. Your student should repeat each phrase and write it in her dictation notebook.

fish shop	**ran with them**	**rub his chin**
this bug	**bad path**	**rich man**
fun hat	**thin moth**	**shut that shed**
wet mop	**hug him**	**has an ox**

Advanced Application

For advanced practice, have your student turn to the Advanced Application sheet on page 98 of the activity book.

"You can spell *fish*. Now spell *catfish*, as in *My dachshund chased a catfish around the pond.*" *Student writes* fish *on the first line.*

Continue with the remaining words. Dictate the full word, read the sentence, and have your student fill in the missing syllable.

1. catfish	My dachshund chased a catfish around the pond.
2. shipwreck	The divers explored the shipwreck.
3. chipmunk	That chipmunk just did three somersaults!
4. richest	Isabel is the richest noblewoman in the kingdom.
5. mathematics	My favorite subjects are music and mathematics.
6. withdraw	The general ordered the troops to withdraw.
7. eyelash	You have an eyelash on your cheek.
8. dashboard	I left my glasses on the dashboard of the car.
9. shopping	Let's go shopping for books!
10. pathway	The narrow pathway led us to a little cottage.
11. chatterbox	Miguel's baby brother is such a chatterbox!
12. mushroom	A mushroom sprouted in the damp grass.
13. dishpan	Please fill the dishpan with clean water.
14. bathtub	Who put fifty rubber duckies in the bathtub?
15. chopsticks	I finally learned how to eat with chopsticks!
16. wishful	Having a pet koala is just wishful thinking!

Track Your Progress

Mark the Progress Chart

Remember that each lesson may require several sessions to complete. Before moving on, ask yourself these questions:

1. Can your student segment words with consonant teams?
2. Has your student mastered eight out of the ten Word Cards?

If the answer to both is yes, have your student mark Lesson 13 on the Progress Chart and move on to the next lesson!

Hello, hello!
The latest buzz is that you are halfway through Level 1. That's ama-zzzz-ing!
Have you been filling out your Progress Chart with stingers? Uh ... I mean stickers?

Lesson 14 Final Blends

Objective

This lesson teaches how to segment and spell words with final blends.

You Will Need

- ☐ four tokens
- ☐ Word Cards 71-80
- ☐ *Zip into Spelling* pages 103-112

Before You Begin

Preview Consonant Blends

A consonant blend consists of two sounds that are said together quickly. For example, the word *lamp* has a consonant blend at the end. The /m/ and /p/ sounds are said in rapid succession, but each consonant keeps its own sound.

A blend at the end of a word is called a **final blend**. Listen for the final blends in the following words.

west **land** **left** **melt** **hint**

> A consonant blend is different from a consonant team. In consonant blends such as s-t, n-d, and f-t, each letter retains its own sound. In consonant teams such as th, sh, and ch, two letters combine to make a completely new sound.

Tips for Teaching Blends

If your student has a difficult time segmenting consonant blends into their individual sounds, consider the following:

- Have your student say the word very slowly. For the word *raft*, for example, elongate the sounds when possible: /rrr/–/ăăă/–/fff/–/t/.
- Don't move on to spelling words with blends until your student is able to segment them. Take as many learning sessions as necessary to master this skill.
- If your student has any difficulties when segmenting blends, use the "Hop to It" activity in Appendix J. This is a great kinesthetic activity for learning to hear each sound in a blend.

Review

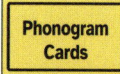

Review a selection of Phonogram Cards from behind the Review divider in your student's Spelling Review Box.

Review a selection of Sound Cards from behind the Review divider. Have your student write the phonograms in his dictation notebook.

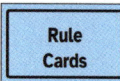

Review a selection of Rule Cards from behind the Review divider.

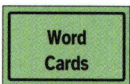

Review a selection of Word Cards from behind the Review divider. Have your student write the words in his dictation notebook.

Read through the Word Bank for Short I.

Alphabetize letter tiles a to z with your student.

New Teaching

Segment Words with Final Blends

Create four gray token boxes on the app or lay four tokens on the table.

Point to the tokens. "Segment the word *tent*." *Student repeats the word and says the individual sounds. As he says each sound, he pulls a token toward himself.*

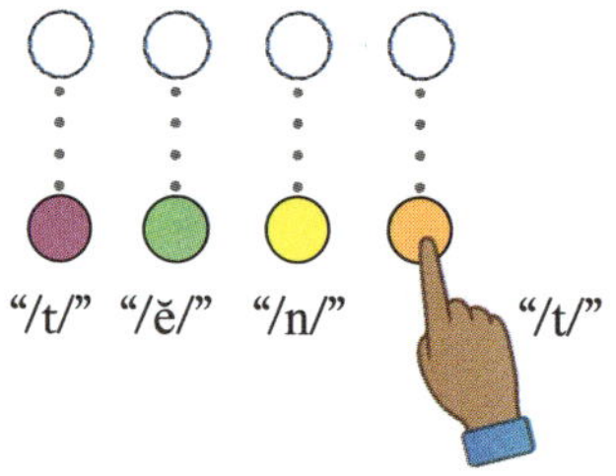

Repeat the activity with the following words.

damp **fast** **mint** **wept**

New Teaching
(continued)

Complete Activity Sheet *(Optional)*

"Let's break some words apart."

Breaking Words Apart: Final Blends

Remove pages 103-105 from the *Zip into Spelling* activity book.

Cut apart the segmenting cards.

Demonstrate the activity by setting the tent card in front of your student. Point to the illustration.

"This is a tent. Say *tent*." *Tent.*

"Watch as I break up the word *tent*." Working from left to right, touch a circle for each sound as you say it: "/t/–/ĕ/–/n/–/t/. Tent."

Have your student repeat the activity using the remaining segmenting cards. Name each item so your student doesn't have to guess what it is.

Answer Key

1. tent	/t/–/ĕ/–/n/–/t/	6. raft	/r/–/ă/–/f/–/t/
2. pond	/p/–/ŏ/–/n/–/d/	7. nest	/n/–/ĕ/–/s/–/t/
3. lamp	/l/–/ă/–/m/–/p/	8. melt	/m/–/ĕ/–/l/–/t/
4. list	/l/–/ĭ/–/s/–/t/	9. jump	/j/–/ŭ/–/m/–/p/
5. hand	/h/–/ă/–/n/–/d/	10. gift	/g/–/ĭ/–/f/–/t/

Spell Word Cards 71-80 with Letter Tiles

Dictate the words and have your student spell them with letter tiles. Use the **Procedure for Spelling with Letter Tiles** in Appendix E.

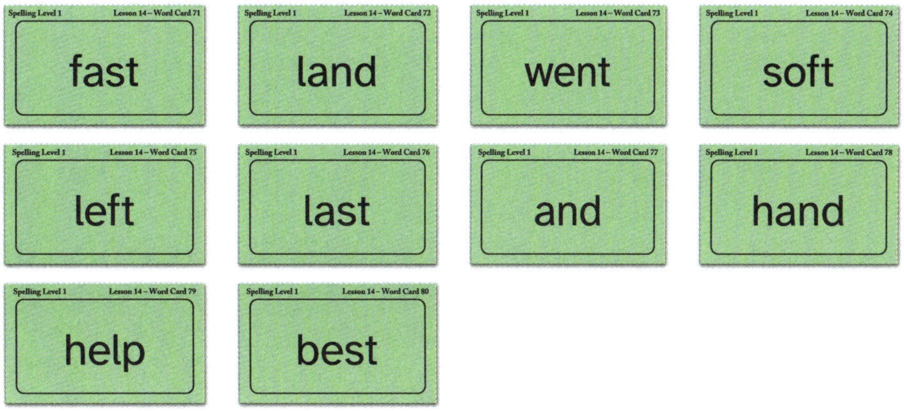

New Teaching
(continued)

Spell on Paper

Once your student is able to spell the words using the letter tiles, have him take out his dictation notebook. Dictate Word Cards 71-80 and have your student spell the words on paper.

File the Word Cards behind the Review divider in the Spelling Review Box.

Practice More Words

The following words reinforce the concepts taught in this lesson. For additional practice, have your student spell some of them in his dictation notebook.

band (marching band)	**gift**	**felt**	**list**
sand	**tent**	**lend**	**west**
pond	**lamp**	**must** (must do)	**jump**
just	**melt**	**hint**	**dust**
raft	**past** (run past)	**send**	**nest**
next	**end**	**test**	**lost**
rest	**hunt**	**wind** (breeze)	**sent**
held	**vent**	**act**	**mint**
damp	**pump**	**bent**	**vest**
pest	**belt**	**limp**	

New Teaching
(continued)

Complete Word Search

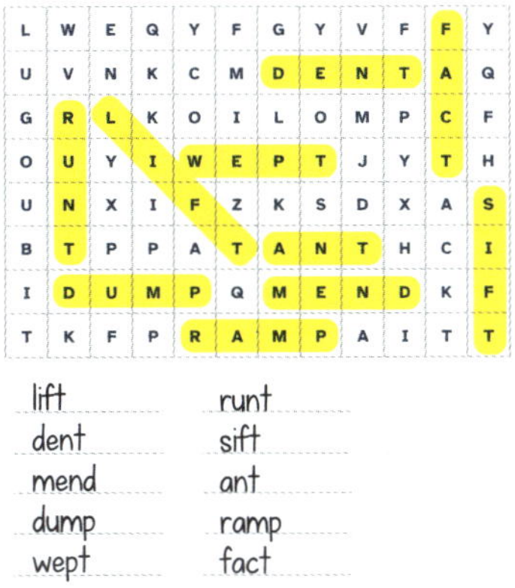

Turn to page 107 in the activity book.

Part 1: Dictate the following words and have your student write them on the lines provided.

lift	**runt**	**dent**	**sift**
mend	**dump**	**ramp**	**wept**
fact	**ant** (ant colony)		

Part 2 ***(Optional)*****:** Have your student find and circle the words hidden in the Word Search.

Complete Activity Sheet *(Optional)*

"Let's pack up to go camping!"

<u>Pitch a Tent</u>

Remove pages 109-112 from the activity book.

Cut out the camping equipment cards and place them in a pile. Cut a slit in the tent as indicated by the dotted line.

Choose nine words from this lesson that you think would most benefit your student to practice. Dictate the words one by one and have your student write each word on the back of an equipment card. After spelling the word correctly, he may place the equipment in the tent.

Continue until all the equipment is in the tent and the student has practiced all nine words.

New Teaching
(continued)

Dictate Phrases

Dictate several phrases each day. Your student should repeat each phrase and write it in his dictation notebook.

best gift	**left hand**	**went past Jim**
ten men	**run and help**	**just rest**
soft sand	**lost ship**	**at an end**
last pet	**fast jog**	**zip it up**

Advanced Application

For advanced practice, have your student turn to the Advanced Application sheet on page 108 of the activity book.

"You can spell *help*. Now spell *helper*, as in *My kitchen helper broke all the spoons." Student writes* help *on the first line.*

Continue with the remaining words. Dictate the full word, read the sentence, and have your student fill in the missing syllable.

1.	**helper**	My kitchen helper broke all the spoons.
2.	**quicksand**	My knapsack sank in the quicksand.
3.	**ventilation**	Our clubhouse needs better ventilation.
4.	**handshake**	A firm handshake is a sign of confidence.
5.	**forklift**	The forklift dropped its load of boxes.
6.	**August**	August days are long, hot, and hazy.
7.	**actor**	The actor blew kisses to his adoring fans.
8.	**lamplight**	We read our stories in a warm ray of lamplight.
9.	**landslide**	I won the talent show by a landslide!
10.	**antidote**	Do you have an antidote for this snakebite?
11.	**absent**	José was absent from our secret meeting.
12.	**headband**	Who bent the antlers on my reindeer headband?
13.	**dustbin**	I accidentally threw your tiara in the dustbin.
14.	**justify**	How does she justify leaving the team?
15.	**jumping**	These baby goats are jumping all over me!

Track Your Progress

Mark the Progress Chart

Remember that each lesson may require several sessions to complete. Before moving on, ask yourself these questions:

1. Can your student segment words with final blends?
2. Has your student mastered eight out of the ten Word Cards?

If the answer to both is yes, have your student mark Lesson 14 on the Progress Chart and move on to the next lesson!

Lesson 15 Initial Blends

Objective

This lesson teaches how to segment and spell words with initial blends.

You Will Need

- ☐ four tokens
- ☐ Word Cards 81-90
- ☐ *Zip into Spelling* pages 113-122

Before You Begin

Preview Initial Blends

A blend at the beginning of a word is called an **initial blend**. Listen for the initial blends in the following words.

glob snip trot flat swim

In blends, each consonant keeps its own sound but is said in rapid succession.

This lesson will give your student practice in segmenting words with initial blends to make them easier to spell. If your student needs additional help in segmenting words with blends, be sure to check out the "Hop to It" activity in Appendix J.

Don't Forget!

Remember that a consonant blend is different from a consonant team. In consonant blends such as s-t, p-l, and f-r, each letter retains its own sound. In consonant teams such as th, sh, and ch, two letters combine to make a completely new sound.

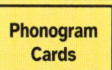

Review

Phonogram Cards

Review a selection of Phonogram Cards from behind the Review divider in your student's Spelling Review Box.

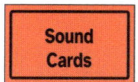

Sound Cards

Review a selection of Sound Cards from behind the Review divider. Have your student write the phonograms in her dictation notebook.

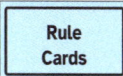

Rule Cards

Review a selection of Rule Cards from behind the Review divider.

Review
(continued)

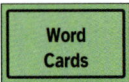

Review a selection of Word Cards from behind the Review divider. Have your student write the words in her dictation notebook.

Read through the Word Bank for Short O.

Alphabetize letter tiles a to z with your student.

Is the daily review helping your student internalize all the concepts she's learned so far? Are the decks behind the Mastered dividers getting bigger? Does your student have a firm grasp on the Rule Card rules for spelling?

Mastered cards will be reviewed again in Lesson 17 to keep them fresh in your student's mind.

New Teaching

Segment Words with Initial Blends

Create four gray token boxes on the app or lay four tokens on the table.

Point to the tokens. "Segment the word *flip*." *Student repeats the word and says the individual sounds. As she says each sound, she pulls a token toward herself.*

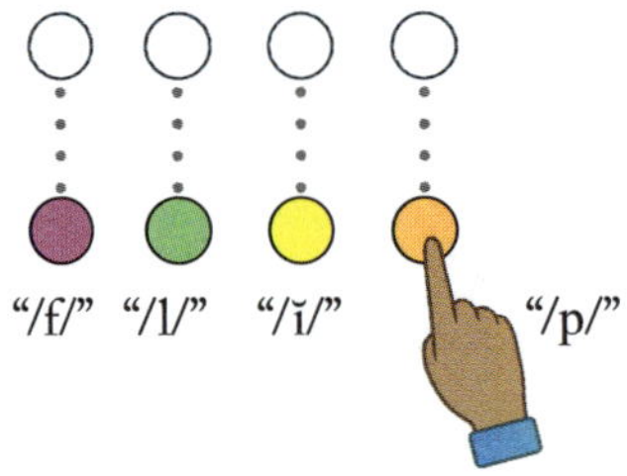

Repeat the activity with the following words.

stem **plug** **slam** **grip**

New Teaching
(continued)

Complete Activity Sheet *(Optional)*

"Let's break some more words apart."

Breaking Words Apart: Initial Blends
Remove pages 113-115 from the *Zip into Spelling* activity book.

Cut apart the segmenting cards.

Demonstrate the activity by setting the drip card in front of your student. Point to the illustration.

"This is a drip. Say *drip*." *Drip*.

"Watch as I break up the word *drip*." Working from left to right, touch a circle for each sound as you say it: "/d/–/r/–/ĭ/–/p/. Drip."

Have your student repeat the activity using the remaining segmenting cards. Name each item so your student doesn't have to guess what it is.

Answer Key

1. drip	/d/–/r/–/ĭ/–/p/	6. flag	/f/–/l/–/ă/–/g/
2. sled	/s/–/l/–/ĕ/–/d/	7. twig	/t/–/w/–/ĭ/–/g/
3. frog	/f/–/r/–/ŏ/–/g/	8. swim	/s/–/w/–/ĭ/–/m/
4. spot	/s/–/p/–/ŏ/–/t/	9. stop	/s/–/t/–/ŏ/–/p/
5. plum	/p/–/l/–/ŭ/–/m/	10. flip	/f/–/l/–/ĭ/–/p/

Spell Word Cards 81-90 with Letter Tiles

Dictate the words and have your student spell them with letter tiles. Use the **Procedure for Spelling with Letter Tiles** in Appendix E.

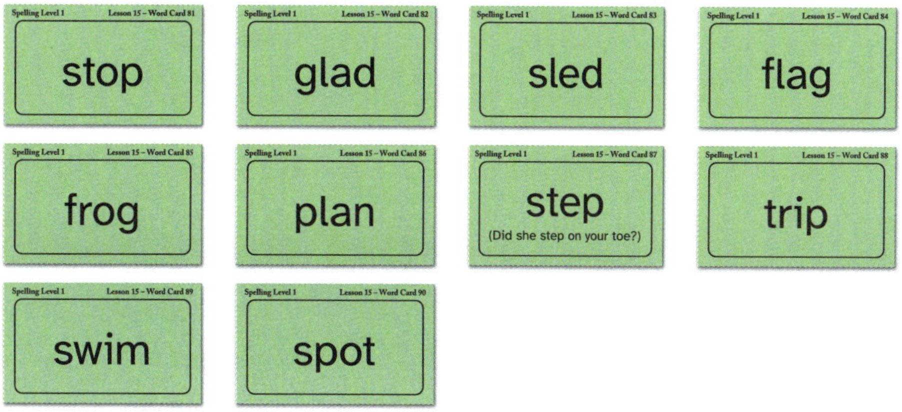

New Teaching
(continued)

Spell on Paper

Once your student is able to spell the words using the letter tiles, have her take out her dictation notebook. Dictate Word Cards 81-90 and have your student spell the words on paper.

File the Word Cards behind the Review divider in the Spelling Review Box.

Practice More Words

The following words reinforce the concepts taught in this lesson. For additional practice, have your student spell some of them in her dictation notebook.

grip	**prop**	**spin**	**flip**
slip	**plug**	**Fran**	**slid**
swam	**snip**	**drip**	**spun**
brag	**sped**	**fled**	**twin**
Greg	**blot**	**grin**	**Brad**
plum (eat a plum)	**twig**	**flat**	**snag**
trap	**snug**	**stem**	**grid**
blob	**prim**	**drop**	**slam**
brim	**slim**	**plod**	**spit**
snap	**Stan**	**Glen**	**plop**
grim	**Fred**	**grab**	**plus**
slap	**drag**	**smug**	

New Teaching
(continued)

> **Tip!**
>
> The Pronounce for Spelling technique may come in handy for two sets of words in this list:
>
> - Words beginning with t-r: *trim, trap,* and *trot*. In these words, many students pronounce the t as /ch/, as in *chrim*.
> - Words beginning with d-r: *drip, drop, drag, drab,* and *drum*. In these words, many students pronounce the d as /j/, as in *jrip*.
>
> Carefully enunciating the initial consonant will help your student spell these words correctly.

Complete Word Search

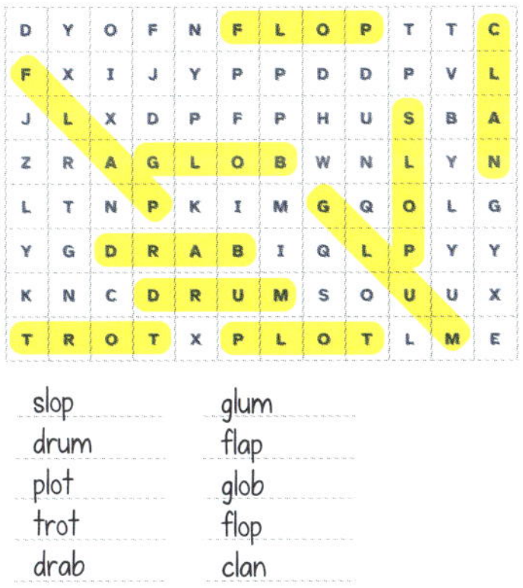

D Y O F N F L O P T T C
F X I J Y P P D D P V L
J L X D P F P H U S B A
Z R A G L O B W N L Y N
L T N P K I M G Q O L G
Y G D R A B I Q L P Y Y
K N C D R U M S O U U X
T R O T X P L O T L M E
slop
drum
plot
trot
drab
glum
flap
glob
flop
clan

Turn to page 117 in the activity book.

Part 1: Dictate the following words and have your student write them on the lines provided.

slop	**drum**	**plot**	**trot**
drab	**glum**	**flap**	**glob**
flop	**clan**		

Part 2 *(Optional)*: Have your student find and circle the words hidden in the Word Search.

Complete Activity Sheet *(Optional)*

"Now it's time to clean up the kitchen!"

Wash the Dishes

Remove pages 119-122 from the activity book.

Cut a slit in the dishwasher as indicated by the dotted line. Cut out the dirty dish cards and place them in a pile with the dirty dishes facing up.

Choose twelve words from this lesson that you think would most benefit your student to

New Teaching
(continued)

practice. Dictate the words one by one and have your student write each word on a dirty dish card. After spelling the word correctly, she may place the dirty dish in the dishwasher.

Continue until all the dirty dishes have been loaded into the dishwasher and the student has practiced all twelve words. Your student may then remove the cards from the dishwasher and flip them over to reveal the clean dishes.

Dictate Phrases

Dictate several phrases each day. Your student should repeat each phrase and write it in her dictation notebook.

must stop	**hid his plum**	**grab them**
pond frog	**west wind**	**drop that sled**
flip and spin	**is glad**	**swam in jam**
step on	**plan this trip**	**then had ham**

Advanced Application

For advanced practice, have your student turn to the Advanced Application sheet on page 118 of the activity book.

"You can spell *sled*. Now spell *bobsled*, as in *Penguin Pete slid down the iceberg on a bobsled." Student writes* sled *on the first line.*

Continue with the remaining words. Dictate the full word, read the sentence, and have your student fill in the missing syllable.

1.	**bobsled**	Penguin Pete slid down the iceberg on a bobsled.
2.	**swimming**	I'm sad that our swimming hole dried up.
3.	**stopwatch**	Carlo timed our race with a stopwatch.
4.	**spotless**	The butler demanded a spotless house.
5.	**pilgrim**	The pilgrim wore shiny buckles on his shoes.
6.	**footstep**	I heard a footstep on the stairs...was it yours?
7.	**snapdragon**	Snapdragon plants painted the garden with color.
8.	**handspun**	Grandma made my scarf with handspun yarn.
9.	**smuggle**	Try to smuggle extra cookies out of the kitchen!
10.	**raindrop**	Emma caught a raindrop on her tongue.
11.	**spinach**	Does anyone love spinach more than Popeye?
12.	**drumstick**	Her drumstick hit the cymbal with a crash.
13.	**earplug**	The music was so loud my earplug popped out!
14.	**primrose**	Anika carried a delicate primrose bouquet.
15.	**trapeze**	The trapeze artists swooped above our heads.

Track Your Progress

Mark the Progress Chart

Remember that each lesson may require several sessions to complete. Before moving on, ask yourself these questions:

1. Can your student segment words with initial blends?

2. Has your student mastered eight out of the ten Word Cards?

If the answer to both is yes, have your student mark Lesson 15 on the Progress Chart and move on to the next lesson!

Wowza, that's quite a list of words with initial blends! Check out these snazzy sentences I wrote with some of them.
Don't slip on the slop.
Feeling glum? Eat a plum!
I'd flip for a drip of honey!
Tee-hee!

Lesson 16 The Soft C Rule

Objective

This lesson teaches when c says /s/ and how to spell words beginning with c and k.

You Will Need

- ☐ Rule Card 3
- ☐ blank blue tile*
- ☐ *Zip into Spelling* pages 123-134
- ☐ Word Cards 91-100

Before You Begin

Preview The Soft C Rule

Remove the Soft C Rule poster from page 123 of the activity book and keep it handy for use in the lesson.

This rule explains that c says its "soft" sound, /s/, before e, i, or y.

Read the following examples and listen for the /s/ sound.

center	**circle**	**fancy**
cycle	**place**	**city**

This is a highly reliable pattern with very few exceptions. The exceptions occur in higher-level words of foreign origin, such as *cello* and *concerto* (in which c followed by e says /ch/) and *Celtic* (in which c followed by e says /k/).

How to Handle Spelling Mistakes

Misspellings happen! And when they do, here are four tips for fixing them.

1. **Ask the student to slowly read exactly what he has written down.** Often your student will see his own error and be able to fix it.

2. **Figure out what caused the mistake.**
   Does he pronounce the word incorrectly?
   Do you need to re-teach something?
   Did he segment the word incorrectly?
   Do you need to review a Rule Card or a Sound Card?

3. **Have your student spell the word again, first with tiles and then on paper.**

4. **Create a Word Card for the misspelled word so it can be reviewed in a later lesson.**

Before You Begin
(continued)

Customizing your student's instruction in this way will help him grow in spelling ability more quickly.

For more tips on correcting spelling mistakes, and what to do when your student makes a mistake *outside* of spelling lessons, see Appendix K.

*Blank blue tiles are included in the Letter Tiles kit. If you are using the Letter Tiles app, you'll find the blank blue tile at the end of the Alphabet tiles category.

Review

Review a selection of Phonogram Cards from behind the Review divider in your student's Spelling Review Box.

Review a selection of Sound Cards from behind the Review divider. Have your student write the phonograms in his dictation notebook.

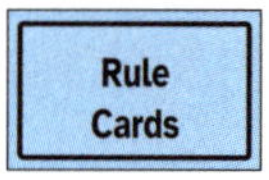

Review a selection of Rule Cards from behind the Review divider.

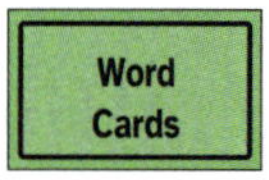

Review a selection of Word Cards from behind the Review divider. Have your student write the words in his dictation notebook.

Always shuffle the Word Cards before reviewing them. By doing so, your student will practice words with a variety of patterns.

Read through the Word Bank for Short E.

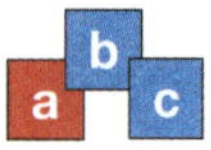

Alphabetize letter tiles a to z with your student.

New Teaching

Teach Spelling Rule 3: The Soft C Rule

Move letter tile c into the workspace.

"Tell me the two sounds of the letter c." */k/–/s/.*

"When c says /s/, we say that the c is **soft**."

"When c says /k/, we say that the c is **hard**."

"Tell me the **hard** sound of c." */k/.*

"Tell me the **soft** sound of c." */s/.*

"We have a way to tell which of these two sounds the c is going to make."

Arrange letter tiles c, e, i, and red y in the workspace as follows.

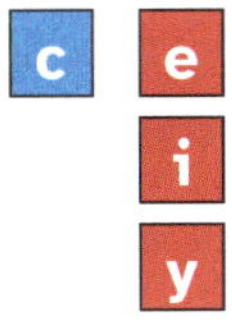

"If c is followed by e, i, or y, it says /s/."

Show the c tile visiting the letters e, i, and y one at a time. "In front of e it says /s/. In front of i it says /s/. And in front of y it says /s/."

"We can say that e, i, and y make the c soft."

Take out the Soft C Rule poster and explore it with your student.

Read the sample words aloud and listen for the /s/ sound: *race, city, cycle.*

You may wish to hang the poster in your lesson area for future reference.

New Teaching
(continued)

Read Rule Card 3 with your student and then file it behind the Review divider.

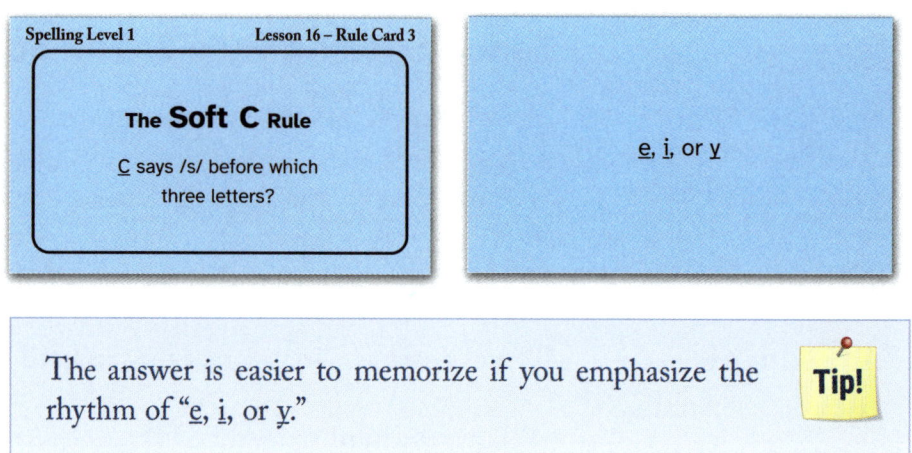

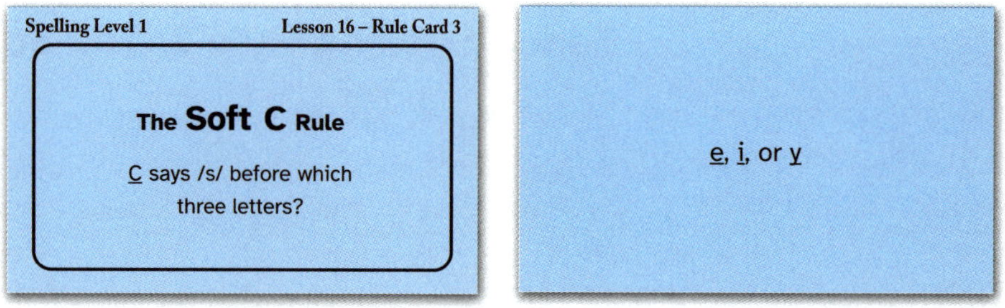

Spelling Level 1
Lesson 16 – Rule Card 3
The Soft C Rule
C says /s/ before which three letters?
e, i, or y

The answer is easier to memorize if you emphasize the rhythm of "e, i, or y."

Tip!

Decide If C Is Hard or Soft

Arrange letter tiles c, a, o, u, l, and r in the workspace as follows.

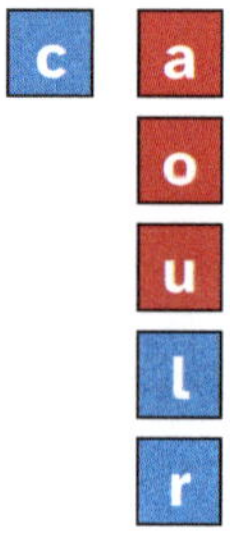

"C says /s/ before e, i, or y, but it says /k/ before everything else."

Show the c tile visiting the letters a, o, u, l, and r one at a time.

"In front of a it says /k/. In front of o it says /k/. In front of u it says /k/." Repeat for l and r.

When your student understands this concept, mix up the e, i, and y with the a, o, u, l, and r and place the c in front of each one. Ask your student to tell you whether the c is hard or soft.

Before moving on, work with the tile activity above until you are confident that your student has mastered it.

New Teaching
(continued)

Choose between C and K

"Today we will spell words that have the sound of /k/ at the beginning. Repeat these words after me and listen for the /k/ sound: *camp, kid, kept, cash.*" *Student repeats the words.*

"Some of these words begin with c and some begin with k."

Move letter tiles **c** and **k** into the workspace.

"Let's spell the word *kid.*"

Build the word *kid*, placing a blank blue tile in place of the /k/ sound.

[ ] i d

"In place of this blank tile, we need to decide whether to use c or k."

"We always try c first." c i d

"Does c work?" *No.*

"Why not?" *The c becomes soft. (Or, the c says /s/ because of the i.)*

"What would this word say?" */sĭd/.*

"So we know that we use k." k i d

Build the following words using a blank blue tile for the /k/ sound. Dictate the word and have your student replace the blank tile with c or k. If necessary, remind him that we always try the c tile first.

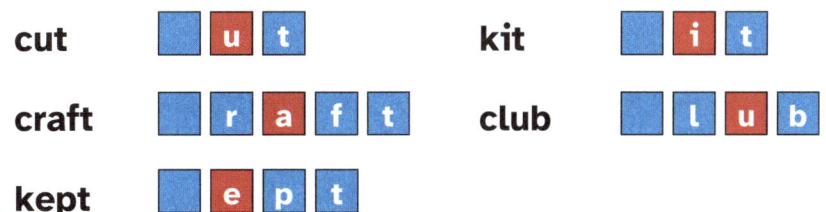

cut	[ ] u t	**kit**	[ ] i t
craft	[ ] r a f t	**club**	[ ] l u b
kept	[ ] e p t		

> **Tip!** Here is an easy way for your student to remember whether to try c first or k first: c comes before k in the alphabet, so try c first.

New Teaching
(continued)

Complete Activity Sheet *(Optional)*

"Let's help these racers cross the finish line."

Race to the Finish!

Remove pages 125-127 from the *Zip into Spelling* activity book.

Cut out the bicycle cards and place them in a pile on the racetrack in numerical order 1-9.

"These racers want to cross the finish line. I'll say a word and you'll decide whether the word needs a c or a k to spell the sound of /k/."

One at a time, dictate the words below and have your student complete the word by writing either a c or a k on the line on the appropriate bicycle card. If he chooses correctly, he may send the bicycle to the finish line.

1. kept	2. camp	3. can
4. cap	5. cut	6. craft
7. kid	8. cup	9. cast

Continue until all the bicycles have crossed the finish line.

Spell Word Cards 91-100 with Letter Tiles

Dictate the words and have your student spell them with letter tiles.

> For each of these spelling words, have your student select the blank blue tile when he hears the sound of /k/. He should spell the rest of the word and then go back and replace the blank with either a c or a k.

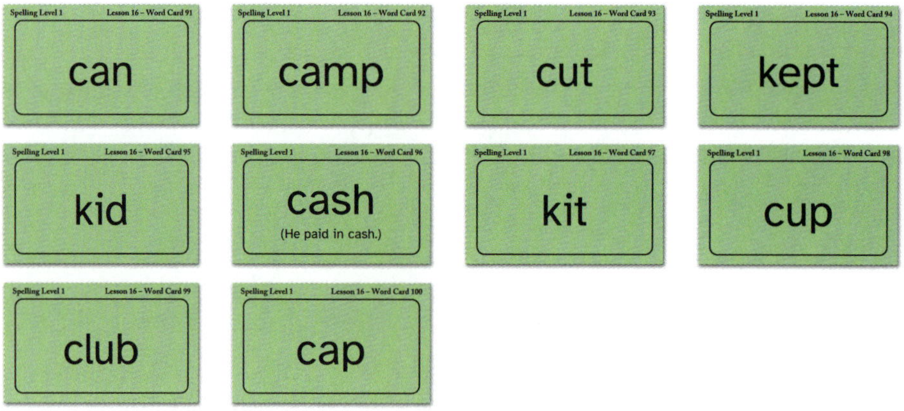

New Teaching
(continued)

Spell on Paper

Once your student is able to spell the words using the letter tiles, have him take out his dictation notebook. Dictate Word Cards 91-100 and have your student spell the words on paper.

File the Word Cards behind the Review divider in the Spelling Review Box.

Practice More Words

The following words reinforce the concepts taught in this lesson. For additional practice, have your student spell some of them in his dictation notebook.

cab	**cast** (plaster cast)	**cub**	**Ken**	**crab**
crash	**crop**	**Kim**	**cost**	**cod**
cat	**cloth**			

> For the word *cost*, you may have to remind your student to "pronounce for spelling." In many regions, it is pronounced *cawst*.
>
> **Tip!**

Complete Word Search

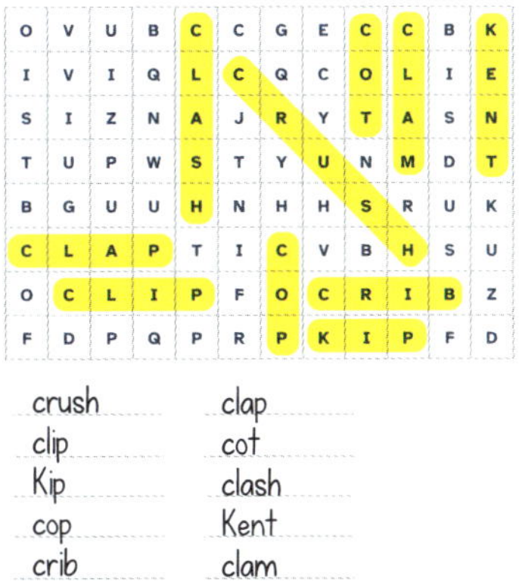

Turn to page 129 in the activity book.

Part 1: Dictate the following words and have your student write them on the lines provided.

crush	**clap**	**clip**	**cot**
Kip	**clash**	**cop**	**Kent**
crib	**clam**		

Part 2 *(Optional)*: Have your student find and circle the words hidden in the Word Search.

New Teaching
(continued)

Complete Activity Sheet *(Optional)*

"Now let's go on a treasure hunt!"

Bike Trail Treasures

Remove pages 131-134 from the activity book.

Cut a slit in the bike basket as indicated by the dotted line. Cut out the treasure cards and place them in a pile with the illustrations facing up.

Choose twelve words from this lesson that you think would most benefit your student to practice. Dictate the words one by one and have your student write each word on the back of a treasure card. After spelling the word correctly, he may put the treasure in the bike basket.

When your student selects a card that says "Lucky Find!," he doesn't need to write a word but instead may put the card directly in the bike basket.

Continue until all the treasures have been added to the basket and the student has practiced all twelve words.

Dictate Phrases

Dictate several phrases each day. Your student should repeat each phrase and write it in his dictation notebook.

Kim sent	**tent kit**	**his club**
kept fit	**last crab**	**such cost**
at camp	**that kid**	**much cash**
drop this cup	**bend and cut**	**Ken can hop**

Advanced Application

For advanced practice, have your student turn to the Advanced Application sheet on page 130 of the activity book.

"You can spell *can*. Now spell *candle*, as in *Don't mishandle the candle, please!*" *Student writes* can *on the first line.*

Continue with the remaining words. Dictate the full word, read the sentence, and have your student fill in the missing syllable.

1.	**candle**	Don't mishandle the candle, please!
2.	**campground**	What a spooky campground this is!
3.	**shortcut**	Let's take a shortcut to the creek.
4.	**cashier**	Why did the cashier smush my marshmallows?
5.	**cupcake**	I decorated my cupcake with sprinkles.
6.	**kitten**	The kitten chewed up my shoelaces!
7.	**clipboard**	Place these forms on your clipboard, please.
8.	**clubhouse**	We painted our secret clubhouse bright yellow.
9.	**capital**	Does Snickerdoodle begin with a capital S?
10.	**costly**	The bungling burglars made a costly mistake.
11.	**codfish**	The fisherman's net was full of codfish.
12.	**cotton**	My bunny's ears are softer than cotton.
13.	**caterpillar**	A caterpillar must spend a fortune on shoes.
14.	**crabapple**	Her horse ate fruit from the crabapple tree.
15.	**washcloth**	Who left this soapy washcloth on the floor?

Track Your Progress

Mark the Progress Chart

Remember that each lesson may require several sessions to complete. Before moving on, ask yourself these questions:

1. Does your student have a firm grasp of the Soft C Rule?
2. Has your student mastered eight out of the ten Word Cards?

If the answer to both is yes, have your student mark Lesson 16 on the Progress Chart and move on to the next lesson!

Lesson 17 The Floss Rule

Objective

This lesson teaches that letters f, l, and s may be doubled at the end of a word.

You Will Need

- ☐ extra f, l, and s tiles
- ☐ *Zip into Spelling* pages 135-146
- ☐ Rule Card 4
- ☐ Word Cards 101-110
- ☐ piece of floss (optional)

Before You Begin

Letter Tile Setup

If you are using physical letter tiles, set out extra f, l, and s tiles so your student can spell words with double letters.

Preview The Floss Rule

Remove the Floss Rule poster from page 135 of the activity book and keep it handy for use in the lesson.

The Floss Rule explains that we often double f, l, and s after a single vowel at the end of a one-syllable word.

The word *floss* is a great example because it follows the rule and contains the letters f, l, and s. Look at these other words that follow the rule.

ff:	**stiff**	**cuff**	**off**
ll:	**bill**	**roll**	**dull**
ss:	**pass**	**miss**	**less**

Now look at these examples of words that do *not* meet all the criteria of the Floss Rule.

until (because it isn't a one-syllable word)
peel (because there is more than one vowel)
shelf (because the f doesn't come right after the vowel)

In addition, the rule does not apply when a final s sounds like /z/, as in *has*, *was*, and *is*.

We double the f, l, and s after a single vowel in hundreds of words, but there are several common words in which we do not double the last letter even though they meet all the criteria. Your student has already learned six of those words: *if, gas, yes, this, us,* and *bus*.

Review

It's time to review the cards behind the Mastered dividers to ensure they stay fresh in your student's mind. Shuffle the cards and choose a selection for review.

Review a selection of Phonogram Cards from behind the **Mastered** divider in your student's Spelling Review Box.

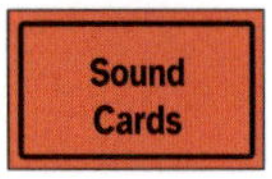

Review a selection of Sound Cards from behind the **Mastered** divider. Have your student write the phonograms in her dictation notebook.

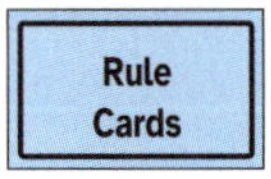

Review a selection of Rule Cards from behind the **Mastered** divider.

Review a selection of Word Cards from behind the **Mastered** divider. Have your student write the words in her dictation notebook.

Read through the Word Banks as necessary.

Alphabetize letter tiles a to z with your student.

New Teaching

Teach Spelling Rule 4: The Floss Rule

"Today we're going to look at an interesting word: *floss*."

Build the word .

Point to the last s. "See how the word ends with two s tiles? Why are there two s's instead of just one? We're going to find out!"

New Teaching
(continued)

Take out the Floss Rule poster and show it to your student.

"The rule says *We often double f, l, and s at the end of a word...*" Point to the end of the word.

"*...after a single vowel...*" Point to the o. "A *single vowel* means just one vowel. There aren't two vowels in a row."

"*...in a one-syllable word.*"

"The word *floss* is a great example of this rule. It follows all the parts of the rule and contains the letters f, l, and s to help remind us."

"Let's look at another word."

Move the t, e, and l tiles into the workspace.

"I want to spell the word *tell*. Let's follow this poster and figure out if we need to double the last letter."

"Is l one of the letters that we often double at the end of a word?" *Yes.*

"Does the l come right after a single vowel?" *Yes.*

"Is *tell* a one-syllable word?" *Yes.*

"Good! So we double the l." Finish building the word. t e l l

Explore the sample words on the Floss Rule poster with your student.

You may wish to hang the poster in your lesson area for future reference.

New Teaching
(continued)

Read Rule Card 4 with your student and then file it behind the Review divider.

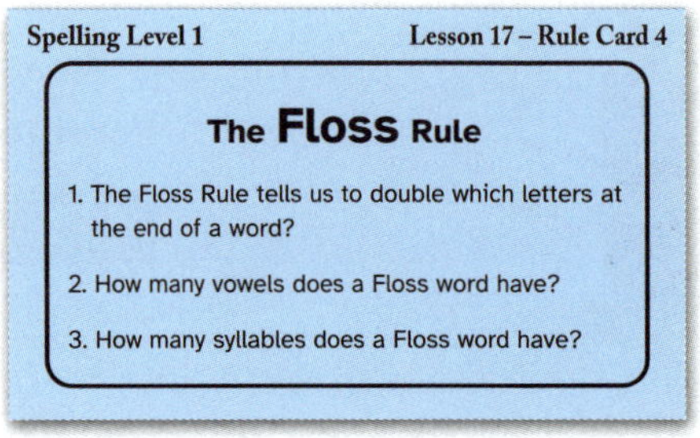

Spelling Level 1
Lesson 17 – Rule Card 4
The Floss Rule
1. The Floss Rule tells us to double which letters at the end of a word?
2. How many vowels does a Floss word have?
3. How many syllables does a Floss word have?

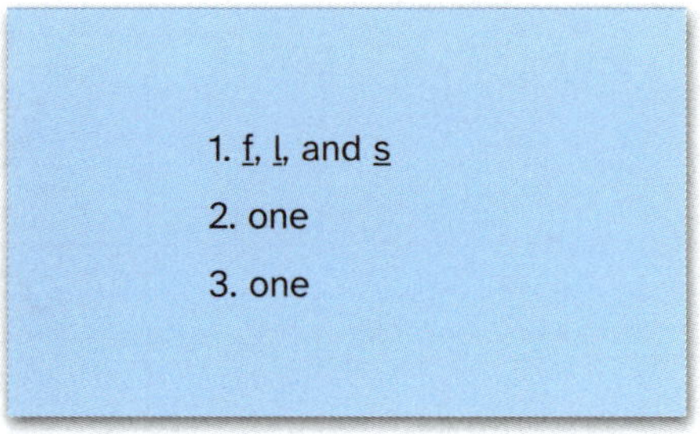

1. f, l, and s
2. one
3. one

Complete Activity Sheet *(Optional)*

"It's time to floss! Let's see if we can find some floss in the cabinet."

Time to Floss

Remove pages 137-140 from the *Zip into Spelling* activity book.

Cut out the medicine cabinet and fold the ends toward the middle to create the cabinet doors. Cut out the object cards and place them in the medicine cabinet with the words facing up.

Have your student open the cabinet and take out a card. She should read the word and explain why the word *is* a floss word (because it ends in a double f, l, or s) or *is not* a floss word (because it ends in a single consonant). She may then turn the card over to reveal either a floss container or another medicine cabinet item. If she has correctly identified the word, she may keep the item; if not, return it to the medicine cabinet for another try.

Continue until the medicine cabinet is empty.

New Teaching
(continued)

Spell Word Cards 101-110 with Letter Tiles

Dictate the words and have your student spell them with letter tiles. Use the **Procedure for Spelling with Letter Tiles** in Appendix E.

For the words *doll* and *off*, you may need to tell your student to "pronounce for spelling." In many regions, the words are pronounced *dawl* and *awf* in conversational speech.

If your student tries to spell *sell* with a c̲ (as in *cell*), tell her to use an s̲ and explain the difference between these homophones.

Spell on Paper

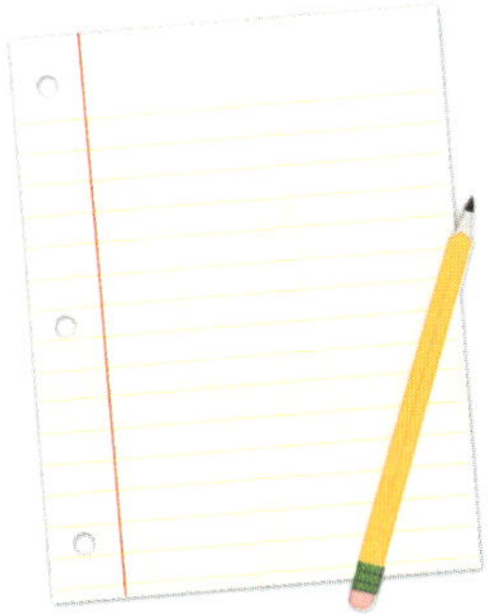

Once your student is able to spell the words using the letter tiles, have her take out her dictation notebook. Dictate Word Cards 101-110 and have your student spell the words on paper.

File the Word Cards behind the Review divider in the Spelling Review Box.

New Teaching
(continued)

Practice More Words

The following words reinforce the concepts taught in this lesson. For additional practice, have your student spell some of them in her dictation notebook.

stuff	**kiss**	**class**	**press**	**pill**
dress	**drill**	**fill** (fill a cup)	**ill**	**mess**
spell	**bill**	**less**	**still**	**Jill**
pass	**cuff**	**cliff**	**shall**	**shell**
well	**kill**	**stiff**	**loss**	**bell**
sniff	**Bess**	**brass**	**Swiss**	**fluff**
chess	**floss**	**boss**	**bliss**	**Bill**
moss	**huff**	**Jess**	**Russ**	**chill**
spill	**bluff**	**Ross**	**cross**	**fuss**
Jeff	**swell**	**gruff**	**Tess**	**muff**

Complete Word Search

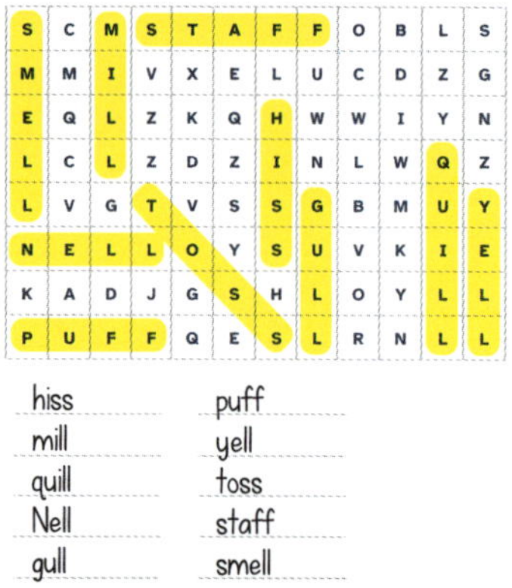

Turn to page 141 in the activity book.

Part 1: Dictate the following words and have your student write them on the lines provided.

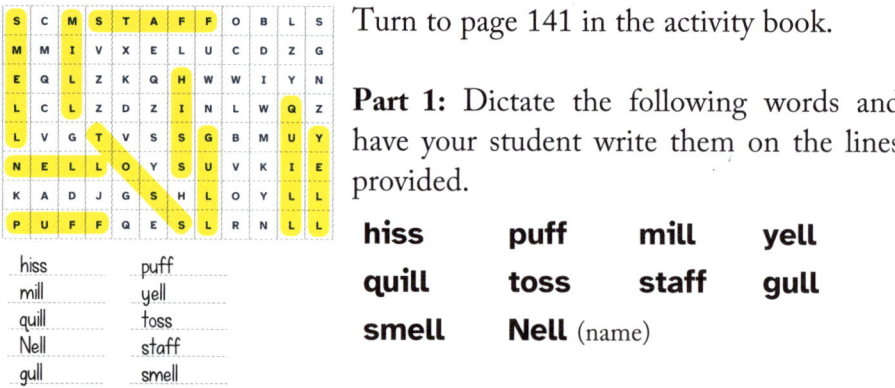

hiss	**puff**	**mill**	**yell**
quill	**toss**	**staff**	**gull**
smell	**Nell** (name)		

Part 2 *(Optional)*: Have your student find and circle the words hidden in the Word Search.

New Teaching
(continued)

Complete Activity Sheet *(Optional)*

"This hippo has been eating lots of sweet and sticky foods! Let's help her floss her teeth."

Hippo Needs to Floss

Remove pages 143-146 from the activity book.

Cut out the floss strand under the hippo illustration. Cut around the hippo's teeth as indicated by the dotted lines. Cut out the food cards and place them in a pile in the hippo's mouth, with the illustrations facing up.

Choose twelve words from this lesson that you think would most benefit your student to practice. Dictate the words one by one and have your student write each word on the back of a food card. After spelling the word correctly, she may set the card aside.

Continue until the hippo's mouth is empty and the student has practiced all twelve words. The student can then floss the hippo's teeth using the illustrated floss strand or a real piece of floss, if desired.

Dictate Phrases

Dictate several phrases each day. Your student should repeat each phrase and write it in her dictation notebook.

fell off	**will sell**	**sniff and smell**
tell Dan	**fill this glass**	**hug and kiss**
math class	**big cliff**	**best dress**
sit still	**rag doll**	**dug that well**

Advanced Application

For advanced practice, have your student turn to the Advanced Application sheet on page 142 of the activity book.

"You can spell *mill*. Now spell *windmill*, as in *A crooked old cat lives in that windmill." Student writes* mill *on the first line.*

Continue with the remaining words. Dictate the full word, read the sentence, and have your student fill in the missing syllable.

1.	**windmill**	A crooked old cat lives in that windmill.
2.	**crossroads**	The bus will pick us up at the crossroads.
3.	**classroom**	Our classroom pet is a gerbil named Gretchen.
4.	**kissing**	My kissing fish don't seem to like each other.
5.	**lesson**	I loved your lesson on ventriloquism!
6.	**seashell**	Sally sells seashell necklaces for six dollars.
7.	**uphill**	Peddling my bike uphill is exhausting!
8.	**spyglass**	The pirate dropped his spyglass in the sea.
9.	**offhand**	I can't think of a funny example offhand.
10.	**dollhouse**	The dog knocked my dollhouse off the table!
11.	**sundress**	Sam sewed a blue sundress for his sister.
12.	**surpass**	You will never surpass my taco-eating record!
13.	**gruffness**	The three billy goats' gruffness was legendary.
14.	**instill**	It's impossible to instill good manners in a hyena.
15.	**earmuff**	Why does Wayne wear only one earmuff?

Tip!

In case your student is wondering: Floss Rule words retain their double f, l, or s even when combined with other words, prefixes, or suffixes. For example, in *crossroads*, the base word *cross* continues to follow the Floss Rule, even when it is combined with *roads*. In *kissing*, the base word *kiss* continues to follow the Floss Rule even when suffix -ing is added.

Track Your Progress

Mark the Progress Chart

Remember that each lesson may require several sessions to complete. Before moving on, ask yourself these questions:

1. Does your student have a firm grasp of the Floss Rule?
2. Has your student mastered eight out of the ten Word Cards?

If the answer to both is yes, have your student mark Lesson 17 on the Progress Chart and move on to the next lesson!

Yikes, that hippo scared the fuzz right off my tummy!
I guess that means I have a buzz-cut now.
Seriously, though, flossing is important. I personally like to use lemongrass (smells so good!). And hey—GRASS is a Floss word! BUZZ!

Lesson 18 CK and the CK Rule

Objective

This lesson introduces consonant team ck and teaches when to use ck and k for the sound of /k/ at the end of a one-syllable word.

You Will Need

- ☐ letter tile ck
- ☐ Phonogram Card 30
- ☐ Sound Card 30
- ☐ Rule Card 5
- ☐ blank blue tile
- ☐ *Zip into Spelling* pages 147-154
- ☐ Word Cards 111-120

Before You Begin

Preview Consonant Team CK

Consonant team ck says /k/ as in *duck*.

When we practice the Phonogram Card for ck, we say "/k/, two-letter /k/." This phrase distinguishes ck from the other ways of spelling /k/, such as c and k.

ck — The ck tile is stored under the Consonant Teams category.

Refer to the Letter Tiles app or Phonogram Sounds app for a demonstration of the ck phonogram sound.

Preview The CK Rule

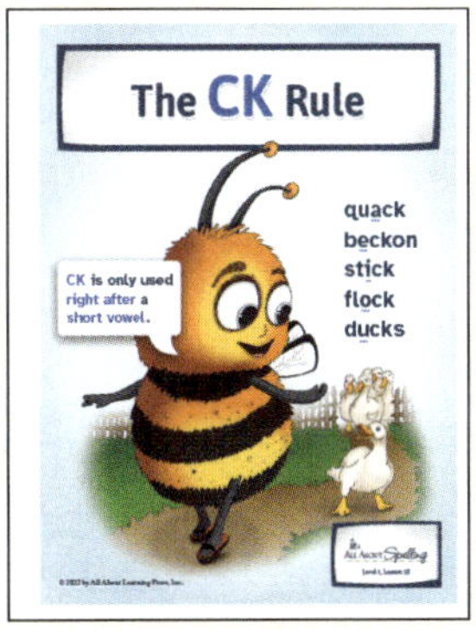

Remove the CK Rule poster from page 147 of the activity book and keep it handy for use in the lesson.

This rule explains that ck is only used right after a short vowel.

Ck comes after short vowels in several hundred words. Read the following sample words.

deck	**muck**	**snack**
pick	**buckle**	**chicken**

Review

Review a selection of Phonogram Cards from behind the Review divider in your student's Spelling Review Box.

Review a selection of Sound Cards from behind the Review divider. Have your student write the phonograms in his dictation notebook.

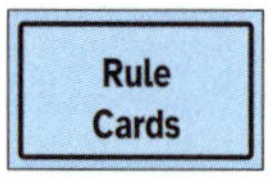

Review a selection of Rule Cards from behind the Review divider.

Review a selection of Word Cards from behind the Review divider. Have your student write the words in his dictation notebook.

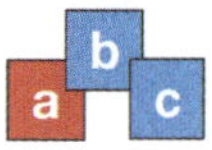

Alphabetize letter tiles a to z with your student.

New Teaching

Teach Consonant Team CK

"We have a new tile today."

Move the **ck** tile into the workspace.

"Repeat after me: /k/, two-letter /k/." *Student repeats the sound.*

"Are the letters on this tile vowels or consonants?" *Consonants.*

"Good. Since the two consonants work together as a team, this tile is stored under the Consonant Teams label." Point to the category label.

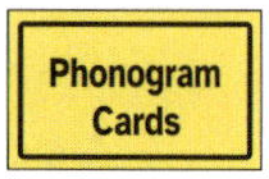

Take out Phonogram Card 30 and practice it with your student. Show the student the card and have him say the sound. Mix in several other Phonogram Cards for mixed review and practice until your student can say the sounds accurately.

New Teaching
(continued)

Teach Sound Card 30

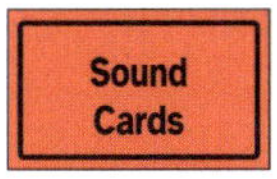

Take out Sound Card 30.

"I am going to dictate a sound. Write the two letters that work together to make that sound."

Dictate the new Sound Card. Practice until your student can easily write the correct phonogram in his dictation notebook. Mix in several other Sound Cards for mixed review.

File the flashcards behind the Review divider in the Spelling Review Box.

Teach Spelling Rule 5: The CK Rule

Move letter tile 

into the workspace.

"Ck is interesting because it only comes after a short vowel."

Build the word *duck*, using a blank blue tile for the /k/ sound.

"I want to build the word *duck*. Let's figure out if we can use ck in place of this blank tile."

Point to the u. "Is this a short vowel?" *Yes.*

"Right! Since it is a short vowel, we can use ck for the sound of /k/."

Replace the blank tile with the ck tile. 

New Teaching
(continued)

Take out the CK Rule poster and explore it with your student.

Read the sample words aloud and listen for the short vowel sound in each. Notice how ck only comes immediately after a short vowel.

You may wish to hang the poster in your lesson area for future reference.

Read Rule Card 5 with your student and then file it behind the Review divider.

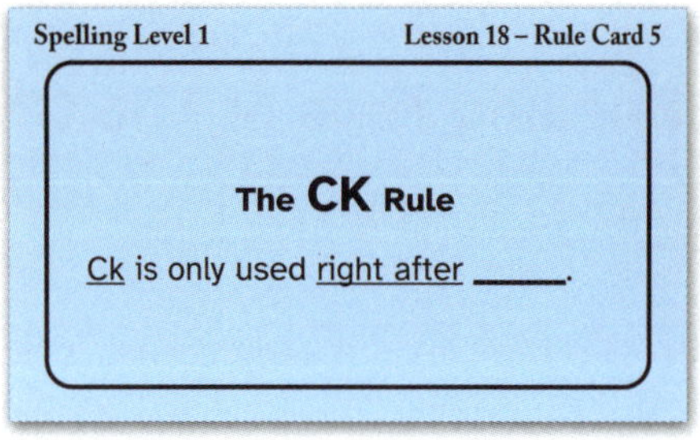

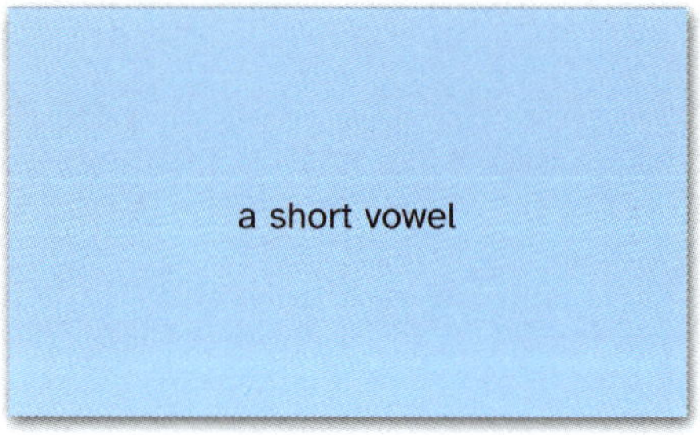

Choose between CK and K

"Now let's spell the word *desk*." Build the word, placing a blank blue tile in place of the /k/ sound. Add tiles ck and k off to the side.

"As you know, ck is only used **right after** a short vowel."

Point to the s. "Is this a short vowel?" *No.*

"Right! Since the letter immediately before it is not a short vowel, we use k."

New Teaching
(continued)

Complete Activity Sheet

"Zack the duck just learned that <u>ck</u> only comes right after a short vowel. Can you help him find out which words end in <u>ck</u> and which end in <u>k</u>?"

Should I Quack?
Turn to page 149 in the *Zip into Spelling* activity book.

One at a time, have your student look at each object and decide whether the word ends with <u>ck</u> or <u>k</u>. The student should then write the letters on the line provided. If the word ends in <u>ck</u>, your student can quack like a duck.

If necessary, remind your student that <u>ck</u> is used only if the letter immediately before it is a short vowel.

Answer Key
<u>Ck</u>: clock, rock, truck, lock, neck
<u>K</u>: desk, milk, mask

Spell Word Cards 111-120 with Letter Tiles

Dictate the words and have your student spell them with letter tiles. Use the **Procedure for Spelling with Letter Tiles** in Appendix E.

New Teaching
(continued)

Spell on Paper

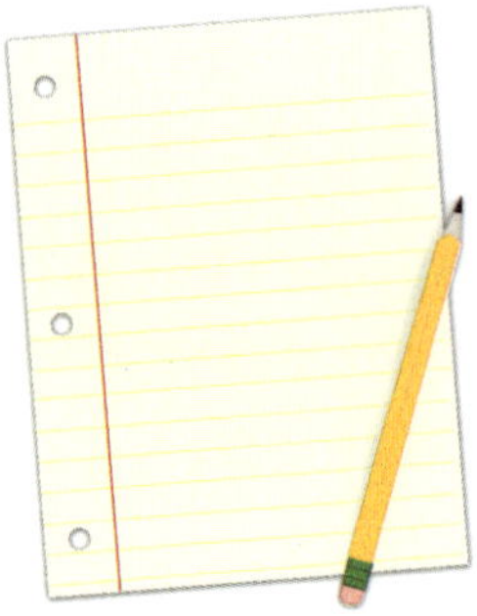

Once your student is able to spell the words using the letter tiles, have him take out his dictation notebook. Dictate Word Cards 111-120 and have your student spell the words on paper.

File the Word Cards behind the Review divider in the Spelling Review Box.

Practice More Words

The following words reinforce the concepts taught in this lesson. For additional practice, have your student spell some of them in his dictation notebook.

back	**husk**	**kick**	**check**	**Rick**
elk	**block**	**quack**	**lock** (lock the door)	**stick**
task	**pack**	**brick**	**quick**	**deck**
risk	**sick**	**luck**	**stuck**	**mask**
bask	**trick**	**dock**	**flock**	**rack**
thick	**speck**	**bulk**	**tuck**	**dusk**
track	**Jack**	**truck**	**cluck**	**silk**
click	**sack**	**musk**	**shack**	**slick**
lack	**fleck**	**slack**	**lick**	**smack**
mock	**stack**	**sock**		

New Teaching
(continued)

Complete Word Search

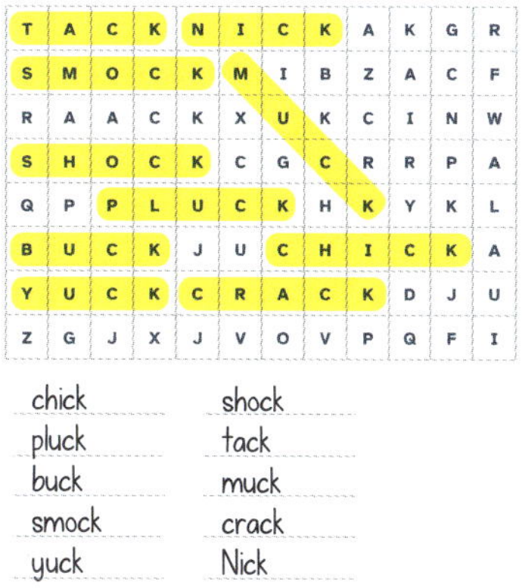

Turn to page 151 in the activity book.

Part 1: Dictate the following words and have your student write them on the lines provided.

chick	**shock**	**pluck**	**tack**
buck	**muck**	**smock**	**crack**
yuck	**Nick**		

Part 2 *(Optional)*: Have your student find and circle the words hidden in the Word Search.

Complete Activity Sheet *(Optional)*

"Let's help these ducklings crack out of their shells."

<u>Hatch Some Eggs</u>
Remove pages 153-154 from the activity book.

Cut out the duck egg cards and place them in a pile.

Choose twelve words from this lesson that you think would most benefit your student to practice. Dictate the words one by one and have your student write each word on a duck egg card. After spelling the word correctly, he may flip the card over to reveal a newly hatched duckling.

Continue until all the eggs have been hatched and the student has practiced all twelve words.

New Teaching
(continued)

Dictate Phrases

Dictate several phrases each day. Your student should repeat each phrase and write it in his dictation notebook.

ask Ben	**fun trick**	**stuck in mud**
pick up	**thick fog**	**hunt elk**
black mask	**stiff neck**	**quick snack**
red brick	**check them**	**sick duck**

Advanced Application

For advanced practice, have your student turn to the Advanced Application sheet on page 152 of the activity book.

"You can spell *clock*. Now spell *clockwork*, as in *My plan is running like clockwork." Student writes* clock *on the first line.*

Continue with the remaining words. Dictate the full word, read the sentence, and have your student fill in the missing syllable.

1.	**clockwork**	My plan is running like clockwork.
2.	**basket**	Agatha found a raccoon in her sewing basket.
3.	**chicken**	Why did the chicken chase the chihuahua?
4.	**cracker**	There's nothing in the cupboard but a cracker.
5.	**unpack**	Did you unpack the box of broken beads?
6.	**silkworm**	My pet silkworm spun me a pair of socks.
7.	**thickness**	Check the thickness of the ice before skating!
8.	**quickest**	What's the quickest way to get to Borneo?
9.	**checkerboard**	I cracked Aunt Gert's antique checkerboard!
10.	**duckling**	A lone duckling waddled around the pond.
11.	**rocket**	Let's ride a rocket to the moon!
12.	**soundtrack**	What's your favorite movie soundtrack?
13.	**milkshake**	Mark's mandarin milkshake was marvelous!
14.	**luckiest**	The luckiest contestant will win a rhubarb pie!
15.	**knapsack**	She hid nine new nickels in her knapsack.

Track Your Progress

Mark the Progress Chart

Remember that each lesson may require several sessions to complete. Before moving on, ask yourself these questions:

1. Does your student have a firm grasp of the CK Rule?
2. Has your student mastered eight out of the ten Word Cards?

If the answer to both is yes, have your student mark Lesson 18 on the Progress Chart and move on to the next lesson!

Lesson 19 NG

Objective

This lesson introduces consonant team ng and teaches how to spell words with this phonogram.

You Will Need

- [ ] letter tile ng
- [ ] Phonogram Card 31
- [ ] Sound Card 31
- [ ] *Zip into Spelling* pages 155-158
- [ ] Word Cards 121-130

Before You Begin

Preview Consonant Team NG

Consonant team ng says /ng/ as in *king*. Listen for the /ng/ sound in the following words.

clang **thing** **song** **stung**

When phonogram ng comes after a and i, the vowels don't say their pure short vowel sound. Instead, the sound falls between the short and long vowel sounds, as in *clang* and *sing*.

Phonogram ng rarely follows e. In fact, there are only four words that have the combination eng: *English*, *England*, *length*, and *strength*.

ng — The ng tile is stored under the Consonant Teams category.

Refer to the Letter Tiles app or Phonogram Sounds app for a demonstration of the ng phonogram sound.

Review

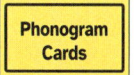

Phonogram Cards — Review a selection of Phonogram Cards from behind the Review divider in your student's Spelling Review Box.

Sound Cards — Review a selection of Sound Cards from behind the Review divider. Have your student write the phonograms in her dictation notebook.

Rule Cards — Review a selection of Rule Cards from behind the Review divider.

Review
(continued)

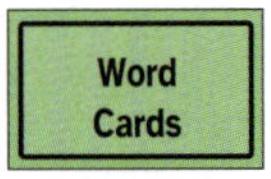

Review a selection of Word Cards from behind the Review divider. Have your student write the words in her dictation notebook.

Read through the Word Banks as necessary.

Alphabetize letter tiles a to z with your student.

How is the daily review going? Are the decks behind the Mastered dividers getting bigger?

Mastered cards will be reviewed in Lesson 22 to keep them fresh in your student's mind.

New Teaching

Teach Consonant Team NG

"We have a new tile today."

Move the  tile into the workspace.

"The letters n-g work together to say /ng/. Repeat after me: /ng/." *Student repeats the sound.*

Move the following tiles into the workspace.

"Ng can come after a." Slide ng next to the a.

"It can come after i." Slide ng next to the i.

"It can come after o." Slide ng next to the o.

New Teaching
(continued)

"And it can come after u." Slide ng next to the u.

"But it rarely comes after e." Remove the e tile from the workspace.

Add an s tile to the workspace. Build the words *sang*, *sing*, *song*, and *sung* one at a time and read them with your student.

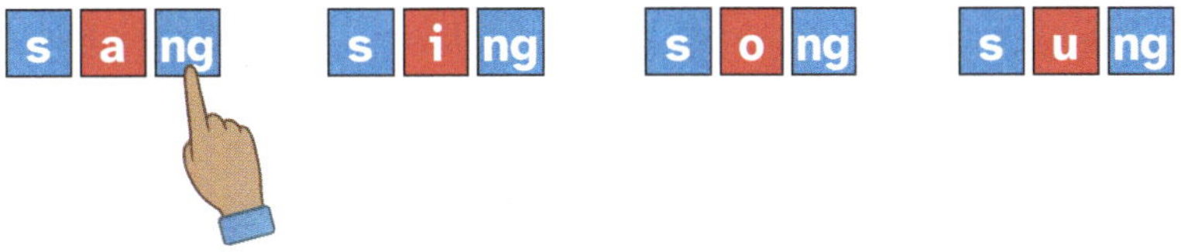

Point to the ng tile.

"Are the letters on this tile vowels or consonants?" *Consonants.*

"Good. Since the two consonants work together as a team, this tile is stored under the Consonant Teams label." Point to the category label.

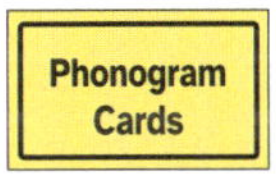

Take out Phonogram Card 31 and practice it with your student. Mix in several other Phonogram Cards for mixed review and practice until your student can say the sounds accurately.

Teach Sound Card 31

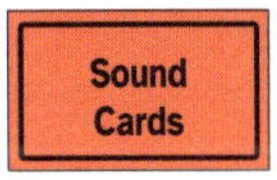

Take out Sound Card 31.

"I am going to dictate a sound. Write the two letters that work together to make that sound."

Dictate the new Sound Card. Practice until your student can easily write the correct phonogram in her dictation notebook. Mix in several other Sound Cards for mixed review.

File the flashcards behind the Review divider in the Spelling Review Box.

New Teaching
(continued)

Spell Word Cards 121-130 with Letter Tiles

Dictate the words and have your student spell them with letter tiles. Use the **Procedure for Spelling with Letter Tiles** in Appendix E.

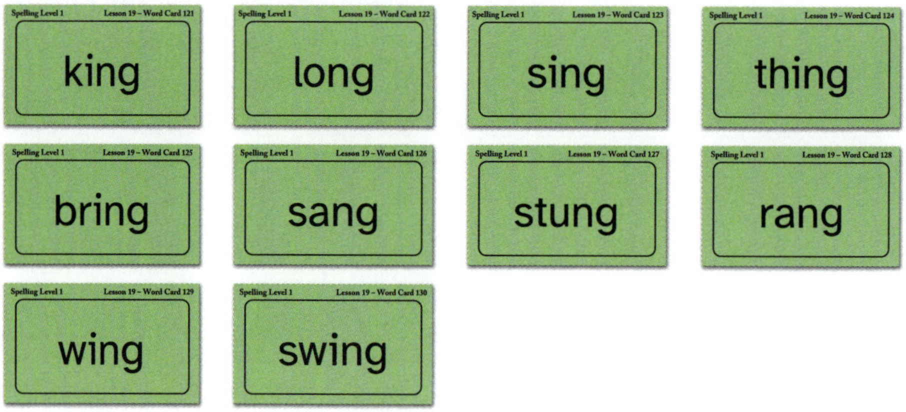

If your student spells *king, sing, thing,* or *bring* with an <u>e</u> instead of an <u>i</u>, remind her that English words rarely contain the combination <u>eng</u>.

In many regions, it does sound as if there is a long <u>e</u>. Your student will need to "pronounce for spelling" and say these words with an /ĭ/ sound.

Spell on Paper

Once your student is able to spell the words using the letter tiles, have her take out her dictation notebook. Dictate Word Cards 121-130 and have your student spell the words on paper.

File the Word Cards behind the Review divider in the Spelling Review Box.

New Teaching
(continued)

Practice More Words

The following words reinforce the concepts taught in this lesson. For additional practice, have your student spell some of them in her dictation notebook.

bang	**song**	**hung**	**ring**	**hang**
pang	**lung**	**sting**		

Complete Word Search

Turn to page 155 in the *Zip into Spelling* activity book.

Part 1: Dictate the following words and have your student write them on the lines provided.

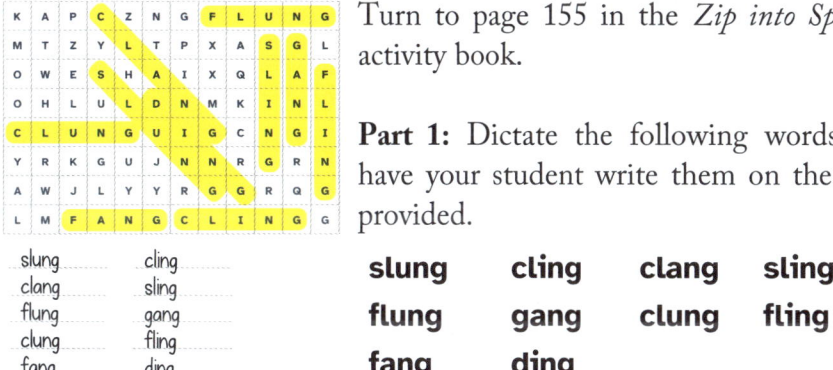

slung	**cling**	**clang**	**sling**
flung	**gang**	**clung**	**fling**
fang	**ding**		

Part 2 ***(Optional)*****:** Have your student find and circle the words hidden in the Word Search.

Complete Activity Sheet *(Optional)*

"Let's see if you can guess whose wings these are."

Things with Wings

Remove pages 157-158 from the activity book.

Cut out the cards and place them in a pile with the wings facing up.

Choose nine words from this lesson that you think would most benefit your student to practice. Dictate the words one by one and have your student write each word on a wing card. After spelling the word correctly, she may turn over the card to reveal whose wing it is.

Continue until all the wings have been identified and the student has practiced all nine words.

New Teaching
(continued)

Dictate Phrases

Dictate several phrases each day. Your student should repeat each phrase and write it in her dictation notebook.

long nap	**shall sing**	**hang up**
sad song	**on this swing**	**bat wing**
bell rang	**bring back**	**King Ed sang**
less risk	**it stung Rick**	**chop that thing**

Advanced Application

For advanced practice, have your student turn to the Advanced Application sheet on page 156 of the activity book.

"You can spell *king*. Now spell *kingfisher*, as in *The kingfisher dove into the marsh." Student writes* king *on the first line.*

Continue with the remaining words. Dictate the full word, read the sentence, and have your student fill in the missing syllable.

1.	**kingfisher**	The kingfisher dove into the marsh.
2.	**longest**	We used the longest sticks to build our fort.
3.	**singer**	The singer opened his mouth—and sneezed.
4.	**earring**	I found your lost earring in the flower bed.
5.	**wingspan**	Falcons have an impressive wingspan!
6.	**everything**	Maya gave everything away when she moved.
7.	**flinging**	Who keeps flinging mud at the windows?
8.	**upswing**	We experienced an upswing in our cookie sales!
9.	**hungry**	My hungry stomach growled like an angry bear.
10.	**gangly**	That gangly man barely fits in his tiny car.
11.	**stingray**	My sister swam with dolphins and a stingray!
12.	**songbird**	A sweet songbird landed on my windowsill.

Track Your Progress

Mark the Progress Chart

Remember that each lesson may require several sessions to complete.

If your student has mastered eight out of the ten Word Cards, have her mark Lesson 19 on the Progress Chart and move on to the next lesson!

Lesson 20 NK

Objective

This lesson introduces consonant team nk and teaches how to spell words with this phonogram.

You Will Need

- ☐ letter tile nk
- ☐ Phonogram Card 32
- ☐ Sound Card 32
- ☐ *Zip into Spelling* pages 159-164
- ☐ Word Cards 131-140

Before You Begin

Preview Consonant Team NK

Consonant team nk says /ngk/ as in *thank*. Listen for the /ngk/ sound in the following words.

blank **wink** **clank** **dunk**

Consonant team nk influences the vowels a and i just as ng does. The vowels don't say their pure short vowel sound. Instead, the sound falls between the short and long vowel sounds, as in the words *rank* and *think*.

Consonant team nk never combines with e to form words. There is no word part enk.

The nk tile is stored under the Consonant Teams category.

Refer to the Letter Tiles app or Phonogram Sounds app for a demonstration of the nk phonogram sound.

Review

Review a selection of Phonogram Cards from behind the Review divider in your student's Spelling Review Box.

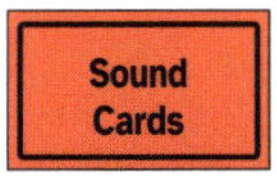

Review a selection of Sound Cards from behind the Review divider. Have your student write the phonograms in his dictation notebook.

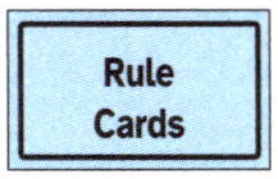

Review a selection of Rule Cards from behind the Review divider.

Review
(continued)

Review a selection of Word Cards from behind the Review divider. Have your student write the words in his dictation notebook.

Alphabetize letter tiles a to z with your student.

New Teaching

Teach Consonant Team NK

"We have a new tile today."

Move the nk tile into the workspace.

"The letters n-k work together to say /ngk/. Repeat after me: /ngk/." *Student repeats the sound.*

Move the following tiles into the workspace.

"Nk can come after a." Slide nk next to the a.

"It can come after i." Slide nk next to the i.

"It can come after o." Slide nk next to the o.

"And it can come after u." Slide nk next to the u.

"But it never comes after e." Remove the e tile from the workspace.

Build the words *bank, sink, honk,* and *junk* one at a time and read them with your student.

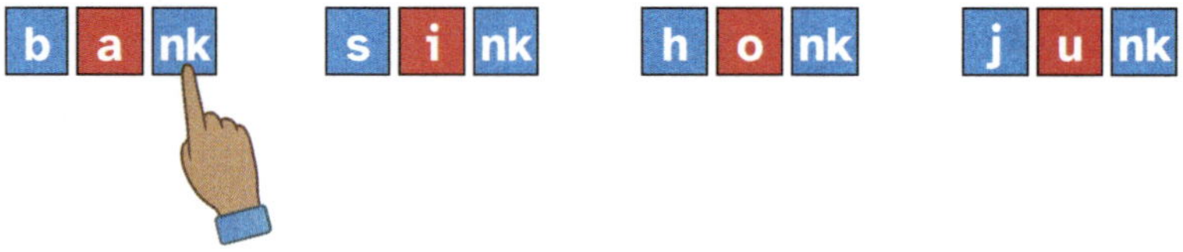

New Teaching
(continued)

Point to the nk tile.

"Are the letters on this tile vowels or consonants?" *Consonants.*

"Good. Since the two consonants work together as a team, this tile is stored under the Consonant Teams label." Point to the category label.

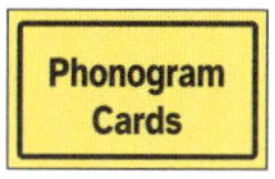

Take out Phonogram Card 32 and practice it with your student. Mix in several other Phonogram Cards for mixed review and practice until your student can say the sounds accurately.

Teach Sound Card 32

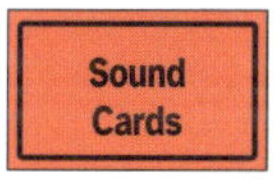

Take out Sound Card 32.

"I am going to dictate a sound. Write the two letters that work together to make that sound."

Dictate the new Sound Card. Practice until your student can easily write the correct phonogram in his dictation notebook. Mix in several other Sound Cards for mixed review.

File the flashcards behind the Review divider in the Spelling Review Box.

Spell Word Cards 131-140 with Letter Tiles

Dictate the words and have your student spell them with letter tiles. Use the **Procedure for Spelling with Letter Tiles** in Appendix E.

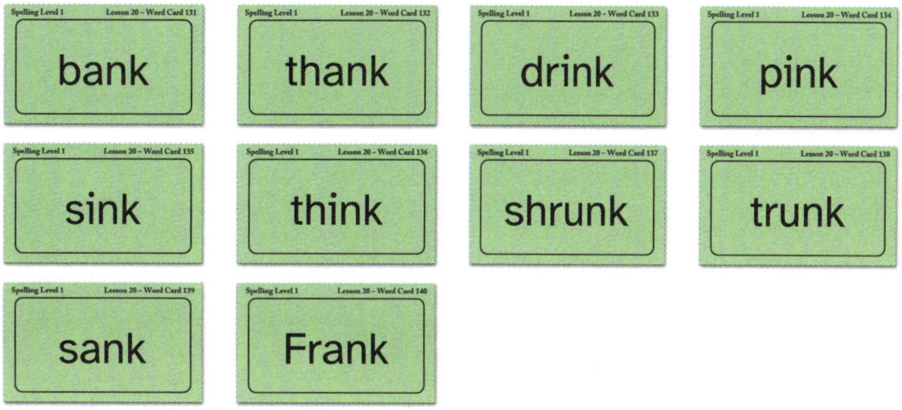

New Teaching
(continued)

As your student spells the words, keep these tips in mind.

drink: Make sure your student pronounces the word carefully and enunciates the d. Many children pronounce the d-r blend as /jr/.

trunk: Your student may need to "pronounce for spelling" to avoid a /ch/ sound at the beginning.

drink, pink, sink, think: If your student spells these words with an e instead of an i, remind him that English words never contain the combination enk. Your student may need to "pronounce for spelling" and say these words with an /ĭ/ sound.

Spell on Paper

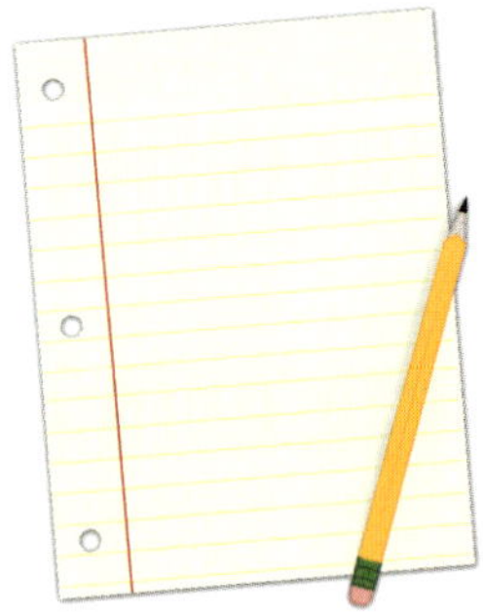

Once your student is able to spell the words using the letter tiles, have him take out his dictation notebook. Dictate Word Cards 131-140 and have your student spell the words on paper.

File the Word Cards behind the Review divider in the Spelling Review Box.

Practice More Words

The following words reinforce the concepts taught in this lesson. For additional practice, have your student spell some of them in his dictation notebook.

stink	**drank**	**flunk**	**ink**	**honk**
blank	**rank**	**dunk**	**Hank**	**shrink**
junk	**chunk**	**rink**	**plank**	**clank**

New Teaching
(continued)

Complete Word Search

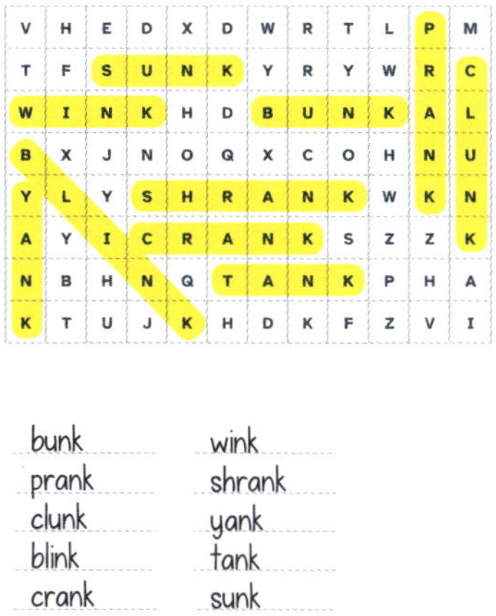

Turn to page 159 in the *Zip into Spelling* activity book.

Part 1: Dictate the following words and have your student write them on the lines provided.

bunk	**prank**	**clunk**	**blink**
crank	**wink**	**shrank**	**yank**
tank	**sunk**		

Part 2 *(Optional)*: Have your student find and circle the words hidden in the Word Search.

Complete Activity Sheets *(Optional)*

"This skunk looks hungry. Let's help her gather some berries!"

Feed the Skunk

Remove pages 161-162 from the activity book.

Cut out the berry cards and place them in a pile. Place the skunk illustration in front of your student.

Choose twelve words from this lesson that you think would most benefit your student to practice. Dictate the words one by one and have your student write each word on the back of a berry card. After spelling the word correctly, he may place the berry on the skunk's plate.

Continue until the skunk has gathered all the berries and the student has practiced all twelve words.

The next activity provides an opportunity for mixed review.

New Teaching
(continued)

"Now let's make our own skunk!"

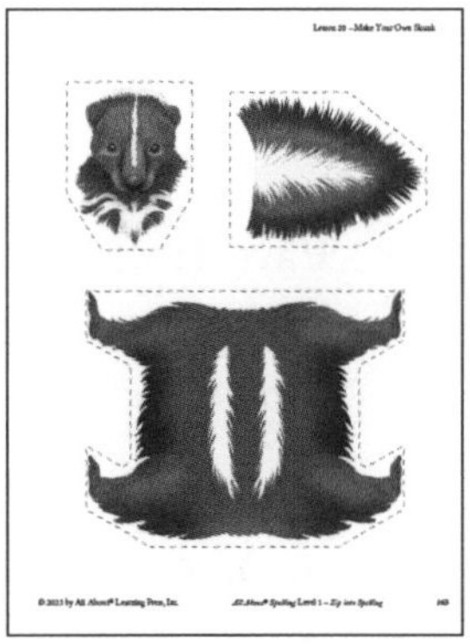

Make Your Own Skunk

Remove pages 163-164 from the activity book.

Cut out the skunk pieces as indicated.

One by one, dictate the words below and have your student write each one on the back of a skunk piece. (There are spaces for six words on the base of the skunk, two words on the tail, and one word on the head.)

stink	**smell**	**musk**
log	**stank**	**quick**
soft	**dig**	**stunk**

After spelling the words correctly, your student may assemble the skunk by folding the base as indicated and using tape to attach the head and tail pieces to the base.

Dictate Phrases

Dictate several phrases each day. Your student should repeat each phrase and write it in his dictation notebook.

pink dish	**truck trunk**	**did not think**
sell junk	**drank milk**	**ship sank**
black ink	**blank spot**	**Frank will win**
thank them	**fish tank**	**kick this rock**

Advanced Application

For advanced practice, have your student turn to the Advanced Application sheet on page 160 of the activity book.

"You can spell *bank*. Now spell *riverbank*, as in *The possum perused the riverbank for food." Student writes* bank *on the first line.*

Continue with the remaining words. Dictate the full word, read the sentence, and have your student fill in the missing syllable.

1.	**riverbank**	The possum perused the riverbank for food.
2.	**thanksgiving**	Oh no! I overbaked the Thanksgiving yams!
3.	**blankly**	My turtle stared at me blankly and walked away.
4.	**honking**	There are fifty-five honking geese on the lawn!
5.	**pinker**	Her cheeks are pinker than cotton candy.
6.	**inkblot**	Have you ever taken an inkblot test?
7.	**blanket**	I love spring when daisies blanket the meadow.
8.	**stinkbug**	"Ew, a stinky stinkbug!" wailed the skunk.
9.	**blinkers**	None of the turning cars used their blinkers.
10.	**crankiest**	Pickles is the crankiest cat in the neighborhood!
11.	**hoodwink**	The spy thought he could hoodwink us!

You may wish to let your student know that the word *thanksgiving* can begin with a capital t or a lowercase t.

When we refer to the holiday, as in the sample sentence, we spell the word with a capital t.

When we use the word as a general noun, we spell it with a lowercase t, as in this sentence: *This is an occasion for great thanksgiving and joy.*

Track Your Progress

Mark the Progress Chart

Remember that each lesson may require several sessions to complete.

If your student has mastered eight out of the ten Word Cards, have him mark Lesson 20 on the Progress Chart and move on to the next lesson!

There I am,
hanging out in the hive,
minding my own beeswax, when ...
I smell a STINK!
So I poke my head out and discover that the
STINK is attached to a SKUNK.
But she was so cute and fluffy, who could
stay upset about a little stink?
Nobody's perfect!
You just have to BEE yourself,
that's my motto!

Lesson 21 Compound Words

Objective

This lesson teaches how to spell compound words.

You Will Need

- ☐ second set of letter tiles a-z
- ☐ Word Cards 141-150
- ☐ *Zip into Spelling* pages 165-168

Before You Begin

Letter Tile Setup

Building compound words will require more letters. If you are using physical letter tiles, add the remaining tiles from the second set of a-z letter tiles to complete your setup.

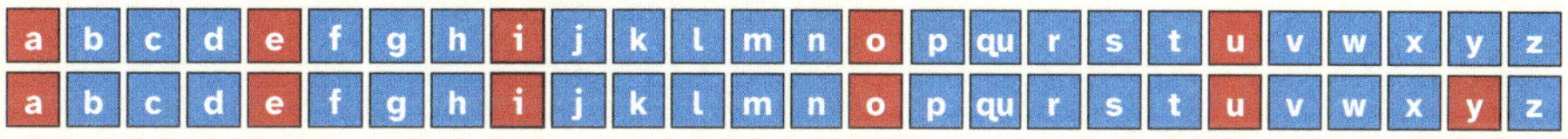

Preview Compound Words

Compound words are special words that are made up of two smaller words, such as *desktop*. Read the following examples and look for the two smaller words.

football	**checklist**	**sandbox**	**cheesecake**
meatballs	**milkshake**	**cupcake**	**toothbrush**

Notice how the meaning of the smaller words is retained: a *football* is a *ball* that you kick with your *foot*. Also note that when forming compound words, the spelling of the two smaller words does not change. For example, in the word *hilltop*, the word *hill* retains the double l even though the l is no longer the last letter in a one-syllable word. The Floss Rule still applies to the base word *hill*.

If your student is a beginning reader, she may not yet have a visual memory of which words are compound words. Is *eggshell* one word or two? How about *sandbox*? This knowledge comes from reading experience. In the meantime, feel free to tell your student at any time if a dictated word is a compound word.

Review

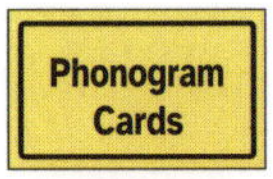

Review a selection of Phonogram Cards from behind the Review divider in your student's Spelling Review Box.

Review a selection of Sound Cards from behind the Review divider. Have your student write the phonograms in her dictation notebook.

Review a selection of Rule Cards from behind the Review divider.

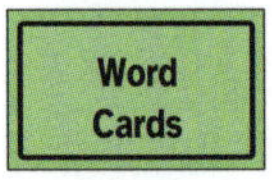

Review a selection of Word Cards from behind the Review divider. Have your student write the words in her dictation notebook.

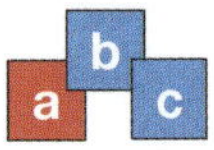

Alphabetize letter tiles a to z with your student.

New Teaching

Teach Compound Words

Build the word s u n s e t.

"A compound word is two smaller words put together. What are the two small words in the word *sunset*?" *Sun, set.*

"How many syllables are in the word *sunset*?" *Two.*

"To spell a two-syllable word, clap it out." Demonstrate how to do this. Clap as you say *sun*, and then clap as you say *set*.

"Spell the first word, s u n."

"Then spell the second word, s e t, right next to it."

s u n s e t

"Then we double-check the word to make sure that we spelled it correctly." Say the word slowly while running your finger under the word.

New Teaching
(continued)

"Now you try it. Spell the word *hilltop*. First, clap the syllables." *Student says* hill *[clap]* top *[clap].*

"Spell *hill*." *Student spells the word.*

"Now spell *top* right next to it." *Student spells the word.*

"Read the compound word." *Hilltop.*

"Good! When we combine two small words to make a compound word, we don't change the smaller words; they stay exactly the same."

Spell Word Cards 141-150 with Letter Tiles

"All of these words are compound words."

Dictate the words and have your student spell them with letter tiles. Use the **Procedure for Spelling with Letter Tiles** in Appendix E.

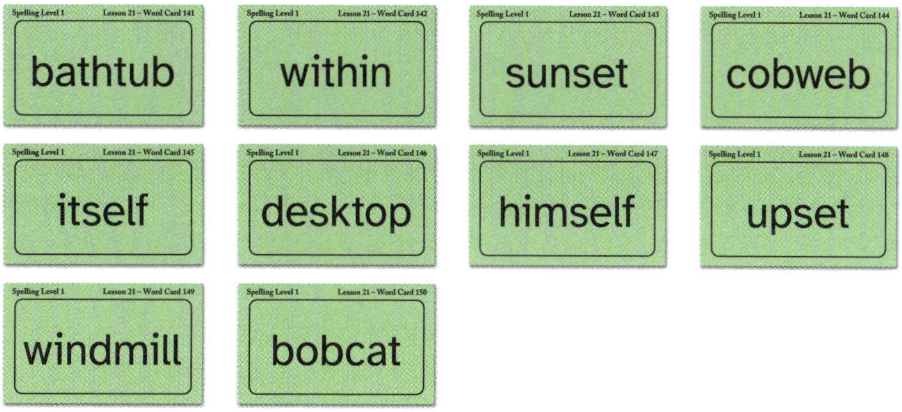

New Teaching
(continued)

Spell on Paper

Once your student is able to spell the words using the letter tiles, have her take out her dictation notebook. Dictate Word Cards 141-150 and have your student spell the words on paper.

File the Word Cards behind the Review divider in the Spelling Review Box.

Practice More Words

The following words reinforce the concepts taught in this lesson. For additional practice, have your student spell some of them in her dictation notebook.

backpack	**handcuff**	**upon**	**catfish**
lipstick	**blacktop**	**dishcloth**	**drumstick**
catnip	**clamshell**	**hilltop**	**locksmith**
quicksand	**cannot**	**milkman**	**pigpen**
anthill	**backdrop**	**sandbox**	**dustpan**
muskrat	**padlock**	**dishpan**	**humpback**
gumdrop	**handbag**	**uphill**	**snapshot**
nutshell	**flapjack**	**handheld**	**bedbug**
inkblot	**checklist**	**shellfish**	**stinkbug**
eggshell			

New Teaching
(continued)

Complete Activity Sheet *(Optional)*

"Now let's play a card game with some of our new compound words."

Stinkbug!

Remove pages 165-168 from the *Zip into Spelling* activity book.

Cut out the playing cards and quietly set aside the Stinkbug card for later use.

Show your student that there are six pairs of matching cards and explain that you will dictate the names of the characters for her to add to the blank lines on one set of cards. Note: When you get to the Humpback card, say "Humpback, as in humpback whale."

After the student has spelled all the words, pull out the Stinkbug card. "Now we get to play a game of Stinkbug! Try not to be left with this card!"

Mix up all thirteen cards and deal an assortment to each player. If any player is dealt a matching pair, set those cards on the table before continuing. Now take turns selecting a single card from another player and setting down any pairs that result.

Continue until all the cards have been matched up and one player is left with the Stinkbug.

Dictate Phrases

> **Tip!**
>
> If your student doesn't have visual memory of compound words yet, tell her which word in the dictated phrase is a compound word. For example: "*Dishcloth* is a compound word. Write *wet dishcloth*."

Dictate several phrases each day. Your student should repeat each phrase and write it in her dictation notebook.

wet dishcloth	**milkman left**	**cannot lock it**
red sunset	**long cobweb**	**in his backpack**
upset the bobcat	**in the pigpen**	**let himself in**
pink lipstick	**upon this hilltop**	**sink in quicksand**

Track Your Progress

Mark the Progress Chart

Remember that each lesson may require several sessions to complete. Before moving on, ask yourself these questions:

1. Does your student have a good grasp of the concept of compound words?

2. Has your student mastered eight out of the ten Word Cards?

If the answer to both is yes, have your student mark Lesson 21 on the Progress Chart and move on to the next lesson!

Lesson 22 Adding S to Make Words Plural

Objective

This lesson teaches how to spell plural words by adding s.

You Will Need

- [ ] *Zip into Spelling* pages 169-174
- [ ] Word Cards 151-160
- [ ] Rule Card 6

Before You Begin

Preview The Add S Rule

Remove the Add S Rule poster from page 169 of the activity book and keep it handy for use in the lesson.

In the *All About Spelling* program, your student will be learning various guidelines for making words plural.

- Add s to make most words plural (taught in this lesson)
- Add e-s to base words that end in ch, sh, s, x, and z (taught in Lesson 23)
- Change single y to i before adding a suffix, as in *fly* to *flies* (taught in Level 3)
- Some plural words are irregular, as in *child* to *children* and *knife* to *knives* (taught in Level 5)

Preview Verbs Ending in S

Many present tense verbs end in suffix *s*, such as *chomps* and *runs*. This lesson doesn't explicitly cover verbs, but the same spelling principles apply. After learning how to spell plural words, your student will be able to spell present tense verbs as well.

Review

It's time to review the cards behind the Mastered dividers to ensure they stay fresh in your student's mind. Shuffle the cards and choose a selection for review.

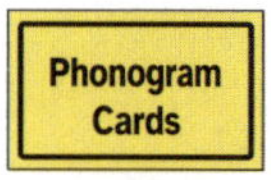

Review a selection of Phonogram Cards from behind the **Mastered** divider in your student's Spelling Review Box.

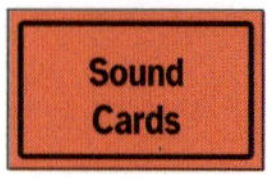

Review a selection of Sound Cards from behind the **Mastered** divider. Have your student write the phonograms in his dictation notebook.

Review a selection of Rule Cards from behind the **Mastered** divider.

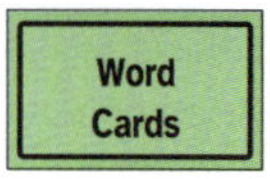

Review a selection of Word Cards from behind the **Mastered** divider. Have your student write the words in his dictation notebook.

Read through the Word Banks for Short I, Short O, and Short E.

Alphabetize letter tiles a to z with your student.

New Teaching

Introduce Plural Words

Build the word b u g s.

"We say one *bug*." Cover the s with your finger.

"And we say two *bugs*."

"*Bugs* is **plural** because it means **more than one**."

"I'll say a word and you make it plural."

"One *cat*, two _____." If necessary, prompt your student to say *cats*.

New Teaching
(continued)

"One *tent*, two ______." *Tents.*

"One *ball*, five ______." *Balls.*

Identify Base Words

"Now we are going to do just the opposite. I will tell you a **plural word** and you will tell me the base word. So if I say *swings*, you'll say *swing*."

"The word is *chairs*." *Chair.*

"*Tents.*" *Tent.*

Practice with the following words until this concept becomes easy for your student. (Note that this is an oral exercise; your student is not writing the words.)

books	**cars**	**trees**	**cakes**
fingers	**paints**	**baskets**	**hugs**

> **Tip!** If your student has any difficulty, have him fill in the sentence "I have one _______ *(book)*." This will help him produce the base word.

Teach Spelling Rule 6: The Add S Rule

"Let's build some plural words. I want to spell the word *maps*."

"First I build the base word, **m a p**."

"Then I add s."

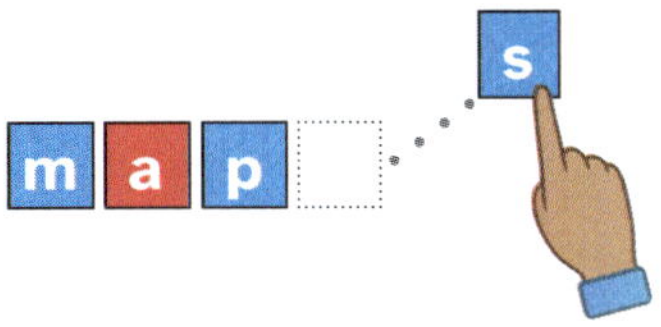

"Adding s to a base word is the most common way to make a word plural."

Leave the word *map* in the workspace.

"Let's spell *frogs*. First I build the base word, **f r o g**."

New Teaching
(continued)

"Then I add s to make it say *frogs*." **f r o g s**

Point to the s in **m a p s**.

"What sound does the s make in *maps*?" */s/.*

Point to the s in **f r o g s**.

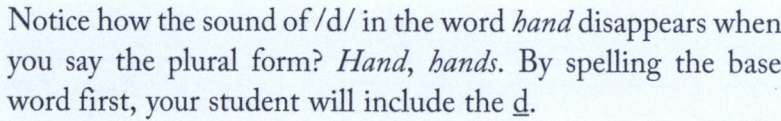

"What sound does the s make in *frogs*?" */z/.*

"Good! Now it's your turn. Spell the word *hands*. Spell the base word first."

Student spells **h a n d**.

"Now change *hand* to *hands*." *Student adds s.* **h a n d s**

> Notice how the sound of /d/ in the word *hand* disappears when you say the plural form? *Hand*, *hands*. By spelling the base word first, your student will include the d.

Take out the Add S Rule poster and explore it with your student.

Read the sample words aloud and have your student tell you the base word for each.

You may wish to hang the poster in your lesson area for future reference.

New Teaching
(continued)

Read Rule Card 6 with your student and then file it behind the Review divider.

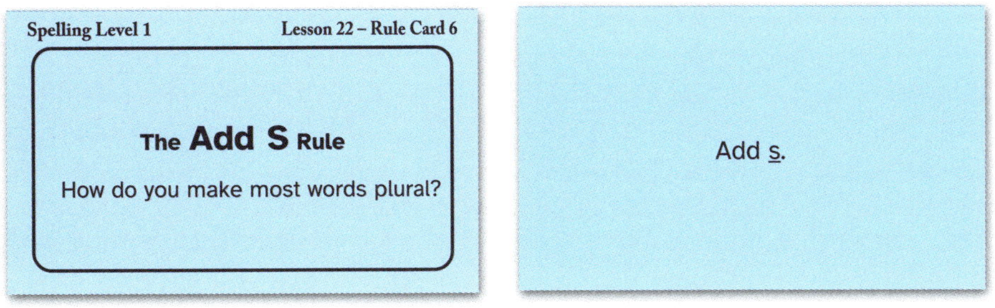

Spell Word Cards 151-160 with Letter Tiles

Dictate the words and have your student spell them with letter tiles. Use the **Procedure for Spelling with Letter Tiles** in Appendix E.

> For each word, have your student spell the base word first and then make it plural. If your student ever uses the z tile to make a word plural (as in *bedz*), let him know that we only use s for the sound of /z/ in plural words.

New Teaching
(continued)

Spell on Paper

Once your student is able to spell the words using the letter tiles, have him take out his dictation notebook. Dictate Word Cards 151-160 and have your student spell the words on paper.

File the Word Cards behind the Review divider in the Spelling Review Box.

Practice More Words

The following words reinforce the concepts taught in this lesson. For additional practice, have your student spell some of them in his dictation notebook.

backpacks	**twigs**	**bats**	**bells**
maps	**banks**	**frogs**	**clams**
ducks	**bugs**	**cats**	**gifts**
bedbugs	**clocks**	**plums** (ate six plums)	**flapjacks**
jobs	**hats**	**dogs**	**hills**
snacks	**kings**	**hens**	**lamps**
ships	**things**	**dolls**	**tracks**
logs	**rams**	**locks** (door locks)	**pets**
trips	**pups**	**wings**	

New Teaching
(continued)

Complete Word Search

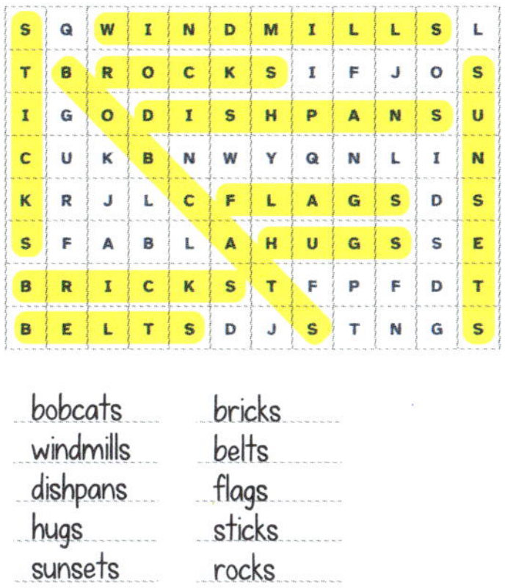

Turn to page 171 in the *Zip into Spelling* activity book.

Part 1: Dictate the following words and have your student write them on the lines provided.

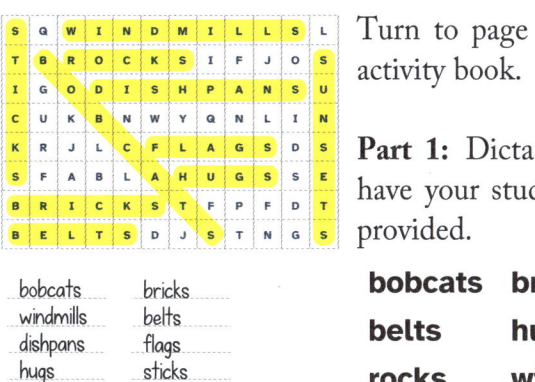

bobcats	**bricks**	**flags**	**sticks**
belts	**hugs**	**sunsets**	**dishpans**
rocks	**windmills**		

Part 2 *(Optional)*: Have your student find and circle the words hidden in the Word Search.

Complete Activity Sheet *(Optional)*

"Let's make some ice cream cones!"

<u>**Serve the Ice Cream!**</u>
Remove pages 173-174 from the activity book.

Cut out the ice cream scoop cards and the ice cream cones.

Choose nine words from this lesson that you think would most benefit your student to practice. Dictate the words one by one and have your student write each word on the back of an ice cream scoop card. After spelling the word correctly, he may add the scoop to one of the ice cream cones. Your student can decide whether to make each cone a single scoop, double scoop, triple scoop, or higher.

Continue until all the ice cream cones have been assembled and the student has practiced all nine words.

New Teaching
(continued)

Dictate Phrases

Dictate several phrases each day. Your student should repeat each phrase and write it in his dictation notebook.

his things	**ten pink pigs**	**get us hats**
bugs in rugs	**hung clocks**	**has snacks**
camp in tents	**Bob has hens**	**fill up cups**
pack the lamps	**cash in banks**	**six sad clams**

Advanced Application

For advanced practice, have your student turn to the Advanced Application sheet on page 172 of the activity book.

"You can spell *cups*. Now spell *buttercups*, as in *Let's tiptoe through the buttercups together." Student writes* cups *on the first line.*

Continue with the remaining words. Dictate the full word, read the sentence, and have your student fill in the missing syllable.

1.	**butterc<u>ups</u>**	Let's tiptoe through the buttercups together.
2.	**sheep<u>dogs</u>**	The shepherd treated his sheepdogs like kings.
3.	**lady<u>bugs</u>**	Eleven ladybugs had tea on the lawn.
4.	**foot<u>hills</u>**	We bought land in the foothills of New Mexico.
5.	**river<u>beds</u>**	The riverbeds in the canyon are dry and sandy.
6.	**cata<u>logs</u>**	Samantha has seed catalogs piled to the ceiling!
7.	**wom<u>bats</u>**	Wombats waddle when they walk.
8.	**car<u>pets</u>**	That nutty ferret tore up all our new carpets!
9.	**sham<u>rocks</u>**	Erin O'Malley wore three shamrocks in her hair.
10.	**egg<u>shells</u>**	Save those eggshells for your potting soil!
11.	**door<u>bells</u>**	We have seven doorbells on our front door.
12.	**wor<u>ships</u>**	Little Andy worships his big sisters!
13.	**snow<u>banks</u>**	We carved a massive fort into those snowbanks.
14.	**copy<u>cats</u>**	Those copycats are wearing identical costumes!

Track Your Progress

Mark the Progress Chart

Remember that each lesson may require several sessions to complete. Before moving on, ask yourself these questions:

1. Does your student have a good grasp of the Add S Rule?

2. Has your student mastered eight out of the ten Word Cards?

If the answer to both is yes, have your student mark Lesson 22 on the Progress Chart and move on to the next lesson!

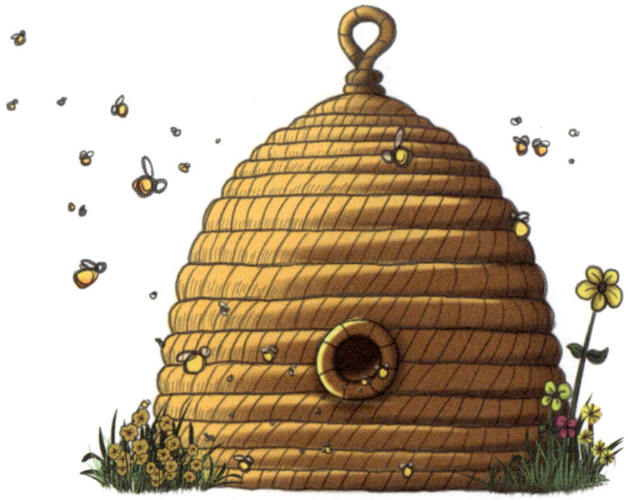

Lesson 23 Adding ES to Make Words Plural

Objective

This lesson teaches how to spell plural words by adding e-s.

You Will Need

- [ ] third s letter tile
- [ ] *Zip into Spelling* pages 175-183
- [ ] Rule Card 7
- [ ] Word Cards 161-170

Before You Begin

Letter Tile Setup

If you are using physical letter tiles, add the third s tile to your letter tile setup so your student can spell plural words with e-s.

Preview The Add ES Rule

Remove the Add ES Rule poster from page 175 of the activity book and keep it handy for use in the lesson.

In Lesson 22, students learned that the most common way to make words plural is by adding s. The second most common way to make words plural is to add e-s.

Read the following words aloud and listen for the /ĭz/ sound that occurs when e-s is added.

-ch	-sh	-s	-x	-z
matches	**wishes**	**buses**	**boxes**	**waltzes**
churches	**brushes**	**glasses**	**hoaxes**	**buzzes**

It is interesting to note that e-s is added when the base word ends in ch, sh, s, x, and z.

Preview Verbs Ending in ES

Many present tense verbs end in e-s, such as *mashes* and *waxes*. This lesson doesn't explicitly cover verbs, but the same spelling principles apply. After learning how to spell plural words, your student will be able to spell present tense verbs as well.

Review

Review a selection of Phonogram Cards from behind the Review divider in your student's Spelling Review Box.

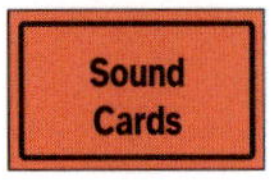

Review a selection of Sound Cards from behind the Review divider. Have your student write the phonograms in her dictation notebook.

Review a selection of Rule Cards from behind the Review divider.

Review a selection of Word Cards from behind the Review divider. Have your student write the words in her dictation notebook.

Alphabetize letter tiles a to z with your student.

New Teaching

Introduce Plural Words Ending in ES

"I'll say a word and you make it plural."

"One *box*, two ________." If necessary, prompt your student to say *boxes*.

"One *glass*, two ________." *Glasses.*

"One *brush*, two ________." *Brushes.*

Teach Spelling Rule 7: The Add ES Rule

Build the word

.

"You know that the most common way to make a word plural is by adding s, as in *rocks*."

"Today you will learn the **second** most common way to make words plural: add e-s."

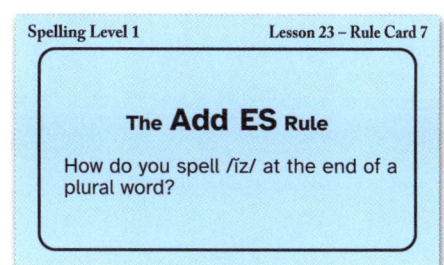

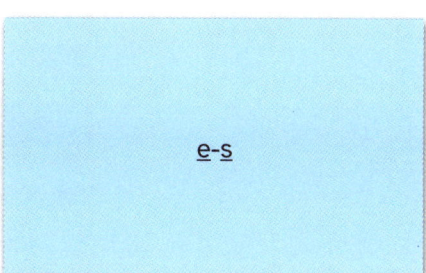

New Teaching
(continued)

Build the word **c l a s s**.

"What is the plural of *class*?" *Classes.*

"Read this word." *Class.*

Add s to form **c l a s s s**.

"This doesn't say *classes*, does it?" *No.*

"Try reading it just as I spelled it." *Classs.*

Remove the s and replace it with e-s to form **c l a s s e s**.

"To spell the plural word, we need to add e-s. Now read the word." *Classes.*

"If you hear /ĭz/ at the end of a plural word, use e-s."

"How many syllables are in the word *classes*?" *Two.*

"Right. E-s forms its own syllable: /clăss–ĭz/."

Take out the Add ES Rule poster and explore it with your student.

Read the sample words aloud and listen for the /ĭz/ sound in the last syllable.

You may wish to hang the poster in your lesson area for future reference.

Read Rule Card 7 with your student and then file it behind the Review divider.

Spelling Level 1 — Lesson 23 – Rule Card 7

The Add ES Rule

How do you spell /ĭz/ at the end of a plural word?

e-s

New Teaching
(continued)

Complete Activity Sheet *(Optional)*

"Uh-oh! This next activity is a mess. Let's see if we can clean it up."

What Makes Messes?

Remove pages 177-178 from the *Zip into Spelling* activity book.

Cut out the object cards and spread them out in front of your student with the words facing down.

"Find the *boxes*. Do you hear /ĭz/ at the end of the word?" *Yes.*

"Flip the card over and write e-s to spell *boxes*." *Student writes e-s.*

"Find the *mops*. Do you hear /ĭz/ at the end of the word?" *No.*

"Flip the card over and write s to spell *mops*." *Student writes s.*

One at a time, name the remaining objects. Have your student fill in s or e-s to spell the plural word.

brushes	**rags**	**dishes**	**dustpans**
lunches	**glasses**	**bathtubs**	

After spelling the words correctly, your student can sort the objects into two piles: "things that are messy" and "things that clean."

Spell Word Cards 161-170 with Letter Tiles

Dictate the words and have your student spell them with letter tiles. Use the **Procedure for Spelling with Letter Tiles** in Appendix E.

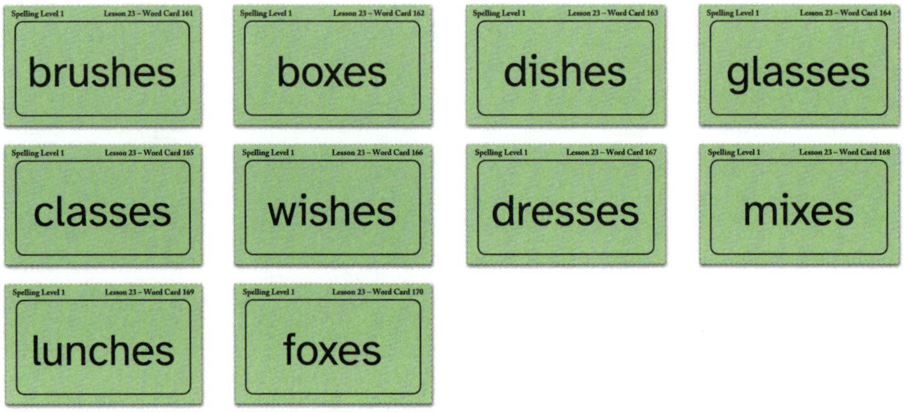

New Teaching
(continued)

Spell on Paper

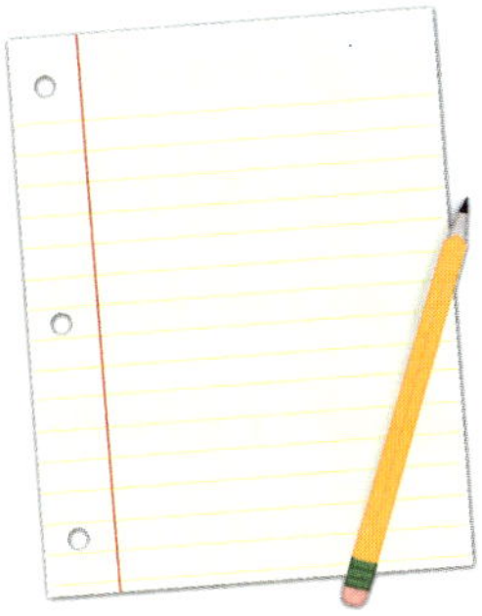

Once your student is able to spell the words using the letter tiles, have her take out her dictation notebook. Dictate Word Cards 161-170 and have your student spell the words on paper.

File the Word Cards behind the Review divider in the Spelling Review Box.

Practice More Words

The following words reinforce the concepts taught in this lesson. For additional practice, have your student spell some of them in her dictation notebook.

lashes	**kisses**	**ashes**	**taxes**
mashes	**riches**	**dashes**	**mosses**
rashes	**benches**	**ranches**	**sandboxes**

Complete Activity Sheet *(Optional)*

"This beach needs to be cleaned up! Let's get to work."

Clean Up the Beach

Remove pages 179-182 from the activity book.

Cut out the object cards and distribute them on the beach scene. Cut out the trash bin, create a cylinder by taping the ends together as indicated, and then tape the bin to the beach scene.

Choose eight words from this lesson that you think would most benefit your student to practice. Dictate the words one by one and have your student write each word on the back of an object card. After spelling the words correctly, your student may wad up the trash and throw it in the trash bin.

Continue until the beach is sparkling clean and your student has practiced all eight words. You may wish to throw the whole trash bin and wadded paper in a real paper recycling bin.

New Teaching
(continued)

Dictate Phrases

Dictate several phrases each day. Your student should repeat each phrase and write it in her dictation notebook.

has glasses	**six kisses**	**red dresses**
dashes fast	**sits on benches**	**cats in boxes**
bun mixes	**math classes**	**lots of riches**
crack the dishes	**ten foxes ran**	**jumps in sandboxes**

Advanced Application

For advanced practice, have your student turn to the Advanced Application sheet on page 183 of the activity book.

"You can spell *dishes*. Now spell *radishes*, as in *The rabbits ate all the radishes." Student writes* dishes *on the first line.*

Continue with the remaining words. Dictate the full word, read the sentence, and have your student fill in the missing syllable.

1.	**ra<u>dishes</u>**	The rabbits ate all the radishes.
2.	**match<u>boxes</u>**	No one can match my collection of matchboxes.
3.	**eye<u>lashes</u>**	Evangeline has the longest eyelashes ever seen.
4.	**tooth<u>brushes</u>**	The hippos require very large toothbrushes.
5.	**out<u>foxes</u>**	That clever mouse always outfoxes our cat!
6.	**work<u>benches</u>**	Mom built two workbenches for her shop.
7.	**eye<u>glasses</u>**	Mister Fly got five new pairs of eyeglasses.
8.	**oak<u>mosses</u>**	What type of tree do oakmosses grow on?
9.	**sub<u>classes</u>**	Squares are subclasses of rectangles.
10.	**over<u>mixes</u>**	Sheldon always overmixes the cookie dough!

Track Your Progress

Mark the Progress Chart

Remember that each lesson may require several sessions to complete. Before moving on, ask yourself these questions:

1. Does your student have a good grasp of the Add ES Rule?

2. Has your student mastered eight out of the ten Word Cards?

If the answer to both is yes, have your student mark Lesson 23 on the Progress Chart and move on to the next lesson!

I love plurals!
I don't want to drone on and on,
but I love them so much that I
wrote you a little rhyme. Ahem.
WONDERFUL THINGS ABOUT BEES
Bees have buzzes
and cuddly fuzzes.
Our stings are great.
Our wings fly straight.
We sneeze cute sneezes—
we're the bee's knees-es!

Lesson 24 The Long Vowel Rule

Objective

This lesson teaches the long vowel sounds and how to spell one-syllable words ending with long vowel sounds.

You Will Need

- ☐ Rule Card 8
- ☐ Word Cards 171-180
- ☐ *Zip into Spelling* pages 185-195

Before You Begin

Preview Long Vowel Sounds

So far, your student has learned to spell hundreds of words with short vowel sounds where the vowel is followed by a consonant. Now your student is ready to spell simple words with long vowel sounds.

When a vowel says its long sound, it says its name.

- **a** The long sound of a is /ā/ as in *acorn*.
- **e** The long sound of e is /ē/ as in *even*.
- **i** The long sound of i is /ī/ as in *ivy*.
- **o** The long sound of o is /ō/ as in *open*.
- **u** The long sound of u is /ū/ as in *unit*.

Preview The Long Vowel Rule

Remove the Long Vowel Rule poster from page 185 of the activity book and keep it handy for use in the lesson.

This rule explains that when a vowel is at the end of a syllable, it usually says its long sound. Read the following examples and listen for the long vowel sounds.

he **no** **baby** **tiger** **music**

Note that the rule says the vowel *usually* says its long sound. There are instances in which the vowel says one of its other sounds at the end of a syllable, such as in *water* (after w, a says its third sound), *soda* (a says its third sound when it is the last letter in the word), *happier* (i often says /ē/ when it comes before a vowel suffix), and *machine* (i often says /ē/ in words borrowed from other languages). In words of Latin origin, vowels at the end of syllables are often short, as in *condition* and *product*. Your student will learn these generalizations later in the *All About Spelling* program.

Before You Begin
(continued)

Preview Dictate Sentences Activity

Your student is ready to start writing complete sentences. Starting with this lesson and continuing in future levels, you will dictate several sentences each day. Like the phrases, the sentences reinforce concepts taught in both current and previous lessons.

You will read the sentences out loud one time. Your student should repeat the sentence and then write it on a line in his dictation notebook. Having your student repeat the phrases and sentences out loud helps him remember them more easily and write them down accurately.

Review

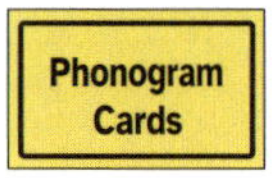

Review a selection of Phonogram Cards from behind the Review divider in your student's Spelling Review Box.

Review a selection of Sound Cards from behind the Review divider. Have your student write the phonograms in his dictation notebook.

Review a selection of Rule Cards from behind the Review divider.

Review a selection of Word Cards from behind the Review divider. Have your student write the words in his dictation notebook.

Alphabetize letter tiles a to z with your student.

New Teaching

Introduce Long Vowel Sounds

Move letter tiles a, e, i, o, and u into the workspace.

Point to the a.

"Tell me the three sounds of this letter." */ă/–/ā/–/ah/.*

"Which of those sounds is the **short** sound?" */ă/ (*or *the first sound).*

"Good. The first sound of a vowel is its short sound. We also have a name for the **second** sound of a vowel. The second sound is called its **long** sound."

"What is the second sound of the letter a?" */ā/.*

Point to the e.

"What are the two sounds of this letter?" */ĕ/–/ē/.*

"What is the long sound of this letter?" */ē/.*

Point to the i.

"What are the three sounds of this letter?" */ĭ/–/ī/–/ē/.*

"What is the long sound of this letter?" */ī/.*

Point to the o.

Your student can probably see the pattern now.

"And what do you think the long sound of o is?" */ō/.*

"And the long sound of u?" */ū/.*

"Good. The long sound of a vowel is the same as its name."

New Teaching
(continued)

Teach Spelling Rule 8: The Long Vowel Rule

Build the word **m** **e**.

"Point to the vowel." *Student points to the e.*

"When a vowel is at the end of a syllable, it usually says its name. Read this word." *Me.*

"Change the word *me* to *he* by switching one of the tiles." *Student exchanges the m tile for an h tile.*

Repeat this activity using the following sets of words. Have your student change the consonant to spell the word you specify.

he → be → we → she

go → no → so

Take out the Long Vowel Rule poster and explore it with your student.

Read the sample words aloud and help your student notice which syllables have long vowel sounds at the end.

You may wish to hang the poster in your lesson area for future reference.

Read Rule Card 8 with your student and then file it behind the Review divider.

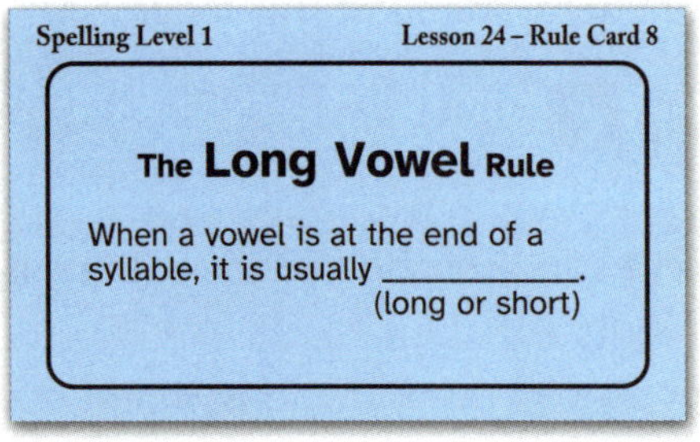

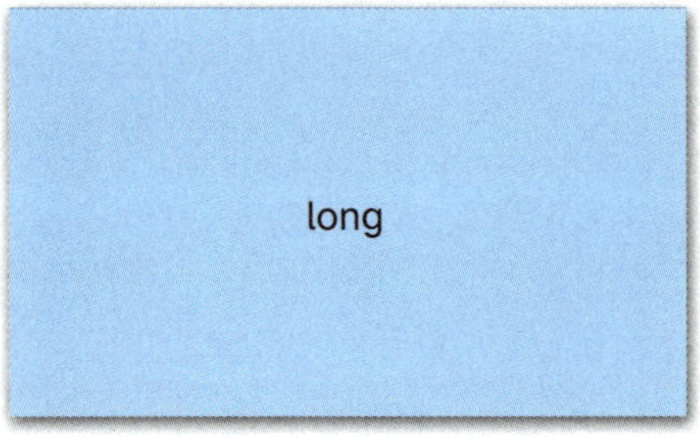

New Teaching
(continued)

Complete Activity Sheet *(Optional)*

"Let's flip some flapjacks!"

Flip the Flapjacks

Remove pages 187-190 from the *Zip into Spelling* activity book.

Cut out the flapjack cards and place them in a pile with the words facing down.

Have your student select a card, flip it over to reveal the word, and determine if the vowel will be long or short. He may then add that flapjack to the appropriate plate.

Continue until all the flapjacks have been flipped and the student has sorted all sixteen words.

Answer Key
long vowels: be, go, we, no, I, he, so, she
short vowels: bed, got, wet, not, it, hem, sock, shed

Teach Two Common Words: *the* and *a*

"Here is an interesting case."

Build the word th e m.

"What is this word?" *Them.*

"If I remove the m, what does it say?" *Student may say /thē/ or /thŭ/.*

"Good. This word can say /thē/ or /thŭ/. Usually, we say /thŭ/."

New Teaching
(continued)

Tip!

We usually pronounce *the* like /thŭ/. But sometimes we pronounce it as /thē/ when:

1. it comes before a vowel sound (*the apple, the open door, the ice cream*).
2. we want to emphasize something (*"You saw THE Queen of England?!"*).

For many children, spelling the word *the* doesn't present difficulties because they have seen it in writing so many times. But if your student does have trouble, tell him to "pronounce for spelling" and say it like /thē/ for spelling purposes.

Build the word a.

"The same thing happens with the word *a*. We can say /ā/ or /ŭh/ when we speak, and we spell it a."

Spell Word Cards 171-180 with Letter Tiles

Dictate the words and have your student spell them with letter tiles. Use the **Procedure for Spelling with Letter Tiles** in Appendix E.

The spelling words in this lesson may be too easy for your student. If so, skip them and move on to Advanced Application on page 226.

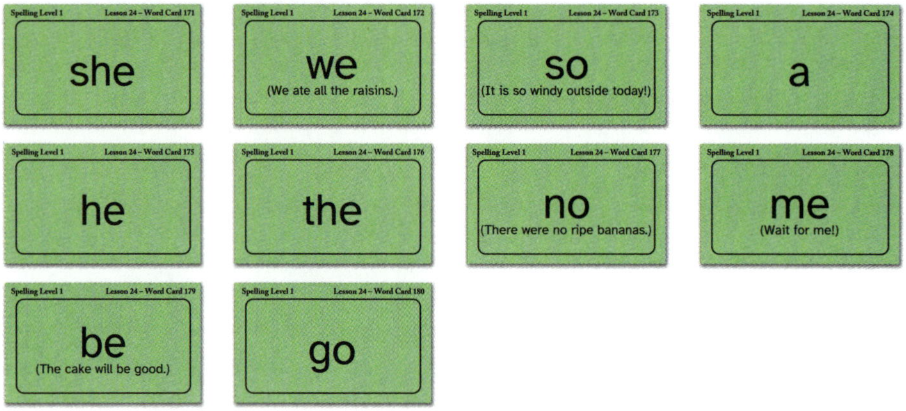

New Teaching
(continued)

Spell on Paper

Once your student is able to spell the words using the letter tiles, have him take out his dictation notebook. Dictate Word Cards 171-180 and have your student spell the words on paper.

File the Word Cards behind the Review divider in the Spelling Review Box.

Practice More Words

The following words reinforce the concepts taught in this lesson. For additional practice, have your student spell them in his dictation notebook.

hi (say hi to someone) **I** (I am)

> You may need to point out to your student that *I* is capitalized. **Tip!**

Complete Activity Sheet *(Optional)*

"It's time to make some toast!"

Let's Make Toast!

Remove pages 191-194 from the activity book.

Cut a slit in the toaster as indicated by the dotted line. Cut out the bread cards and place them in a pile with the bread slices facing up.

Choose twelve words from this lesson that you think would most benefit your student to practice. Dictate the words one by one and have your student write each word on a bread card. If he spells the word correctly, he may put the bread in the toaster for a moment and then pop it up to reveal the finished piece of toast on the back.

Continue until all the bread has been toasted and the student has practiced all twelve words.

New Teaching
(continued)

Dictate Phrases

Dictate several phrases each day. Your student should repeat each phrase and write it in his dictation notebook.

so much gum	**no bells**
fell with a thud	**in the bathtub**
grass on the hill	**a bad smell**

Dictate Sentences

Dictate several sentences each day. Your student should write the sentences in his dictation notebook. If necessary, explain that each sentence will begin with a capital letter and end with a period.

She had six hats.
We sang songs.
He has spots.
Get me a jug.
Go with me.
It will be fun.

Advanced Application

For advanced practice, have your student turn to the Advanced Application sheet on page 195 of the activity book.

"You can spell *no*. Now spell *domino*, as in *The last domino finally fell down.*" *Student writes* no *on the first line.*

Continue with the remaining words. Dictate the full word, read the sentence, and have your student fill in the missing syllable.

1.	**domino**	The last domino finally fell down.
2.	**hibernate**	I wish I could hibernate like a hedgehog.
3.	**mango**	Our parrot can eat a mango in five minutes.
4.	**adobe**	An old adobe wall surrounds the town.
5.	**epitome**	Meerkats are the epitome of cute animals.
6.	**also**	Penguins and pandas are also adorable!
7.	**helium**	All the helium balloons are stuck on the ceiling.
8.	**ironic**	It's ironic that nosy Ned doesn't like gossip!

Track Your Progress

Mark the Progress Chart

Remember that each lesson may require several sessions to complete. Before moving on, ask yourself these questions:

1. Does your student have a firm grasp on the long vowel sounds and the Long Vowel Rule?
2. Has your student mastered eight out of the ten Word Cards?

If the answer to both is yes, have your student mark Lesson 24 on the Progress Chart and move on to the next lesson!

What?
Only one lesson to go?
Are you pollen my leg?
Well, dip me in honey
and stick me to a daisy!
Come on, now, get in here and give me a
HIVE-FIVE!
We're almost there!

Lesson 25 Putting It All Together

Objective

This lesson provides cumulative review of all concepts taught in Level 1.

You Will Need

☐ *Zip into Spelling* pages 197-205

Before You Begin

Evaluate Your Student's Progress

This is the final lesson!

No new concepts are taught in this lesson; instead, it is designed as a motivating way for your student to practice everything she has learned. At the same time, it provides you with a comprehensive way to evaluate whether your student needs reinforcement in any specific concepts before moving on to Level 2. As you complete the activities, determine which concepts, if any, your student still needs to practice.

Congratulations to you and your student on finishing Level 1. You may want to plan a little celebration!

Final Review

Complete Activity Sheets

"Have you ever eaten a s'more?" *Discuss your student's experience.* "Today you get to describe what a s'more is like!"

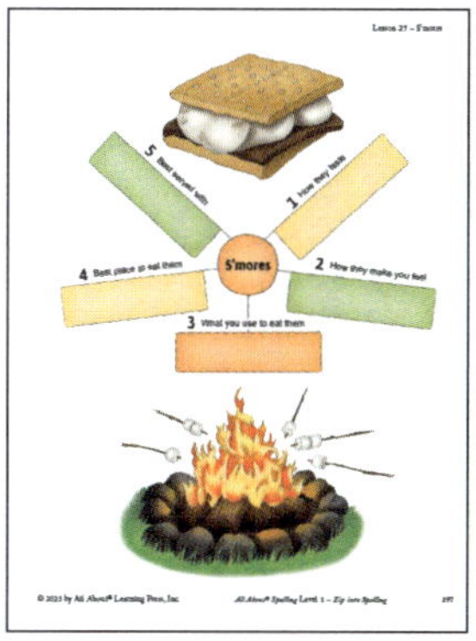

S'mores

Turn to page 197 in the *Zip into Spelling* activity book.

Point to the first space. "First describe how s'mores taste. In the blank space, write either *yum* or *yuck*."

"For number 2, describe how s'mores make you feel. Write either *so glad* or *so sad*."

"For number 3, describe what you use to eat them. Write either *hands* or *chopsticks*."

"For number 4, write the best place to eat them: *in a sandbox, at camp,* or *on an anthill.*"

Final Review
(continued)

"For number 5, write what they are best served with: *plums, a glass of milk,* or *flapjacks.*"

"Good! Now let's talk about gifts."

"Has anyone ever surprised you with a gift and it wasn't even your birthday or a holiday?" *Discuss your student's experience.*

"In this next activity, you'll write six silly reasons to give someone a chocolate bar."

Who Gets Chocolate?

Remove pages 199-201 from the activity book.

Cut out the strips along the dotted lines. Assemble the sentence strips in numerical order 1-6, place the cover sheet on top of the pile, and staple where indicated to create a booklet.

Have your student flip the booklet open to sentence 1. "I'll dictate a sentence and you'll fill in the missing words. *Hank sang the birthday song under water.*"

Continue with the remaining sentences.

2. Chad posted a sign at lunch that said, "No Peas Allowed."
3. Six of his socks pass the sniff test.
4. Nick can quack like a duck while he hops on one foot.
5. Mel can spit watermelon seeds farther than anyone else.
6. Beth gave me a box of frogs just for fun.

"What other random reasons are there to share a chocolate bar?" *Discuss your student's ideas.*

"And now you're going to write the steps for how to catch a moose."

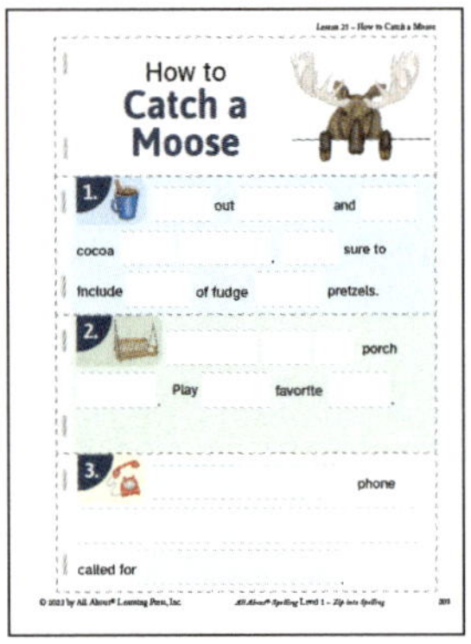

How to Catch a Moose

Remove pages 203-205 from the activity book.

Cut out the strips along the dotted lines. Assemble the sentence strips in numerical order 1-6, place the cover sheet on top of the pile, and staple where indicated.

Final Review
(continued)

One by one, dictate the following sentences and have your student lift the flaps and fill in the missing words. When completed, she will have all the steps for catching a moose.

1. Set out snacks and hot cocoa to drink. Be sure to include lots of fudge and pretzels.
2. Hang up a porch swing. Play his favorite song.
3. Hand him a phone and tell him his mom called for a quick chat.
4. Ask him if he would like to see your latest card trick.
5. Buy a big truck and offer him a ride to visit his cousin.
6. Get your camera. Snap his picture. (He will want to brush his hair first.)

Track Your Progress

Mark the Progress Chart

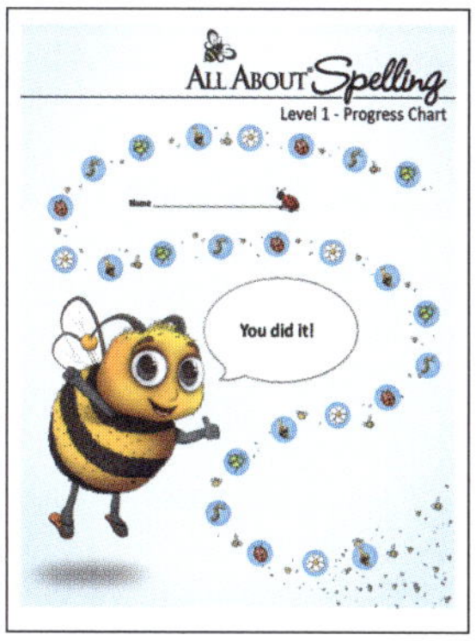

Did your student ace this review lesson? Do you feel your student has mastered all the concepts in Level 1?

If so, have your student mark Lesson 25 on the Progress Chart and then ... celebrate!

Celebrate!

Present Your Student with the Certificate of Achievement

YOU DID IT!
You zipped through Level 1 like a boss bee and I couldn't be prouder! In fact, the whole hive is abuzz with excitement.
You deserve a big slurp of nectar!
And on behalf of all the bees, I extend my swarmest wishes as you wing your way to Level 2!
ZIP, ZIP, BUZZ-AY!

3

Appendices

APPENDIX A
Scope and Sequence of Level 1

Your Student Will:	Lesson
Learn and master the first 26 phonograms	1
Identify the first and last sounds in a word	2
Segment words with two and three sounds	3
Learn the Vowels Rule, alphabetize the letter tiles, and distinguish between vowels and consonants	4
Write the phonograms from dictation	5
Learn short vowel sounds, the Short Vowel Rule, and choose the correct vowel for a word	6
Segment words with letter tiles, learn the procedure for spelling with tiles, spell words containing short a, and spell words from dictation	7
Spell words containing short i	8
Learn how to capitalize names and spell words containing short o	9
Spell words containing short u	10
Understand what a syllable is, count syllables in a word, and spell words containing short e	11
Learn the second sound of s and spell words containing s, x, and qu	12
Learn the concept of consonant teams, learn phonograms th, sh, and ch, and spell words with those phonograms	13
Segment words with consonant blends at the end and spell words with final blends	14
Segment words with consonant blends at the beginning and spell words with initial blends	15
Learn the Soft C Rule, choose between c and k for the sound of /k/ at the beginning of a word, and spell words with the sound of /k/ at the beginning	16
Learn the Floss Rule for doubling letters f, l, and s and spell words ending in ff, ll, and ss	17
Learn consonant team ck and the CK Rule for spelling /k/ at the end of a word, spell words with ck or k at the end	18
Learn consonant team ng and spell words containing ng	19
Learn consonant team nk and spell words containing nk	20
Spell compound words	21
Learn what a plural word is, identify base words, learn the Add S Rule, and spell plural words by adding s	22
Learn the Add ES Rule and spell plural words by adding e-s	23
Learn long vowel sounds and the Long Vowel Rule and spell words ending with long vowel sounds	24
Review all concepts learned in Level 1	25

APPENDIX B
Phonograms Taught in Levels 1-7

Phonograms are letters or letter combinations that represent a single sound. For example, the letter <u>b</u> represents the sound /b/ as in *bat*. The letter combination <u>sh</u> represents the sound /sh/ as in *ship*.

Card #	Phonogram	Sound	For the Teacher's Use Only (example of word containing the phonogram)	Lesson/ Level
Phonograms Taught in Level 1				
1	m	/m/	moon	1
2	s	/s/–/z/	sun, has	1
3	p	/p/	pig	1
4	a	/ă/–/ā/–/ah/	apple, acorn, father	1
5	n	/n/	nest	1
6	t	/t/	tent	1
7	b	/b/	bat	1
8	j	/j/	jam	1
9	g	/g/–/j/	goose, gem	1
10	d	/d/	deer	1
11	c	/k/–/s/	cow, city	1
12	y	/y/–/ĭ/–/ī/–/ē/	yarn, gym, my, happy	1
13	h	/h/	hat	1
14	k	/k/	kite	1
15	r	/r/	rake	1
16	i	/ĭ/–/ī/–/ē/	itchy, ivy, radio	1
17	v	/v/	vase	1
18	f	/f/	fish	1
19	z	/z/	zipper	1
20	o	/ŏ/–/ō/–/o͞o/–/ŭ/	otter, open, to, oven	1
21	l	/l/	leaf	1
22	w	/w/	wave	1
23	u	/ŭ/–/ū/–/o͝o/	udder, unit, put	1
24	e	/ĕ/–/ē/	echo, even	1
25	qu	/kw/	queen	1
26	x	/ks/	ax	1
27	th	/th/–/~~th~~/	three, then	13

Card #	Phonogram	Sound	For the Teacher's Use Only (example of word containing the phonogram)	Lesson/ Level
28	sh	/sh/	ship	13
29	ch	/ch/–/k/–/sh/	child school chef	13
30	ck	/k/, two-letter /k/	duck	18
31	ng	/ng/	king	19
32	nk	/ngk/	thank	20
Phonograms Taught in Level 2				Level 2
33	ee	/ē/, double <u>e</u>	feed	
34	wh	/hw/	while	
35	er	/er/ as in *her*	her	
36	ar	/ar/	car	
37	or	/or/–/er/ as in *work*	corn work	
38	oy	/oy/ that we **may** use at the end of English words	toy	
39	oi	/oy/ that we **may not** use at the end of English words	oil	
40	aw	/aw/ that we **may** use at the end of English words	saw	
41	au	/aw/ that we **may not** use at the end of English words	pause	
42	ow	/ow/–/ō/	cow low	
43	ou	/ow/–/ō/–/ōō/–/ŭ/	mouse soul soup touch	
Phonograms Taught in Level 3				Level 3
44	ay	/ā/, two-letter /ā/ that we **may** use at the end of English words	day	
45	ai	/ā/, two-letter /ā/ that we **may not** use at the end of English words	rain	
46	ur	/er/ as in *nurse*	nurse	
47	oa	/ō/, two-letter /ō/ that we **may not** use at the end of English words	boat	

Card #	Phonogram	Sound	For the Teacher's Use Only (example of word containing the phonogram)	Lesson/ Level
48	oo	/o͞o/–/o͝o/–/ō/	food book floor	Level 3
49	ea	/ē/–/ĕ/–/ā/	leaf bread great	
50	ed	/ĕd/–/d/–/t/	wanted snowed dropped	
51	ir	/er/ as in *first*	first	
52	igh	/ī/, three-letter /ī/	light	
Phonograms Taught in Level 4				Level 4
53	tch	/ch/, three-letter /ch/	watch	
54	dge	/j/, three-letter /j/	badge	
55	or	/or/–/er/ as in *work*	corn work	
56	ew	/o͞o/–/ū/	grew few	
57	ie	/ē/–/ī/	field pie	
58	wr	/r/, two-letter /r/ used **only** at the beginning of a word	write	
59	kn	/n/, two-letter /n/ used **only** at the beginning of a word	know	
60	eigh	/ā/, four-letter /ā/	eight	
61	ear	/er/ as in *early*	early	
62	ph	/f/, two-letter /f/	phone	
63	ti	/sh/, tall-letter /sh/	nation	
64	ey	/ē/–/ā/	key they	
65	oe	/ō/, two-letter /ō/ that we **may** use at the end of English words	toe	
Phonograms Taught in Level 5				Level 5
66	si	/sh/–/zh/	mission vision	
67	ough	/ō/–/o͞o/–/ŭff/–/ŏff/–/aw/–/ow/	though through rough cough thought bough	
68	ei	/ā/–/ē/ that we **may not** use at the end of English words	vein ceiling	
69	ui	/o͞o/	fruit	

Card #	Phonogram	Sound	For the Teacher's Use Only (example of word containing the phonogram)	Lesson/ Level
70	gn	/n/, two-letter /n/ used at the beginning or end of a word	gnat	Level 5
71	our	/er/ as in *journey*	journey	
Phonograms Taught in Level 6				Level 6
72	mb	/m/, two-letter /m/	lamb	
73	gu	/g/, two-letter /g/	guide	
74	augh	/aw/, four-letter /aw/	daughter	
Phonograms Taught in Level 7				Level 7
75	ci	/sh/, short-letter /sh/	special	
76	rh	/r/, two-letter /r/	rhyme	

APPENDIX C

Spelling Rules Taught in Level 1

Rule #	Rule	Lesson
1	 **The Vowels Rule** Every word has at least one vowel. The vowels are a, e, i, o, u, and sometimes y.	4
2	 **The Short Vowel Rule** When a single vowel is followed by a consonant, it usually says its short sound.	6
3	 **The Soft C Rule** C says /s/ before e, i, or y.	16
4	 **The Floss Rule** We often double f, l, and s at the end of one-syllable words when they come right after a single vowel.	17
5	 **The CK Rule** Ck is only used right after a short vowel.	18
6	 **The Add S Rule** Add s to make most words plural.	22
7	 **The Add ES Rule** Add e-s to make words plural if you hear /ĭz/ at the end.	23
8	 **The Long Vowel Rule** When a vowel is at the end of a syllable, it is usually long.	24

APPENDIX D
How to Review the Flashcards

In each teaching session, choose a mix of **no more than twenty** Phonogram, Sound, Word, and Rule Cards to review. The following procedures will help you make the most of your review time.

Phonogram Cards

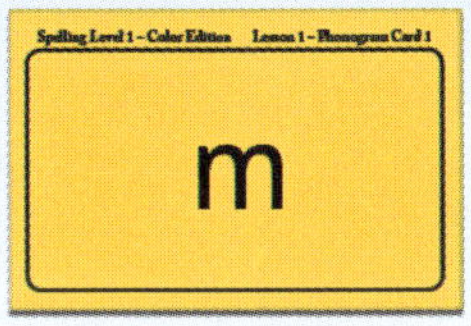

1. Shuffle the cards behind the Review divider before starting. If there are no cards behind the Review divider, either skip that part of the review or choose cards from behind the Mastered divider, according to your student's needs.
2. Choose a small number of cards, between 4-12 depending on your student's age, ability, or attention span.
3. Show the front of the Phonogram Card to your student.
4. Have the student say the sound or sounds.
5. If a phonogram has several sounds, you can give your student a hint by holding up the appropriate number of fingers.

Alternatively, you may wish to use one of the review activities in Appendix M.

When do I move a Phonogram Card behind the Mastered divider?

Look for these signs. If you see all three, the card is mastered!

- Your student responds quickly and easily when you hold up the card.
- Your student says the pure, clipped sound(s) without adding /uh/ at the end (for example, he says /p/, not /puh/).
- You have no doubt that your student knows the card thoroughly.

Sound Cards

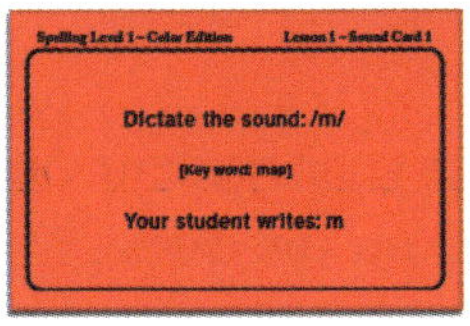

1. Shuffle the cards behind the Review divider before starting. If there are no cards behind the Review divider, either skip that part of the review or choose cards from behind the Mastered divider, according to your student's needs.
2. Choose a small number of cards to review, depending on your student's age, ability, or attention span.
3. Dictate the sound(s) listed on the flashcard. If there is more than one sound, pause briefly between them. Do not read the key words.
4. Your student will write the phonogram that makes the sound(s).

When do I move a Sound Card behind the Mastered divider?

If your student does not hesitate when writing the phonogram, the card is mastered!

Word Cards

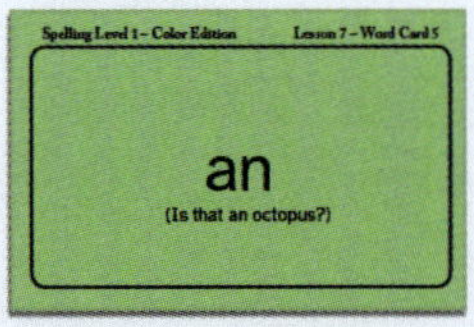
an
(Is that an octopus?)

1. Shuffle the cards behind the Review divider before starting. If there are no cards behind the Review divider, either skip that part of the review or choose cards from behind the Mastered divider, according to your student's needs.
2. Choose a small number of cards, between 4-12 depending on your student's age, ability, or attention span.
3. Dictate the word and have your student spell it. Alternatively, use one of the review activities in Appendix N.

When do I move a Word Card behind the Mastered divider?
If your student does not hesitate when spelling the word, the card is mastered!

A good practice is to keep no more than twenty Word Cards behind the Review divider at a time: the ten cards from the most recent lesson, plus several cards that have not yet been mastered.

If you find that the Word Cards for review are stacking up too much, or that your student is misspelling a lot of words during daily review, slow down the pace of the lessons and spend more time on review. Move on to the next lesson only when you are sure your student has mastered the previous one.

See also Appendix K: How to Handle Spelling Mistakes.

Rule Cards

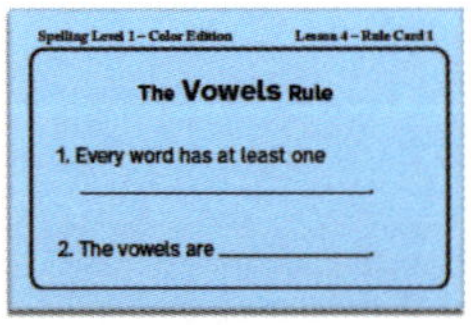
The Vowels Rule
1. Every word has at least one
2. The vowels are

1. Shuffle the cards behind the Review divider before starting. If there are no cards behind the Review divider, either skip that part of the review or choose cards from behind the Mastered divider, according to your student's needs.
2. Choose a small number of cards to review, depending on your student's age, ability, or attention span.
3. Read the Rule Card to your student, pausing so that your student can verbally fill in the blank(s) or answer the question(s) on the card.

When do I move a Rule Card behind the Mastered divider?
If your student does not hesitate when filling in the blanks or answering the questions, the card is mastered!

APPENDIX E

Procedure for Spelling with Letter Tiles

The following routine is very effective and is used throughout the *All About Spelling* program.

1 **Dictate the word, then point to the tiles.**

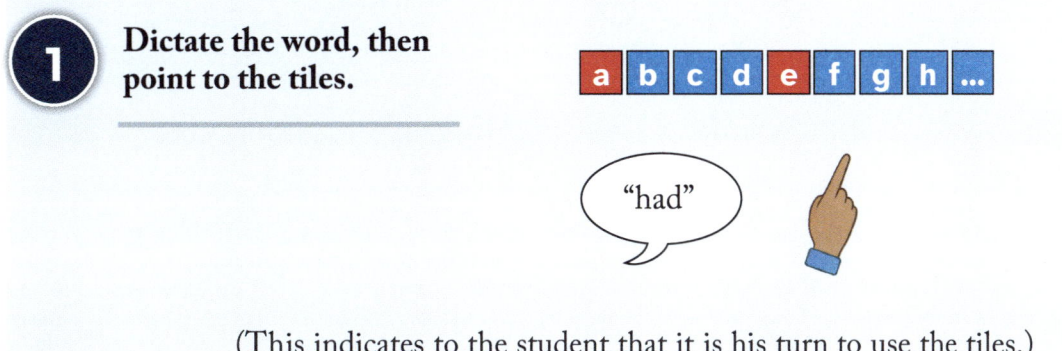

(This indicates to the student that it is his turn to use the tiles.)

2 **The student segments the word aloud, selecting the correct tile for each sound.**

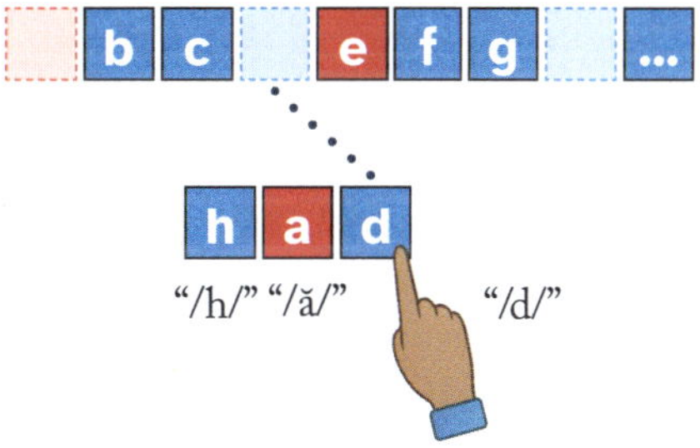

(Segmenting aloud helps the student represent each sound with a phonogram.)

3 **The student reads the word he just spelled.**

(Reading the word enables the student to self-correct if he has made a mistake.)

4 **After each word, the student puts the tiles back in order (physical tiles) or clears the workspace (app).**

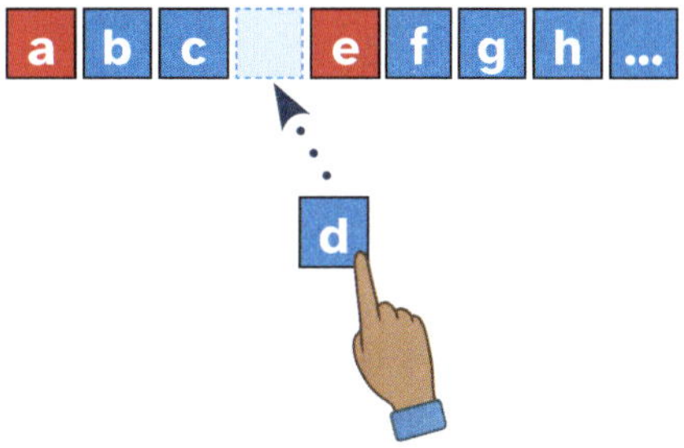

APPENDIX F
Solving Letter Reversal Problems

Most of the letters of the alphabet have unique shapes, so no matter which way you turn them, they can't be confused with any other letters. For example, the letter m looks quite different from the letter x, and f is not likely to be confused with z.

There are a few notorious troublemakers, however, particularly b and d, the letters that students most often have trouble with.

It is easy to see where the confusion comes in: flip the b and it becomes a d. The beginning student may not realize that the direction of the letter matters, or he may not be able to remember which letter is which.

Letters and numbers that can be flipped include:

bd pq pd nu 69

What is considered normal?

If your student is between the ages of three and seven, is just starting to read and spell, and makes occasional reversal errors when reading or writing, it's perfectly normal. It doesn't mean that your student has dyslexia or a reading disability. Make a gentle correction and move on.

But if your student is eight years or older, has had prior reading and spelling instruction, and is making frequent letter reversal errors, it is important to take action to solve the reversal problems.

As teachers, we have two jobs to do regarding reversals:

1. Try to prevent confusion.
2. Where confusion exists, resolve it.

Try to prevent letter confusion before it begins.

The *All About Spelling* program is carefully structured to minimize the likelihood of letter reversals. We teach the sounds of potentially confusing letters like b and d in separate lessons. The student's task is simplified because he only has to make one new visual discrimination at a time.

When your student is learning to print, be sure to teach correct letter formation. Doing so is critical to prevent confusion.

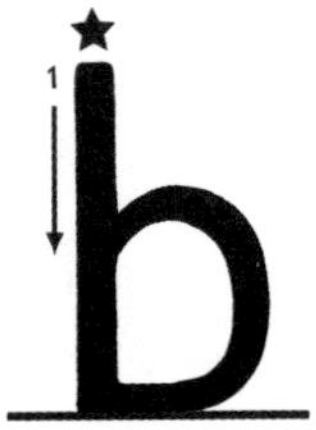

When forming the letter b, start with the stick first, followed by the circle. To write the letter d, start with the circle first, followed by the stick.

Have your student use lined paper so it is clear where the circle is in relation to the stick. Also be sure your student does not lift the pencil from the paper when writing any of the confusable letters.

What to do if your student already reverses letters.

If you are working with older learners, it may be too late to prevent confusion. They may have had a few false starts in spelling and reading and may have already confused these troublemakers. They may encounter the letter b and misinterpret it as the letter d. They may read or spell the word *bad* as *dab* or *fad* as *fab*. You might give a gentle correction and re-teach the letters separately, but your student still mixes them up.

Below are four effective methods to clear up tough reversal problems.

The demonstrations are for correcting b and d reversals, but the same concepts can be applied to any letter or number. You may only need to use one of these methods, but for really resistant cases, you will need to use all four methods.

Please note that it's important to concentrate on just one letter per session. Wait until that letter is completely mastered before teaching another letter.

Method 1: Teach the letters b and d using tactile surfaces.

Have a variety of tactile surfaces for your student to choose from. Possibilities include flannel fabric, corrugated cardboard, very fine sandpaper, fluffy fur fabric, or a carpet square. Ask your student which surface reminds him of the letter b, and then cut a large lowercase b out of the chosen tactile surface.

Using the pointer finger of his dominant hand, have your student trace the letter b on the textured surface. Be sure he starts and ends in the correct place. Practice until he can easily write the letter b.

When your student is ready to go on to a new letter, choose a different textured surface. If fine sandpaper was used for the letter b, perhaps furry fabric can be used for the letter d.

Method 2: Use "air writing" to reinforce proper letter formation.

Another simple but powerful method for correcting reversals is "air writing." Using the dominant hand, the student uses his entire arm to write letters in the air as he says the sound of the letter. The whole arm should be involved, and the student should pretend that his pointer finger is a pen.

Brain research shows that two ideas practiced at the same time can permanently bond the ideas together. In this case, the large movements of the arm combined with saying the sound of the letter helps link these two concepts together in your student's brain. Additionally, this multisensory activity takes advantage of the fact that the muscles in the shoulder and in the jaw have muscle memory, and this makes it easier for your student to recall the shape and sound of the letter.

Method #3: Teach the letters b and d using analogies.

Explain that the letter b is made up of two shapes: a bat and a ball. Using the tactile surface, demonstrate how you write the bat part of the letter first, followed by the ball.

As you write the letter b, say "bat-ball-/b/," like this:

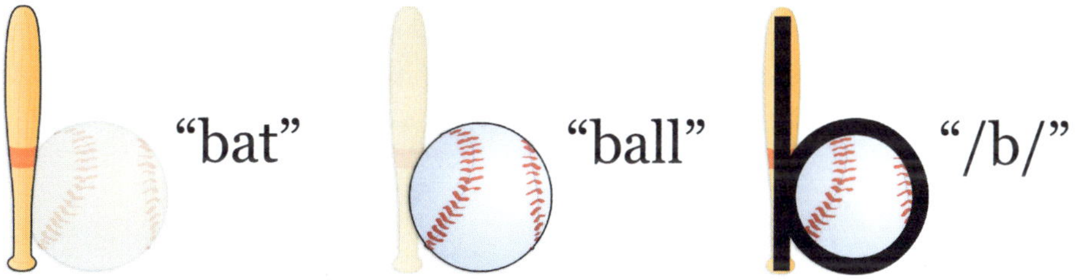

To further clarify which side of the letter the straight line is on, tell your student that *first you grab the bat and then you hit the ball.*

Have your student practice this motion and chant many times over a two-minute time period. Repeat the exercise several times a day.

Show your student that when you are reading and writing from left to right, you encounter the bat part of the letter first. If he is ever unsure of the sound this letter makes when he sees it, he should think to himself, "bat-ball-/b/." This will help him recall the sound of the letter b.

To teach the letter d, you can use the analogy of a doorknob and a door. The doorknob represents the circle part of the letter and the door represents the straight line, like this:

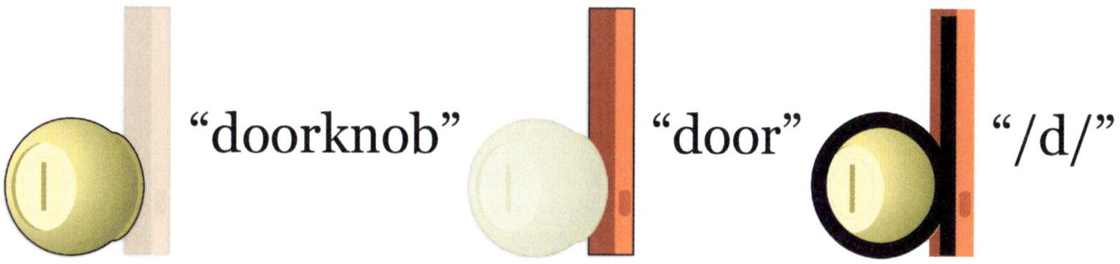

To clarify which side of the letter the straight line is on, tell your student that *first you grab the doorknob and then you open the door.*

Again, practice the motion and chant many times over a two-minute period. Repeat the exercise several times a day.

Show your student that when you are reading or writing from left to right, you encounter the doorknob part of the letter first. If he is ever unsure of the sound this letter makes when he sees it, he should think to himself, "doorknob-door-/d/." He will now be able to recall the sound of the letter d.

Another common analogy to help with b and d is a bed. Though this analogy may help some kids, for others it may require more thought, and for many kids it may not become automatic.

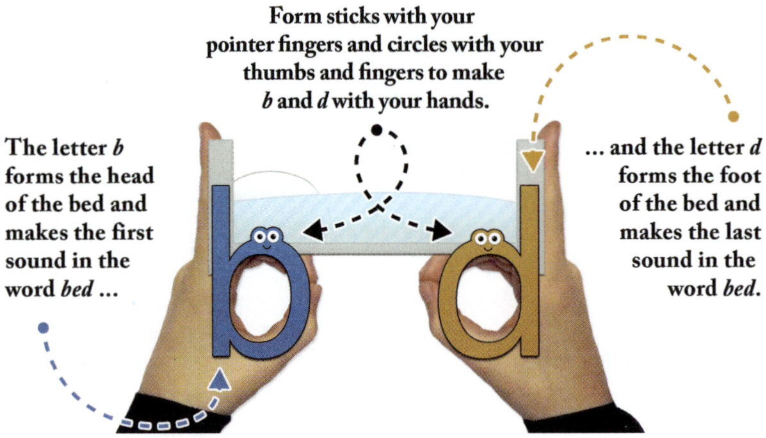
Form sticks with your pointer fingers and circles with your thumbs and fingers to make *b* and *d* with your hands.
The letter *b* forms the head of the bed and makes the first sound in the word *bed* ...
... and the letter *d* forms the foot of the bed and makes the last sound in the word *bed*.
b
d

Method #4: Help your student notice the shape of the mouth while saying the letter sounds.

When we say /b/, our lips come together in a straight line. Point out that the straight line comes first when you write the letter b.

When we say /d/, our lips are open. Coincidentally, the circle comes first when you write the letter d.

If your student misreads or mispells a b as a d, refer back to the tactile surface activity and air writing that you did together. Point to the misread or mispelled letter and say, *If you wrote this letter, what would this letter say?*

If your student can't answer easily, ask him to draw the letter b using air writing. The sound of the letter (/b/–bat) should come more easily this way. Then have your student read the word again.

APPENDIX G
The Pin-Pen Merger

If your student has a hard time spelling words with the sounds of short i and short e, he may be struggling to differentiate between these two vowel sounds. This common spelling problem, called the Pin-Pen Merger, often arises due to regional differences in pronunciation. In *All About Spelling*, short i and short e are taught in different lessons, which gives your student the chance to master one set of words before new (and potentially confusable) words are introduced.

Here are five ways to help your student spell words with short i and short e.

1 Provide extra practice

Download the activity at downloads.allaboutlearningpress.com/downloads/Distinguishing-Between-Short-I-and-Short-E.pdf to give your student extra practice in distinguishing between short i and short e.

2 Pronounce for spelling

Use the procedure in Appendix H. Vowel sounds are often muffled in the normal rhythm of speech, so when it's time to spell, it's important to slow down and drag out the pronunciation so your student can hear the vowel sound very clearly.

3 Watch your mouth

Have your student watch your mouth as you make the sounds /ĭ/ and /ĕ/. The mouth should be open taller when you say the short e sound than when you say the short i sound. Now have your student make the sounds while watching himself in the mirror. For some kids, it may be easier to feel this with their mouth than to see it.

4 Use Word Banks

Lessons 8 and 11 include Word Banks for short i and short e. Word Banks help students develop a visual memory for how words are spelled. As your student reads through these Word Banks, he should use his normal dialect.

5 Treat some words as homophones

In some regions, word pairs like *sit* and *set* are pronounced the same. If this is the case in your area, dictate the word in a sentence so your student has the additional help of hearing the word used in context.

Learning to discriminate between the /ĭ/ and /ĕ/ sounds will help your student immensely in spelling. Working on this skill is well worth the time spent.

APPENDIX H

The Pronounce for Spelling Technique

The Pronounce for Spelling technique is an excellent tool for preventing spelling errors. We refer to it often in the *All About Spelling* program.

When you pronounce for spelling, you exaggerate the pronunciation of a word to make it easier to spell. For example, in casual speech we often pronounce the word *different* as *difrent*, leaving out the second syllable. When we pronounce for spelling, we carefully enunciate each syllable (*dif-fer-ent*), making it much easier to spell.

The Pronounce for Spelling technique is particularly useful in these three situations:

- **Unaccented syllables:** *separate (sep-rit), chocolate (choc-lit), camera (cam-ra)*
- **Regional accents** in which different words are pronounced the same: *than/then, pin/pen, marry/merry*
- **Silent letters:** *friend, Wednesday, muscle*

If your student stumbles into one of these situations, have her follow the two simple steps of the Pronounce for Spelling technique.

1. Exaggerate the pronunciation of the word.
2. Spell each sound you hear.

Here are some additional tips:

- Notice that the first step in this technique is to *exaggerate* the pronunciation. We're not advocating that your student go around saying words like *separate* with ultraprecision—just during spelling lessons.
- If your student isn't aware of the correct pronunciation, model it for her. For example, if she regularly pronounces *camera* as *cam-ra*, carefully pronounce the word for her: *cam-er-a*. When she can hear each syllable, she'll be less likely to gloss over the unaccented syllables.
- It can be endearing when young children mispronounce words—*aminals* for *animals* or *pasghetti* for *spaghetti*. At this stage, it isn't necessary to interrupt a student to correct her pronunciation. We want to keep a positive environment for speaking and communicating. Instead, practice purposeful modeling: if a child says, "I'd like some more pasgetti," you could respond with, "More spaghetti, coming up!"
- Where silent letters can be pronounced (as in *Wed-nes-day*), it's helpful to do so when first learning how to spell those words. There will be times in which the technique won't work, such as in the word *could* where the silent l can't be pronounced. Beginning in Level 2, we introduce additional techniques for spelling these words.

Any time your student *fergets* how to spell a word, simply remind her not to *forget* to pronounce for spelling.

APPENDIX I

Methods for Counting Syllables

Knowing how to recognize and count syllables is an important part of your student's spelling progress and is immensely useful when it comes to encoding multisyllable words.

If your student needs help with counting syllables, choose one of the engaging methods below.

Method	What to Say	What to Do	Example
 The Hum Method	Say the word.	Hum each syllable.	*el – e – phant* (hum) (hum) (hum)
 The Clap Method	Say the word.	Clap each syllable.	*win – dow* (clap) (clap)
 The Robot Method	Say the word in a robotic tone.	Listen to the separation of the word chunks.	*pres – i – dent* (pause) (pause)
 The Jump Method	Say the word.	Jump on each syllable.	*mon – key* (jump) (jump)
 The Name Method	Say your student's name.	Emphasize each syllable.	*Em – i – ly* *Cae – den* *Mad – i – son* *Bryce*

Tip! Practice counting syllables using the One Banana, Two Bananas activity in Lesson 11. You can use any multisyllable words.

APPENDIX J

"Hop to It" Activity for Segmenting Words with Blends

Segmenting words is the foundation of good spelling. Your student must learn to hear the individual sounds in words; otherwise, she is just going to be memorizing strings of letters.

If your student has problems segmenting blends, teach the skill in a concrete way. The following activity can be used to practice both initial and final blends.

Setup

Put four sheets of paper on the floor, lined up in a row. Each sheet should be a different color or, if you don't have colored paper, color a big square on each sheet with crayons. You want to be able to differentiate between the four papers.

1. Think of a word, like *fast*. Don't tell your student the word. Step on the first paper and say /f/. Step on the second paper and say /ă/. Step on the third paper and say /s/, and then on the fourth and say /t/. Have your student guess the word.

2. When your student can easily guess the word, change the game a little. After you've stepped on each piece of paper and said the /f/–/ă/–/s/–/t/ sounds in quick sequence, jump back to the first paper and ask, "What sound was this?" Jump to each paper in turn and have the student identify the corresponding sound. Repeat this with other words until it becomes easy. Go back to the beginning of the word and blend the first two sounds together.

3. Next, have your student segment the word herself. Give her a word that you have already done and have her model your example. She will step on the papers, each paper representing one sound.

4. Now your student should have a good grasp of what is required to segment blends. If your student ever gets stuck when you dictate words to segment, model how it should be done and have her imitate you.

APPENDIX K

How to Handle Spelling Mistakes

The way you handle spelling errors can make a huge difference in your student's ability and confidence. Here are some tips on how to approach errors both during and outside of the spelling lesson.

Steps for Handling Mistakes Made *During* a Lesson

When you're in the middle of a spelling lesson, a mistake might seem like a reason for concern. Instead, every spelling mistake is a chance for your student to learn.

It's best to correct errors right after your student indicates that he is done spelling the word or sentence. Don't wait until after class to check his work.

1. **Ask your student to carefully read exactly what he has written down.**

   Often, he will be able to see and correct his own error.

2. **Determine the cause of the spelling mistake.**

   For example, perhaps your student left out a sound or added an extra one, or perhaps he didn't apply a rule, made a visual error, or forgot to think through syllables or root words. Talk through the reasons the word is misspelled instead of simply correcting the mistake without explanation. If you need to review a phonogram or a rule, now is the time to do it.

3. **Have your student spell the word again.**

   Have him spell the word with the letter tiles and then once again on paper.

4. **Add the word to your student's Spelling Review Box.**

   Leave the word in the review box until your student can spell it quickly and easily. Regular review of challenging words allows the correct spelling pattern to become ingrained in your student's mind.

If your student misspells many words during spelling lessons, it's a sign that you should slow down the pacing of your lessons. You want to make sure he masters the current spelling patterns before you add more.

Steps for Handling Mistakes Made *Outside* a Lesson

Outside of spelling lessons, your student is no longer working with controlled word lists, and he is probably using words that contain spelling concepts he hasn't learned yet. This situation calls for a different approach.

1. **If you haven't taught the spelling concepts related to the word yet, ignore the misspelling.**

   You don't want your student to limit his word choices to avoid being corrected. Instead you want to encourage creativity and freedom. The one exception is if it is a word that your student will be using frequently. In this case, you can teach the word as a sight word.

2. **If you *have* already taught the spelling concepts, write a private note to yourself.**

   Tuck the note in your teacher's manual so you remember to review those concepts during your next spelling lesson. Don't mark up your student's paper with spelling corrections, and don't require him to correct it.

3. **If your student asks how to spell a word that he has not learned yet, go ahead and tell him the spelling.**

   This encourages your student to expand his writing vocabulary and increases his motivation to learn higher-level spelling words.

APPENDIX L

Procedure and Troubleshooting for Spelling Dictation

Dictation is a great tool for teaching spelling because it allows students to use their spelling skills in a "real world" application. That's why we include dictation in every lesson of *All About Spelling.*

The five steps to spelling dictation are explained below. Although the instructions are for dictating sentences, the steps are the same whether you are working with words, phrases, or sentences.

1 **Dictate a sentence.**

Words, phrases, and sentences are provided for you in the lessons, so you will be using only words that your student has already learned to spell. Choose several of each to dictate each day. Let your student know that he needs to focus his attention since you will only be saying the sentence once.

2 **Your student repeats the sentence.**

Repeating the sentence will help your student retain it in short term memory long enough to write it down.

3 **Your student writes the sentence.**

Don't correct your student as he writes out the sentence, even if you see him start to make a spelling mistake. In fact, it's best to look away while he's writing! This will allow him to concentrate on what he's doing without feeling like he's being monitored or judged, and it allows him to "own" the process of spelling. There will be time for correcting spelling after the next step.

4 **Your student proofreads the sentence he just wrote.**

In this step, your student reads his writing aloud or to himself. This is a good time for your student to practice self-correction. He should check himself by asking these questions: *Am I satisfied that I spelled everything correctly? Did I use capital letters and punctuation properly?*

5 **Finally, check the sentence before dictating the next one.**

If you identify a misspelled word, swing into action with the steps listed in Appendix K: How to Handle Spelling Mistakes.

If your student still struggles with dictation after following these steps, try some of the troubleshooting recommendations on the following pages.

Troubleshooting

My student can't repeat the sentence I dictated.
It may be helpful to do some exercises to strengthen your student's working memory. At this stage, instead of doing spelling dictation—which will only be frustrating for both of you—spend some time working on *oral* dictation.

Here's how oral dictation works:

1. Say a short sentence and have your student repeat it back to you.
2. As your student grows in ability, gradually increase the number of words in the sentences.
3. When oral dictation becomes easier for her, go back to the spelling dictation exercises.

My student forgets the sentence before she is done writing it.
If your student was able to repeat the sentence back to you but then forgets it before she's done writing, it may be because she is working so hard to spell the words correctly. As spelling becomes more automatic, it will be easier for her to remember the sentence long enough to write it.

In the meantime, break up the sentences into phrases. Encourage your student to repeat the phrase in her head (or out loud) several times as she's writing. Gradually lengthen the phrases until she's able to remember entire sentences long enough to write them.

My student writes down the wrong word.
Sometimes this happens because of short-term memory issues, but other times it is because the student is creative and embellishes the sentence. Students who are easily distracted often substitute words, too.

If your student is changing the words in the sentence, try saying something like this: "I've noticed that you change some of the words in the sentences that I dictate. Today I want you to write the sentence without changing any of the words. In fact, let's make it a challenge. If you can write *two* sentences correctly today, the dictation section will be over. Sound good?"

My student is overwhelmed by the amount of dictation.
Try doing just one or two sentences per day (or whatever feels like a good number without being overwhelming) and spread the lesson out over more days. Or try making dictation into a game: have your student roll a die to determine the number of sentences to write.

My student doesn't like dictation exercises.
Consider outside-the-box methods that will keep your student engaged, such as writing on a hand-held whiteboard so it's easy to make changes. Be sure to be as encouraging as possible, celebrating your student's achievements, even the small ones.

My student looks to me for approval after each word.
Let your student know that you won't be looking at the sentence until she is completely done writing and reviewing it. The best practice is to look down at your teacher's manual or out the window as your student writes from dictation. Resist the urge to look at her paper until she proofreads the sentence and says, "Done!"

My student doesn't know which ending punctuation to use.
To give your student practice with choosing the correct ending punctuation, turn it into a game. Write a question mark, a period, and an exclamation point on a piece of paper. Read sentences and have her point to the correct punctuation. Show how you make it clear through your intonation. Then switch roles.

APPENDIX M
Activities for Reviewing Phonograms

Tactile and kinesthetic activities help ingrain learning into the long-term memory by turning a lesson into an experience. Here are a few ideas to help your student learn and to make learning fun.

Games and Activities

Play Fun with Phonograms. Go to info.allaboutlearningpress.com/fun-with-phonograms to download five free folder games to use for reviewing Phonogram Cards.

Get gooey! Fill a zip-top bag with shaving cream, whipped cream, liquid soap, glue, or pudding. Seal the bag and have your student write phonograms on the bag.

Trace raised letters. Write phonograms on an index card with liquid glue. After the glue dries, have your student trace the shape of the glue with her index finger as she says the sound. To create a rougher surface, sprinkle sand on the glue before it dries.

Play Phonogram Bingo. Download our Phonogram Bingo cards at blog.allaboutlearningpress.com/phonogram-bingo, or make your own bingo cards with a selection of review phonograms.

Play Phonogram Go Fish. Choose ten to fifteen phonograms to practice. Use index cards to make up two identical sets of cards. Play according to the regular rules.

Play Phonogram Snowball Fight. Write a selection of review phonograms on index cards and tape them to the wall. As you call out phonograms, have your student locate the phonogram on the wall, say the sound(s), and throw a snowball at it. Use Ping-Pong balls, Nerf balls, styrofoam balls, or even crumpled paper for snowballs.

Jump on it! Write a selection of review phonograms on index cards and spread them around the floor. Have your student locate and jump to the correct phonogram as you call out the sound(s).

Play Phonogram Hopscotch. Write a different phonogram in each square of a hopscotch grid. Gather a different marker for each student, such as a beanbag, stone, or bottle cap. Follow the standard rules, but when the student stops to pick up his marker, he says the sound(s) of the phonogram in that square.

Play Phonogram Ball. Use a marker to write phonograms on a large beach ball. Have the student throw the ball in the air, catch it, and then say the sound(s) of the phonograms closest to her thumbs.

Replay the games from Lesson 1. Choose phonograms your student needs to review and play Try Not to Moo, Splash!, or Climb the Mountain.

Practice air writing. Have your student use his index finger to "write" the phonograms in the air in big letters.

Art and Creative Play

Stamp it. If you have rubber stamps with letters, use them to reinforce the phonogram of the day. After teaching a phonogram, use the stamps to stamp the phonogram on the back of your student's hand. Refer to it throughout the day, asking what the phonogram is, what sound(s) it makes, and so on.

Color it. Look for coloring book pages with big spaces and write review phonograms in those spaces. Have the student say the sound(s) of each phonogram. If she says the sound(s) correctly, she may color that space. Continue until the picture is complete.

Build a Phonogram Card city. Create a city in your living room by arranging the Phonogram Cards face up on the floor and furniture so that every Phonogram Card is a building. Have your student drive around the city, saying the sound(s) of the phonograms as he arrives at each building. If he says the sound(s) correctly, turn that card face down. The game continues until all the cards have been turned face down.

Make a salt tray. Fill a baking pan, jelly roll pan, or other shallow container with salt or sand. Have your student write phonograms in the salt tray with the pointer finger of the dominant hand. Gently shake the salt tray to "erase" phonograms. For added fun, experiment with different colors and scents. Go to blog.allaboutlearningpress.com/salt-trays for recipes.

Snacks and Rewards

Play Phonogram Cup Hunt. Choose five to seven review phonograms, write them on mailing labels, and attach the labels to plastic cups. Under one of the cups, place a small wrapped treat, like a few raisins or chocolate chips in plastic wrap, and then have your student close her eyes as you mix up the cups. Have your student open her eyes, choose a cup, say the sound(s) of the phonogram on the cup, and lift the cup. Continue playing until she finds the treat.

Play Snack Track. Use the Phonogram Cards to make a snack track on your floor. Place a small snack next to each card. Starting at the beginning of the track, have your student hop forward one space and say the sound(s) of the phonogram. If he says the sound(s) correctly, he gets to eat the snack and advance to the next card. If incorrect, he must move back two spaces and try again.

Make an ABC Snack. Go to abc-snacks.com, the home of all our ABC Snacks recipes. Choose the phonogram you are working on and make a yummy snack for it.

APPENDIX N

Activities for Reviewing Spelling Words

Games and Activities

Tic-tac-toe. Play the traditional way, but ask your student to spell a dictated word before placing an X or an O on the board.

Write outdoors. Is it winter? Your student can go outside and stomp dictated words in the snow. Live near the beach? He can trace words in the sand. Is it raining? He can use a stick to write in the mud.

Write everywhere! Your student can try writing words in any of the following tactile ways.

- on a dry-erase board or chalkboard
- with magnet letters on a cookie sheet
- on a long adding-machine tape
- with felt letters on a flannel board
- in the driveway with sidewalk chalk
- with alphabet cereal letters
- on an old-fashioned typewriter
- with alphabet stamps
- with paint and paintbrush
- with finger paint
- with a cotton swab dipped in water
- with a label maker
- with Scrabble or Upwords tiles

Bounce and spell. Have your student spell words while jumping on a trampoline, bouncing a ball, or playing catch. She can yell out one letter for every jump, bounce, or toss.

Spell with bendable items. Your student can form playdough, pipe cleaners, or Wikki Stix into letters and then spell words with them.

Make a recording. Have your student dictate words and the correct spelling into a computer. Then he can listen to the recording and write the words.

Art and Creative Play

Letter beads. Have your student practice spelling words by threading letter beads onto pipe cleaners to spell the words.

Create a colorful word cloud. Choose a selection of review words and have your student spell each one several times, each time using a different color marker. Create the cloud on a light-colored piece of construction paper. Encourage your student to vary the size of each word.

Watercolor words. Your student can write the spelling words on white paper with a white crayon and then paint the paper with watercolors. Watch the words appear!

Make a word collage. Have your student cut letters from a magazine and use them to spell words. Glue them to a larger piece of paper to create an artistic collage.

Illustrate words. Select a few words and have your student spell each one and draw a picture for it. She may then make a collage of the words and pictures.

Create a racetrack. Line up blank index cards or squares of paper to form a "track." Place a toy car on the first card. Dictate a word to your student and have him spell it on the index card. If he spells it correctly, he can drive his car to the next card, and so on until he arrives at the finish line.

Spelling flowers. Have your student draw a flower with large petals. Dictate some words and have your student write one word in each petal. If spelled correctly, she may color the petal. Continue until the flower is complete.

Scratch it. Cover white card stock with fun, colorful patterns using wax crayons, and then paint the entire page with black acrylic paint. Grab a wooden stick or toothpick and have your student spell words by scratching them into the paper to reveal the colors.

Snacks and Rewards

Snack stacks. Select fifteen words to practice. Place five index cards in a row in front of your student, each with three spaces to write spelling words. Place some chocolate chips, marshmallows, M&Ms, popcorn, granola, fruit, or other favorite treat next to each index card. Dictate three words, one at a time, and have your student write them on the first index card. If she spells them correctly, she may enjoy the snack next to that card. Do the same for the next three words on the next index card and so on until all the words have been spelled correctly and all the snacks eaten!

Play Yucky Snacks. Select fifteen review words. Dictate three at a time and have your student spell them. Then use them to make up "Silly Recipes for Yucky Snacks." For example, the recipe might be to add three cups of *grass*, mix in a tablespoon of *hat*, and garnish with some *bells*.

APPENDIX O

Choosing Which Letter Tile Format to Use

You have the option to use either the Letter Tiles app or the physical letter tiles. Here are some considerations to help you decide between the two formats.

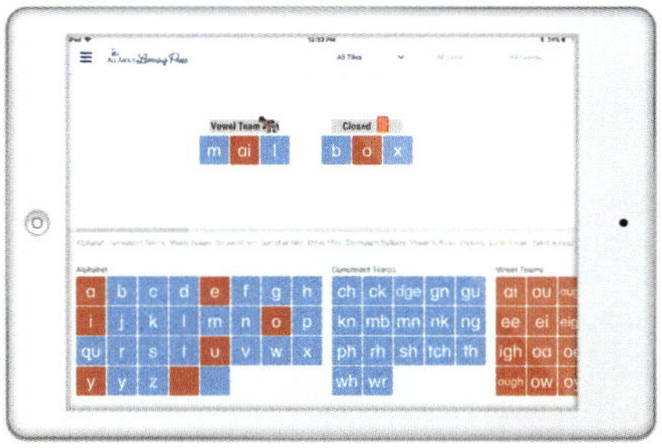

With the Letter Tiles app:

- It's easy to capitalize words.
- You can hear the sounds of the phonograms as you teach.
- No more worries about lost letter tiles.
- Lessons are easy to teach "on the go."
- It's easy to switch between students. Simply select your current lesson in *All About Reading* or *All About Spelling* and you're ready to begin.

The Letter Tiles app is very popular, but the physical letter tiles have devoted fans as well.

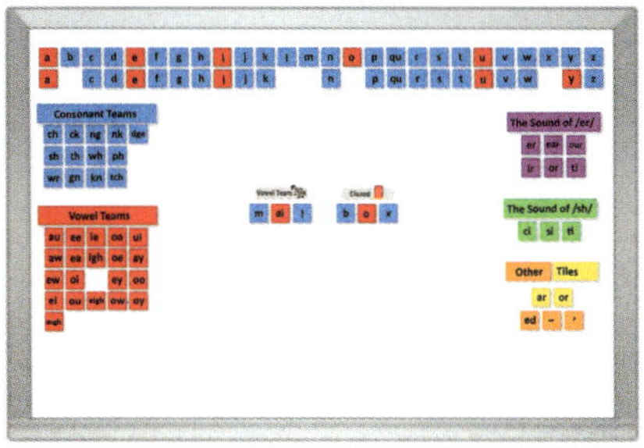

With the Letter Tiles kit:

- No tablet is required to complete the lessons.
- Larger tiles are easy to read.
- Timeless and traditional educational tool.
- Some children benefit from using the gross motor skills necessary for making the larger movements the physical letter tiles require.

Can't decide which tool to use? Consider which one would be most engaging for your student based on his current preferences. For example, does your student prefer colored pencils, or does she like video games? Is your student used to using technology for learning, or is he more comfortable with traditional methods of learning? Does she prefer e-books or paper books?

And don't forget to consider *your* preferences as well. Do you like the larger format of the magnetic whiteboard and physical tiles? Or do you like the more compact nature of the app?

You really can't go wrong with either the app or the physical letter tiles since they both make spelling concepts more concrete for your student. Choose one (or both) methods for working with letter tiles.

APPENDIX P

Magnet Board Setup at the End of Level 1

In Level 1, your student will learn the twenty-six alphabet phonograms as well as six consonant team phonograms. If you are using a magnetic whiteboard instead of the Letter Tiles app, you will add the letter tiles to your board as they are taught and as indicated in the lessons.

At the end of Level 1, your whiteboard will look like the illustration below. This is also how your whiteboard will be set up when you begin Level 2.

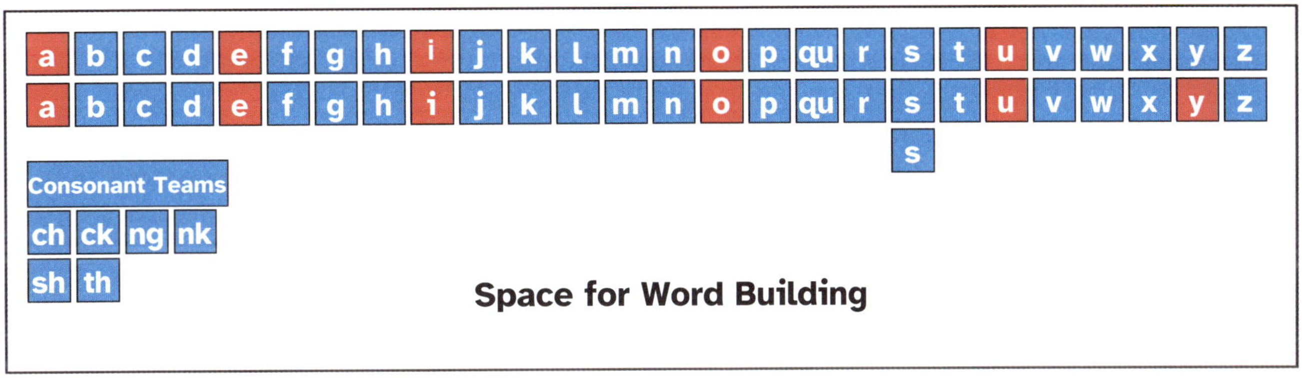

In future levels, more letter tiles will be added to the board and organized under the following categories:

APPENDIX Q

Tips on Purchasing and Using a Magnetic Whiteboard

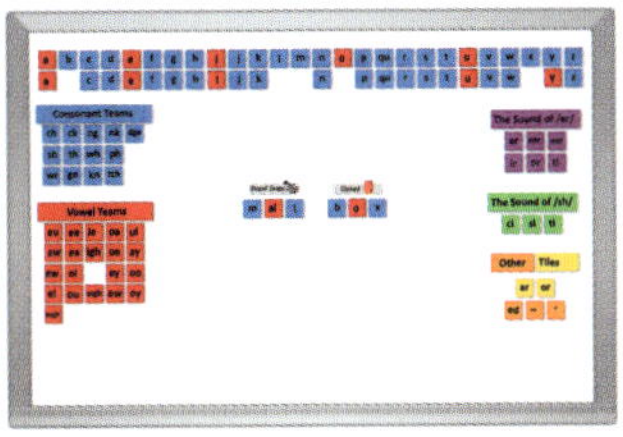

If you will be using the physical letter tiles, a magnetic whiteboard is a great way to keep the tiles organized between lessons and to save time, too.

Here are some tips for preparing and using the letter tiles on a magnetic whiteboard.

- Before purchasing a board, check the product description to be sure it's actually magnetic. Boards may go by several names—magnet board, magnetic board, dry-erase board, whiteboard, marker board—but magnets will not necessarily stick to all of them. Consider purchasing a board with a dry-erase feature—a nice addition to your daily lessons that offers yet another tactile way for your students to practice their spelling words.

- The magnetic whiteboard should be a minimum of 2' high by 3' wide. That will give you enough room for the full set of letters, plus plenty of open space to work in. You can go larger, of course, but it's not necessary.

- To magnetize your letter tiles, simply peel off the paper backing and center one magnet on the back of each letter tile and two magnets on the back of each category label. (The category labels are the longer tiles with names such as Consonant Teams, Vowel Teams, and Sound of /er/.)

- You can work with the letter tiles right on the magnetic whiteboard, or remove just the letter tiles you need for the lesson and arrange them on the table.

- **Whether you work on the table or on a magnetic whiteboard, the letter tiles should be set up in the same arrangement for each lesson.** This will enable you and your student to quickly locate the letter tiles you need. When the letter tiles make their first appearance in Lesson 4, the setup consists of a single row of the letters a to z. More phonograms are introduced in this book and later in the series, and you will soon see the need for the category labels.

Magnetic whiteboards can be purchased at office supply stores, department stores, and online. **Tip!**

APPENDIX R

Words Taught in Level 1

The number listed corresponds with the lesson in which the word is first introduced.

A

a ... 24
act ... 14
ad ... 7
am ... 7
an ... 7
and ... 14
ant ... 14
anthill ... 21
as ... 12
ash ... 13
ashes ... 23
ask ... 18
at ... 7
ax ... 12

B

back ... 18
backdrop ... 21
backpack ... 21
backpacks ... 22
bad ... 7
bag ... 7
bam ... 7
ban ... 7
band ... 14
bang ... 19
bank ... 20
banks ... 22
bash ... 13
bask ... 18
bat ... 7
bath ... 13
bathtub ... 21
bats ... 22
be ... 24
bed ... 11
bedbug ... 21
bedbugs ... 22
beds ... 22
beg ... 11
bell ... 17
bells ... 22
belt ... 14
belts ... 22
Ben ... 11
benches ... 23
bent ... 14
Bess ... 17
best ... 14
bet ... 11
Beth ... 13
Bev ... 11
bid ... 8
big ... 8
bill ... 17
Bill ... 17
bin ... 8
bit ... 8
black ... 18
blacktop ... 21
blank ... 20
blink ... 20
bliss ... 17
blob ... 15
block ... 18
blot ... 15
bluff ... 17
Bob ... 9
bobcat ... 21
bobcats ... 22
bog ... 9
boss ... 17
box ... 12
boxes ... 23
Brad ... 15
brag ... 15
brass ... 17
brick ... 18
bricks ... 22
brim ... 15
bring ... 19
brushes ... 23
buck ... 18
bud ... 10
bug ... 10
bugs ... 22
bulk ... 18
bun ... 10
bunk ... 20
bus ... 10
but ... 10

C

cab ... 16
camp ... 16
can ... 16
cannot ... 21
cap ... 16
cash ... 16
cast ... 16
cat ... 16
catfish ... 21
catnip ... 21
cats ... 22
Chad ... 13
chat ... 13
check ... 18
checklist ... 21
chess ... 17
chick ... 18
chill ... 17
chin ... 13
chip ... 13
chop ... 13
chug ... 13
chum ... 13
chunk ... 20
clam ... 16
clams ... 22
clamshell ... 21
clan ... 15
clang ... 19
clank ... 20
clap ... 16
clash ... 16
class ... 17
classes ... 23
click ... 18
cliff ... 17
cling ... 19
clip ... 16
clock ... 18
clocks ... 22
cloth ... 16
club ... 16
cluck ... 18
clung ... 19
clunk ... 20
cobweb ... 21
cod ... 16
cop ... 16
cost ... 16
cot ... 16
crab ... 16
crack ... 18
crank ... 20
crash ... 16
crib ... 16
crop ... 16
cross ... 17
crush ... 16
cub ... 16
cuff ... 17
cup ... 16
cups ... 22
cut ... 16

D

dab ... 7
dad ... 7
damp ... 14
Dan ... 9
dash ... 13
dashes ... 23
Deb ... 11
deck ... 18
den ... 11
dent ... 14
desk ... 18
desks ... 22
desktop ... 21
did ... 8
dig ... 8
dim ... 8
ding ... 19
dip ... 8
dish ... 13
dishcloth ... 21
dishes ... 23
dishpan ... 21
dishpans ... 22
dock ... 18
dog ... 9
dogs ... 22
doll ... 17
dolls ... 22
Don ... 9
dot ... 9
drab ... 15
drag ... 15
drank ... 20
dress ... 17
dresses ... 23
drill ... 17
drink ... 20
drip ... 15
drop ... 15
drum ... 15
drumstick ... 21
duck ... 18
ducks ... 22
dug ... 10
dump ... 14
dunk ... 20
dusk ... 18
dust ... 14
dustpan ... 21

E

Ed ... 11
eggshell ... 21
elk ... 18
end ... 14

F

fact ... 14
fad ... 7
fan ... 7
fang ... 19
fast ... 14
fat ... 7
fed ... 11
fell ... 17
felt ... 14
fig ... 8
fill ... 17
fin ... 8
fish ... 13
fit ... 8
fix ... 12
flag ... 15
flags ... 22
flap ... 15
flapjack ... 21
flapjacks ... 22
flat ... 15
fleck ... 18
fled ... 15
fling ... 19

plank 20
plod 15
plop 15
plot 15
pluck 18
plug 15
plum 15
plums 22
plus 15
pod 9
pond 14
pop 9
pot 9
prank 20
press 17
prim 15
prop 15
puff 17
pug 10
pump 14
pun 10
pup 10
pups 22

Q

quack 18
quick 18
quicksand 21
quill 17
quit 12

R

rack 18
raft 14
rag 7
ram 7
ramp 14
rams 22
ran 7
ranches 23
rang 19
rank 20
rap 7
rash 13
rashes 23
rat 7
red 11
rest 14
rib 8
rich 13
riches 23
Rick 18
rid 8
rim 8
ring 19
rink 20
rip 8
risk 18
rob 9
rock 18
rocks 22
rod 9
Ron 9
Ross 17
rot 9
rub 10
rug 10
rugs 22
run 10
runt 14
rush 13
Russ 17
rut 10

S

sack 18
sad 7
sag 7
Sam 9
sand 14
sandbox 21
sandboxes 23
sang 19
sank 20
sap 7
sash 13
sat 7
sell 17
send 14
sent 14
set 11
Seth 13
shack 18
shall 17
she 24
shed 13
shell 17
shellfish 21
shells 22
shin 13
ship 13
ships 22
shock 18
shop 13
shot 13
shrank 20
shrink 20
shrunk 20
shut 13
sick 18
sift 14
silk 18
sing 19
sink 20
sip 8
sit 8
six 12
slack 18
slam 15
slap 15
sled 15
slick 18
slid 15
slim 15
sling 19
slip 15
slop 15
slung 19
smack 18
smell 17
smock 18
smug 15
snack 18
snacks 22
snag 15
snap 15
snapshot 21
sniff 17
snip 15
snug 15
so 24
sob 9
sock 18
sod 9
soft 14
song 19
songs 22
speck 18
sped 15
spell 17
spill 17
spin 15
spit 15
spot 15
spots 22
spun 15
stack 18
staff 17
Stan 15
stem 15
step 15
stick 18
sticks 22
stiff 17
still 17
sting 19
stink 20
stinkbug 21
stop 15
stuck 18
stuff 17
stung 19
such 13
sun 10
sunk 20
sunset 21
sunsets 22
swam 15
swell 17
swim 15
swing 19
Swiss 17

T

tack 18
tag 7
tan 7
tank 20
tap 7
task 18
tax 12
taxes 23
Ted 11
tell 17
ten 11
tent 14
tents 22
Tess 17
test 14
than 13
thank 20
that 13
the 24
them 13
then 13
thick 18
thin 13
thing 19
things 22
think 20
this 13
thud 13
Tim 9
tin 8
tip 8
Tom 9
top 9
toss 17
tot 9
track 18
tracks 22
trap 15
trick 18
trip 15
trips 22
trot 15
truck 18
trucks 22
trunk 20
tub 10
tuck 18
tug 10
twig 15
twigs 22
twin 15

U

up 10
uphill 21
upon 21
upset 21
us 10

V

van 7
vent 14
vest 14
vet 11

W

wag 7
wax 12
we 24
web 11
well 17
went 14
wept 14
west 14
wet 11
wig 8
will 17
win 8
wind (breeze) 14
windmill 21
windmills 22
wing 19
wings 22
wink 20
wish 13
wishes 23
wit 8
with 13

Y

Z

Index for Level 1

SPELLING RULES AND STRATEGIES

TEACHING TIPS

WORDS AND WORD PARTS

– NOTES –

- NOTES -

– NOTES –

- NOTES -

- NOTES -

- NOTES -

– NOTES –